Marketing for the Non-marketing Manager

Marketing for the Non-marketing Manager

Colin V. Sowter

McGRAW-HILL BOOK COMPANY

London · New York · St Louis · San Francisco · Auckland
Bogotá · Caracas · Lisbon · Madrid · Mexico
Milan · Montreal · New Delhi · Panama · Paris · San Juan
São Paulo · Singapore · Sydney · Tokyo · Toronto

Published by McGraw-Hill Book Company Europe
Shoppenhangers Road, Maidenhead, Berkshire, SL6 2QL, England
Telephone 01628 23432
Fax 01628 770224

British Library Cataloguing in Publication Data

Sowter, Colin
  Marketing is Too Important to be Left to the Marketing Department
  I. Title
  658.8

  ISBN 0–07–707964–7

Library of Congress Cataloging-in-Publication Data

Sowter, Colin V.,
  Marketing for the non-marketing manager: marketing is too important to be
  left to the marketing department / Colin V. Sowter.
    p. cm.
  Includes index.
  ISBN 0–07–707964–7 (pbk. : alk. paper)
  1. Marketing. I. Title.
HF5415.S6964 1995
658.8–dc20

                                                                95--8795
                                                                    CIP

12345 BL 98765

Typeset by Computape (Pickering) Ltd, North Yorkshire
Printed and bound in Great Britain by Biddles Ltd, Guildford, Surrey
Printed on permanent paper in compliance with ISO Standard 9706.

Contents

Author's preface

Towards the end of the 1980s the marketing director of a well-known company asked if I would give a seminar on marketing to the whole of his research and development department. He was concerned that the engineers should be more market oriented in their dealings with customers, and that they should be able to interface more effectively with their full-time marketing colleagues.

The seminar went well, and I felt that the whole concept of marketing for the non-marketing manager was so worth while that I ventured to advertise an open seminar. This was oversubscribed, and the series is now entering its sixth year. By now, over three hundred companies have made use of these seminars, and an increasing number of them have requested 'tailor-made' sessions on their own premises.

The question I ask is 'Why is there such a thirst for knowledge about marketing?' Is it because people in hitherto successful companies are finding that they have to be more proactive in their marketing efforts? Is it because there is confusion about the difference between marketing and selling? Is it because they wonder whether marketing compromises their intellectual, moral or professional integrity? Is it because they think that 'marketing does not work in our kind of business', and yet they are uneasy about this conclusion? Is it because they do not believe that marketing represents a 'serious' intellectual discipline? This book, which arises directly out of the seminars, aims to address these and many other issues.

The benefit of studying marketing begins to be apparent when we start to apply the principles. Every time we decide to buy or not to buy something in our personal or business life there is an opportunity to further our understanding of the marketing function. Why did we buy from that particular shop or company? Why did that salesman fail to get an order from us?

I am not an academic, and this is not a theoretical study of marketing. It represents the fruit of 35 years' experience in a wide variety of companies. The lessons come from seeing marketing performed well and badly under UK, American and Continental management styles. I have experienced the interface with marketing while working in manufacturing; I have undertaken the task of marketing in seven marketing positions, three of them at board level; I have wrestled with the role of marketing in the organization from a general management perspective. These are the lessons that I am seeking to share through the medium of this book.

Acknowledgements

While no material has knowingly been copied from other sources without acknowledgement, I am indebted to the large number of authors whose books I have read over the years, the consultants whose seminars I have attended, the directors and managers under whom and with whom I have worked in various appointments in a variety of industries, and the delegates who have participated in my own seminars. Their combined wisdom has led to the experience which is the subject of this book, and I would like to acknowledge my gratitude to each one of them.

Introduction

To most people, marketing is about communications. They have an image which has been formed as a result of many people trying to sell to them. They are bombarded with messages from all directions—by post, telephone, fax, television, posters and so on. This must be what marketing is all about!

The danger is that we confuse the message with the vehicle by which the message is communicated. There is no point in having an expensive vehicle if it is carrying the wrong goods! People assume that if they pay enough to have an advertisement written or a brochure designed, all will be well. What they forget is that they are probably the only people who can create the right message.

We cannot start thinking about communicating until we have answered some key questions. What audience do we want to address? What are the key factors which will influence their buying decisions? What do we want to say to them? What is the competitive environment within which we are working? What price are they prepared to pay?

Once we have considered these fundamental business issues in Part I of this book, we can move on to think about the various forms of communication in Part II. Key aspects of international marketing are also discussed, because many companies do not have a coherent international strategy and fail to exploit the opportunities which are open to them; distributorships and agencies often do not work as well as they should.

In Part III we look at market research leading on to the crucial subject of innovation. Why is it that new product development is so ineffective in many organizations? Having been part of the team which moved into newly acquired companies on several occasions, I have probably closed down more development projects than I have opened. This book argues that innovation is not something which takes place solely or even mainly in the R&D department; the marketing component of innovation is at least as significant. Finally, we consider some key aspects of marketing management which are often badly handled.

We live in times of change, and we have to react accordingly. For example, if we are moving from the defence to the civil applications of our products, we have to realize that the competitive factors and the way in which buying decisions are made are entirely different in the new situation. The same is true for an accountant or lawyer moving into the promotion of broader financial or legal services, an industrial supplier moving into consumer marketing (and vice versa), a university or consultancy needing to expand its customer base, a former government-owned operation becoming privatized or achieving agency status, and for most businesses facing new situations.

Every one of us who interfaces with customers or who is concerned with innovation is involved in marketing whether we like it or not. Marketing is much too important to be left to the marketing department—especially if there isn't one!

Notes on the exercises and follow-up

As with the seminars on which it is based, this book is intended to be strongly action-oriented. The issue throughout is 'if we agree with it, what are we going to do about it?'. For this reason, each chapter ends with some very practical 'Exercises' and 'Follow-up'. These are noted for reference at the appropriate points in the text. Readers are urged to select those which are most relevant to their needs. Most of them will be even more useful if they are done with a colleague or a small group.

Part I
THE ROLE OF MARKETING

What is marketing?

A way of thinking about business

Key business issues	*Section*
■ Marketing should be the means of generating profit. If it is not, there is something wrong.	1.1
■ Marketing is a rational process which need not compromise our intellectual, professional, technical or ethical integrity.	1.2
■ Marketing does not always require large budgets or extra staff— it is a way of thinking about business.	1.3
■ We cannot assume that people know or want what we sell, or that they are prepared to find out.	1.4
■ Marketing should be proactive not reactive.	
■ The 'best' product is not always the most commercially successful.	
■ Becoming market-led involves a shift of focus away from 'what we do' to 'what they need'.	1.5
■ Nobody, not even our best customer, actually wants our product or service; they want what it will do for them.	1.6
■ Marketing starts with identifying customer needs, and then organizes the whole company operation to satisfy those needs in a profitable way.	1.7
■ Marketing is too important to be left to the marketing department. Key staff in all functions must be market-led.	1.8
■ Marketing professionalism should be recognized and sought. Many senior managers set their sights too low in recruitment and appointment.	1.9

- Marketing addresses three components of profit—market share,   1.10
  market size and margin. Two of them are often ignored.

- Marketing and selling have an entirely different focus and   1.11
  should not be confused.

- Marketing is not telling people what we do.   1.12

- Marketing is not persuading people to buy things they
  don't need.

- Marketing should not be equated with brochures, advertising,
  customer support or customer service.

- Being market-led does not mean following every whim of every   1.13
  customer.

1.1   Marketing should be the means of generating profit

'The trouble with marketing is that it is a debit against profit.' This remark, made to me at one of my recent seminars, reveals volumes about people's attitudes to marketing. It suggests that it is some sort of disease which needs to be eradicated! Unfortunately this is a commonly held view, and it is based on a complete misunderstanding of what marketing is there to do.

Everything we do is a debit against profit, and marketing is no exception. However, if it is not the means of *generating* profit there is something wrong, either with the product, the market demand or the way in which we are doing our marketing. The problem needs to be dealt with, and this may involve a change in the whole operating philosophy of the company. The fact is that, in a soundly market-led operation, the money spent on marketing is an investment from which we expect a positive return. The short-term negative profit and cash flow is the price we have to pay for long-term success. Inept and inappropriate marketing is certainly a debit against profit!

Sadly, people venture tentatively into some form of marketing which they have seen elsewhere, are disappointed with the results, and conclude that marketing does not work in their particular business. It is not the fault of marketing but of the way in which they are trying to apply it. Wherever there is competition and customers do not spontaneously demand our product, marketing is essential. It is not enough to have a good product—these days, excellence is expected. Whether we like it or not, the product itself may not be the major factor in the buying decision, and success goes to those who are best at marketing. This is equally true whether the 'product' is a tangible item such as a computer or something intangible such as a professional service. Throughout this book both will be described as 'products'.

We are not suggesting that money should be poured aimlessly into a bottomless marketing pit. The thesis is that, intelligently applied, time and money spent on marketing can be the biggest single factor contributing to profitable growth (see Exercise 1.1).

1.2 Marketing is a rational process which need not compromise our integrity

Until relatively recently, one could obtain qualifications, degrees, further degrees and so on in almost every subject except marketing. A consequence of this is the widespread feeling that marketing is not quite as 'professional' as other disciplines. Doubts about some of the highly emotive activities such as advertising and promotion even lead some people to regard marketing as a rather inferior and irrational process.

The aim of this book is to demonstrate emphatically that, properly applied to each particular situation, marketing does not need to compromise our intellectual, professional, technical or ethical integrity in any way. The attempt to persuade people to buy products or services which they do not really need might be described as marketing, but it is not the subject of this book.

1.3 Marketing does not always require large budgets or extra staff

Marketing is an attitude of mind which can transform the way in which existing staff carry out their normal tasks. It does not always require additional staff or large budgets.

In circumstances where the rewards for success are very high, leading companies spend a large percentage of turnover on marketing in its various forms—market research, marketing strategy, market-led innovation, selling, sales support, customer service and so on. This makes good business sense. If millions of pounds are to be spent on new product development, it is essential to establish potential customer demand before committing to the development (but how many companies don't do this?!). If a large salesforce is to be employed, their activities must be prioritized on the basis of marketplace needs. If large budgets are to be spent on television advertising, it is worth commissioning substantial market research to test the advertisements before committing to the campaign.

While this book is absolutely relevant to these high-spending scenarios, we particularly address the situation where a large budget is not available and would not be appropriate. Many of the delegates to my seminars come from organizations which don't even have a marketing department. For many of us, the opportunity to test everything by formal market research is simply not realistic, and we have to make judgements in the absence of information that we would really like. This is one of the reasons why a marketing management post demands abilities of the highest calibre.

Marketing is not primarily a series of separate, specialist and costly activities; it is a way of running a business, a management style, an attitude of mind. As such, it need not, in the first instance, cost anything. The salaries and expenses of the staff concerned are already being paid. A market-orientated management style should saturate every part of our daily decision-making process, so that the main factors influencing strategic and tactical decisions are the needs of the customer rather than the needs of the company.

Having said this, many companies which have historically survived with very low levels of marketing expenditure would be able to achieve greater profitability and growth if they were prepared to take marketing more seriously. This will undoubtedly involve spending more money on appropriate aspects of marketing, and, of course, there is a time lag between investment and return, but this is true of many aspects of business and is not a valid reason for not engaging in marketing.

1.4   'Better mousetraps' do not work; 'better doors' do!

'If a man ... make a better mousetrap than his neighbour, though he build his house in the woods, the world will make a beaten path to his door' (attributed to Emerson). This statement is often seen on the walls of company entrance halls or development departments. It contains a number of dangerous fallacies.

First, we cannot assume that people know what we make or what services we provide. Many companies base their operating procedures on a philosophy of 'enquiries received'; it is a much healthier starting-point to assume that we shall not receive a single enquiry which we ourselves have not generated. Many companies are diversifying out of their historic core business into new fields where they are unknown. Their name would not even be on a 'long-list' of potential suppliers to this marketplace, let alone a 'short-list'; it is the task of marketing to overcome this.

Second, we cannot assume that people want what we are selling, in the sense that they already have it on their 'shopping list'. A prime task of marketing is to stimulate or generate a demand which may be only latent or potential.

Third, we cannot assume that people will 'beat a path to our door'. We need to be proactive, not reactive. 'Order-taking' has little place in a positive marketing strategy. Of course we will take orders when they are presented to us, but the whole emphasis should be to go out, find potential customers, demonstrate that we have what they are looking for, and generate the orders by our own initiatives.

Fourth, there is the whole question of whether people want 'better mousetraps'. Superficial thought suggests that the better the product, the more likely we are to sell it. A little more thought suggests that people are not prepared to pay for 'gold plating', overengineering, or superfluous features. There are some thought-provoking acronyms to describe this situation: JEE—'just enough engineering', and AIP—'adequate is perfect'! Different segments of the market (see Chapter 4) will want different degrees of sophistication. It is by no means obvious that the maximum profit will be achieved by addressing only the top segment of a particular market. This can raise culture problems for people who have been trained in technical or professional excellence, and feel that there is something inferior about the suggestion of 'compromise', but every sale is a balance between price and perceived value. The art is to pitch the level appropriately for any particular buying situation, giving the customer the product that is 'fit for purpose'.

In contrast to the quotation from Emerson, it has been said that 'If we make a better door, people will beat a path to our mousetrap'! This is a much better expression of marketing philosophy. In many companies, the need is not so much to improve the product as to improve the contact with the marketplace. Curiously, some managers seem to regard money spent on development as an investment but money spent on marketing as a waste (see Exercise 1.2).

1.5 Becoming market-led involves a shift of focus

Becoming a market-led operation requires a deliberate shift of focus, away from *what we do* to *what they need*, or want, or might want, or might reasonably be persuaded to want. It encourages us to get out of our ivory tower and into the real world. This is a problem for those who live in a culture of specifications, definitions, standards or professional methodologies. Scientific and professional education encourages us to seek for perfection, to search for excellence, and to devote all our attention to our product or service. It is essential to recognize that people's real needs do not necessarily coincide with our view of what we would like them to have.

Part of this shift of focus involves us in learning the customers' language and jargon, identifying with the issues which concern them, and generally showing that we understand their business. It also requires us to make a deliberate effort to suppress those parts of our own language and jargon which might be a 'turn-off'. This is particularly necessary when we are trying to diversify into a new area; we have to leave behind the old culture and learn to understand a completely new one.

Many companies pay excessive attention to their past achievements, extolling the length of time they have been in business, the fact that they were first in the field with a particular product and so on. The key point as far as customers are concerned is what the supplier is able to do for them in the future. Again, this may require a shift of focus.

1.6   Nobody actually wants our product—they want what it will do for them!

Nobody, not even our best customer, actually wants our product or service. This sounds a drastic statement to make in a book about marketing, but it is worth thinking through its implications. The thing the buyers want is not the product itself but what the product will *do for them*. Making things or developing capabilities do not of themselves achieve anything. These activities do not win the race; all they do is to get us to the starting-point!

People do not want drills—they want holes. People do not want cars— they want a means of getting somewhere, or something to boost their image and give them feelings of pleasure, pride, satisfaction or whatever else they are seeking. They do not want consumer products, equipment or professional services—they want the personal or business benefits which result from them. In other words, a product is a means to an end, not an end in itself.

Failure to realize this can be seen in many of the brochures, advertisements, sales claims and so on with which people are daily bombarded. The emphasis is far too much on telling them what the product or service does, and far too little on what benefits they can gain from it. This is why we have to start with our customers and their needs, not with ourselves and what we sell.

This means that we must be prepared to work hard at our marketing. It is easier and much less disrupting to live in our own world—we understand it and we are comfortable with its culture. We can comprehend and measure what we are doing, whereas the outside world is made up of unquantifiable mysteries. The fact is, however, that the prizes go to those who are prepared to launch out into the unknown world of the customer, with all the risks, frustrations and hard work that this involves (see Exercise 1.3).

1.7 Marketing starts with identifying customer needs

A 'definition' of marketing is that it starts with identifying customer needs and then goes on to organize the whole company operation to satisfy those needs in a profitable way. In some cases the need will be expressed; in others it is potential or latent and has to be developed. It may not have occurred to the customers to buy what we are selling—they may not even have heard of it. We may have to sell a concept before we can begin to sell an actual product. For example, people did not go to the electronic manufacturers and ask for video recorders. The manufacturers first had to determine that, if they could produce a device which would enable people to record programmes and view them later, the demand would be forthcoming. If they had sat back and waited for people to send in enquiries, which is what many companies do, they would still be waiting!

The next part of the definition—'organize the whole company operation to satisfy those needs in a profitable way'—often causes problems. It seems to imply that the marketing department is more important than other departments, and can go round instructing the rest of the company what to do. This is a misunderstanding. All major departments in a company are essential, just as a table needs all its legs.

The point we are beginning to develop is that marketing is not something which takes place solely or even primarily in the marketing department. It is a way of thinking about business which must saturate management thinking at all levels and in all departments. It is this *marketing philosophy* which must be the prime input to company strategy, and this philosophy is too far-reaching to be confined to one department.

If the objective of marketing is to generate profit, does this refer to short- or long-term profit, and do these two not conflict? The answer to these three questions is 'yes, yes, and yes'! A company with a very short-term orientation is often very bad at marketing; managers are obsessed with making profit this year, this quarter or even this month, to the detriment of all else. Obviously there are times when we have to 'batten down the hatches and survive the storm', but short-term cost savings are not a formula for achieving long-term strategic growth.

Successful start-up businesses often begin by investing a large proportion of their initial profit in marketing, in order to build a market position, create an image and buy a market share. Having done this, they are able to reduce the percentage expenditure on marketing and enjoy the sustained growth in profit which they deserve.

We are not suggesting that money should be poured unthinkingly into marketing activities. What we are advocating is a careful evaluation of the market opportunities, an informed estimate of the amount of business which can be obtained, a sensible assessment of the amount of marketing money required to gain that business, a detailed comparison of the various ways in which the money might be spent (selling, advertising, literature, exhibitions, etc.), and firm commitment to a positive marketing programme.

One deficiency of the above definition is that it does not refer to the competition. This crucial aspect of marketing is considered in Chapter 5.

1.8   Marketing is too important to be left to the marketing department

A major myth about marketing is that it is something that goes on in the marketing department. Well-dressed and highly paid individuals seem to carry out mysterious functions, use jargon understood only by themselves, and take little interest in what goes on in the rest of the company. They regard themselves as a race apart from, and distinctly above, all the other functions. This leads some people to come to the conclusion that 'marketing does not work in our business' or 'we can't afford to employ people like that'.

Marketing should start with the chief executive, be a key focus of the whole senior management team, and percolate down to virtually everyone at senior and middle management level in the organization. Apart from those who are required to be proactive in getting or helping to get orders, there are many others who are involved in reactive marketing. They include a switchboard operator, a credit control clerk, a driver—anyone who has any contact with customers. These people may not be able to win an order but they can certainly *lose* one!

In some organizations there is a designated function called 'marketing', which is allocated certain specific tasks such as researching the market, developing strategy, preparing marketing programmes, selling to the marketplace and supporting customers. In others there is no separate function. In every case, the essential marketing tasks still have to be performed.

Marketing could be seen as:

- Customer oriented
- Financially sound
- International
- Business management

■ *Customer oriented*   because it is the customer who pays our salary.

■ *Financially sound*   because, at the end of the day, the main thing we are selling is usually a financial benefit, either to our immediate customers or to their customers or both. Training in key financial concepts may need to be a part of training in marketing, so that soundly based financial arguments can be presented.

■ *International*   because, in most businesses, the potential from the UK market is insufficient to meet corporate growth aspirations.

■ *Business management*   because this is really what it is. I was once asked to give a talk to a group of marketing managers in a 'blue-chip' fast-moving consumer goods company. My session was after lunch on the fourth day of a one-week course; the delegates were beginning to tire, and I feared that the unglamorous subject of 'Industrial Marketing' would be a complete turn-off. After the session, one of the delegates said 'it's a good job *you* came to speak to us; we've been here for four days learning about gimmicks and techniques and jargon, but you're the first person to use the word "management" in connection with marketing'.

Marketing is much too important to be left to the marketing department—especially if there isn't one (see Exercise 1.4).

1.9   Professionalism in marketing should be recognized and sought

Companies often correctly diagnose the need for a marketing function but fail to get the benefits because they set their sights far too low in terms of marketing professionalism. This is usually because senior managers have never seen marketing work the way it should. They often regard marketing as part of selling, and staff the marketing department with former salespeople. In high-technology companies, the most common mistake is to transfer a technical expert into marketing without any training, on the grounds that 'marketing is common sense'. The same company would not put a taxation specialist in charge of chemical engineering plant development; why should they think a comparable transfer will work in the case of marketing?!

Marketing is now a profession which can be learned, studied and experienced. Where a company or an industry is not renowned for training heavyweight marketing staff, it may well be worth bringing in at least a proportion of them from a company or industry which is. The immediate reaction to such a suggestion is often 'you can't understand our business until you have been in it for twenty years'. The reverse—bringing in a sense of objectivity which is not hampered by past practices and attitudes—might actually be just what is needed.

The fallacy of making do with unprofessional and inexperienced marketing staff is that very little cost is saved. The salary may be less than one would have to pay for a professional, but all the other expenses—car, office, secretary, administration, etc.—are exactly the same. One heavyweight can be worth several lightweights in terms of influence on the business.

In theory, the ideal recruit would have a knowledge of both the marketplace and the product range, and would have had a good marketing track record. If such a person can be found, that is fine. However, the much more normal situation is that candidates possess only two or even one of these three qualifications. In these circumstances, which should be regarded as essential? Although this is not the natural instinct of many managers involved in recruitment, it is suggested that the three factors should be ranked in the following order:

1. Knowledge and experience of marketing in a heavyweight marketing environment.

2. Knowledge of the marketplace.

3. Knowledge of the product range.

Knowledge of the marketplace and the product can be learned relatively quickly. New marketing people recruited from a totally different industry can adapt very quickly to the new situation. They have learned to ask the right questions and will largely train themselves. They will instinctively set about finding out the size and trends in the marketplace, the activities of the competition, the reasons why people do and do not buy the new company's products and so on. I have seen such people chairing a meeting with great authority within about two months of joining. Of course they are better after two years, but the alternative—appointing people who have never seen marketing properly used—is incomparably worse (see Follow-up 1.1).

1.10   Marketing addresses three components of profit

Marketing addresses three components which combine to make up the profitability of an enterprise. These are:

- Market share
- Market size
- Percentage margin

The instinct of many people is to concentrate on the first component—market share. For them, the marketing battle is about competing for a limited amount of business and trying to capture sales from the competition. While this is clearly an important part of marketing, it is only one part and greater rewards may actually come from the other two.

Market share

The starting point for any business plan or marketing plan is the sales forecast. The problem is that this forecast is often not expressed in terms of market share and it therefore lacks external validation. Any manager who is asked to approve a set of sales figures should insist on knowing the market share which it represents.

Figures 'plucked out of the air' are a dangerous self-delusion and may be wildly optimistic. They are often based on the level of orders which the factory needs to keep it in production, or which fee-earning consultants need to keep them occupied. This is a sign of marketing at its most amateur. An annual growth rate of 10 per cent may be pessimistic if the market is growing by 15 per cent, but impossibly optimistic if the market is static or declining. In spite of this, immature managers feel that they must build growth into their forecasts irrespective of what is happening in the marketplace. The truth is often that they need this growth in order to justify the increases which they are planning in their own empire. Similarly, senior managers often demand growth figures because they think it will create an incentive. Realistically stretching targets can be motivating, but targets which are unachievable have the reverse effect and simply defer the time when difficult management decisions have to be faced.

I blame laser printers for many of today's business problems! Figures which have been neatly printed and bound into a nice-looking report acquire a legitimacy which people are reluctant to question. In fact, they have no more validity than the back of the restaurant menu on which they were originally written!

We must consider whether a market share figure is really achievable. If we are selling a new product concept, how do we know that sales will 'take off' so quickly? If we are entering an established market dominated by other suppliers, why should the customers buy this hitherto unknown brand? Why should the competitors allow a new entrant to make these gains at their expense? Unless we can answer these questions, we should reconsider the sales forecast.

Market size

The second component of profit—increasing the size of a market—may initially involve selling a concept rather than a product. For example, persuading people to eat turkeys on occasions other than Christmas did not involve proving that one brand of turkey was better than another; the task was to persuade people that the turkey was a viable alternative to a weekend joint, and then that other turkey dishes could be eaten on any day of the week. A patent agent might carry out an audit on the way in which a client protects intellectual property. The result might be to create an increased demand for patenting. This is quite different from sitting back and responding reactively to enquiries received.

There are several ways of expanding the market for an existing product or service, such as broader application, new uses and addressing underexploited potential. Some of the most dramatic case histories are those in which a whole new market has been created, which is sometimes larger than the original market from which it was derived. Customers did not spontaneously demand home computers, camcorders, take-away hamburgers or balloon flights, but entrepreneurs recognized and exploited the opportunities. This is sheer marketing creativity. The process can be even easier in the case of intangible services such as consultancy and training; the market is what we make of it!

Percentage margin

The third component of profit—the percentage margin—should be a major concern of marketing. It is based on two elements—price and cost. In practice, pricing is often carried out by the financial department, and cost is regarded as something which arises mainly in R&D, purchasing and manufacturing. In contrast to this, we argue that both price and cost are strongly related to the situation in the marketplace, and cannot be handled by people living in an 'ivory tower' which insulates them from the realities of customers and competitors.

Price is what the customer is prepared to pay for the value which is perceived in the product; it has much less to do with cost than most people realize. This is so important that the whole of Chapter 6 is devoted to the subject. The impact of price on profitability is enormous. If our net profit is 2 per cent of turnover, an average price increase of 1 per cent would increase the return on capital employed by 50 per cent!

Professional marketeers will try to justify a premium price by promoting the value of the product. They will be aware of the prices charged by the competition, which may have a major influence on the price which people are prepared to pay for their product. If this is true, prices cannot be set by accountants alone (unless they spend about three days a week in the marketplace!). It is, of course, assumed that the marketing staff are mature managers who understand the financial realities of business and who see their task as generating profit rather than turnover.

Cost is also strongly influenced by the marketing function. Of course, there are some major aspects which are outside the control of marketing—buying efficiency, manufacturing productivity and so on— but marketing decisions can often mean the difference between profit and loss. Marketing is responsible for defining the product specification, which has a direct impact on product cost. On the negative side, incremental features which are not really essential may kill the profit margin if the cost cannot be recovered in the price. On the positive side, a product with a higher specification may be a vehicle for increased market share or a higher price. A marketing specification is not a 'wish list'; it calls for a responsible appraisal of an infinite number of options, and a willingness to say 'no' to some interesting product features.

These are the three key components of profit which are influenced by marketing, and we neglect any of them at our peril (see Exercise 1.5).

1.11   Marketing and selling have a different focus

Words are used differently in different organizations, but the most common approach is to describe the whole discipline as marketing and then to subdivide aspects of sales and marketing within this overall umbrella. Various organizational options are discussed in Section 13.1.

A sales emphasis is that we have a product which we need to sell. A marketing emphasis is that the market has a need which we can arrange to meet. The product is the result of the marketing effort rather than the reason for making the marketing effort. Excellence in selling is not sufficient if it is not accompanied by excellence in marketing.

Selling

Selling should have the highly focused short-term objective of winning today's orders, achieving this month's sales forecasts, and generating the income required to meet the annual plan. This activity is totally essential, but it should not be seen as representing the whole of the marketing operation as it appears to do in some companies.

Strategic marketing and product management

This is a highly demanding activity which should be undertaken by staff with the necessary calibre and experience (see Chapter 13). The task of the marketing strategist is to identify the long-term needs of the market-place, to gain an informed view of the probable long-term actions of the competition, and then to propose a strategy which will enable the company to exploit these opportunities profitably.

Arising from the overall marketing plans will be detailed plans for specific marketing programmes such as the development of new products, product launches and relaunches, entry into new market segments, entry into new geographical areas, changes in pricing strategy, and all other activities which will enable the company to progress in a market-led manner. Marketing is making the future happen!

Marketing services

An ancillary aspect of the marketing function is to provide tools which will enable the salesforce to achieve their objectives. These include literature, advertising, exhibitions, sales aids, sales manuals, training packages, product support packages and so on. This is the one area where marketing might legitimately be regarded as a support function to selling.

Calibre and experience of marketing staff

The various areas within the sales and marketing function clearly require very different types of experience, qualifications and motivation. Good marketing managers should be able to sell, and indeed should have had some experience 'on the road' to ensure that they are not abstract theoreticians, but selling would probably not provide sufficient job satisfaction in the long term.

Good sales staff do not necessarily transfer successfully to marketing positions. Their whole culture is based on the achievement of short-term results, and it is this which makes them successful. They may not be very good at longer-term conceptual thinking, and they should not be expected to do it. They may have valuable insights into the marketplace and the competition, but it is probably better if the strategic thinking resulting from their input is carried out by staff with longer-term objectives. This is not to suggest that salespeople are in any way inferior to marketing strategists; they are both totally essential, but they have different strengths. The aim should be to recruit, train or appoint the right people for each task (see Exercise 1.6).

1.12   What marketing is not!

While we are exploring the question of what marketing is, it is important to understand what it is not. Many companies set their sights far too low in terms of what marketing is there to do. They seem to believe certain myths about marketing and thereby bring the whole concept into disrepute.

Myth 1: Marketing is telling people what we do.   This point has already been discussed, but it is included here as possibly the most widespread myth of all.

Myth 2: Marketing is persuading people to buy things they don't need. People come to our homes, uninvited and unwelcome, and try to persuade us to buy products or services against our will. Their only interest is in achieving a sale and gaining their commission. They probably only sell once in a lifetime to a particular customer, and they have nothing to lose by taking a very aggressive sales approach.

Myth 3: Marketing is about brochures, advertising and PR. These activities, although essential, represent only the tip of the iceberg of marketing. The key point is the message to be communicated. Without proper attention to the message, the money spent on communication is largely wasted. This involves a great deal of time and thought which can only be done by staff with a mature understanding of marketing.

Myth 4: Marketing is about customer support and customer service. These activities are totally necessary, but they are not a substitute for strategic marketing. In one company where this attitude had prevailed, I had to set up an entirely separate customer service function, so that customers could be properly supported and marketing managers could get on with what they were really there to do without constantly having to respond reactively to unplanned demands on their time.

Myth 5: Marketing is about trendy clothes and expensive lunches. Those who give this impression have only themselves to blame if their form of marketing is not taken seriously by hard-working managers in other functions whose only perk is an occasional company sandwich! Marketing is one of the most crucial disciplines in the company, and those who practise it should be ambassadors for the seriousness of their profession.

To summarize, senior marketing staff have the great privilege of pointing the company in the future direction in which it should go. This privilege carries with it an enormous degree of responsibility. If they cannot meet the high demands placed upon them, they should be replaced by people who can (see Exercise 1.7).

1.13 Being market-led does not mean following every whim of every customer

So far we have urged that the needs of the marketplace should be the dominant factor influencing strategic and tactical business decision making. Internal needs, such as wanting to keep our factory busy or our fee-earning consultants gainfully employed, must ultimately be subservient to the needs of customers. Our own desire to run a prosperous business depends critically upon having satisfied customers, at least in any situation where repeat purchases and customer loyalty are important.

These arguments seem to suggest that we should fall over backwards to do anything a customer asks us. This is emphatically not the case, and an attempt to do so will lead to disaster.

Being market-led does not mean following every whim of every customer. There is some business we do not want, and there are some terms and conditions which it would not be wise for us to accept. There are some minority requests for product features which it would be folly to build into the majority of our offerings.

We have to 'manage' our customer base to achieve our objectives. We have to be 'market-driving' as well as 'market-driven'. This is a paradox. The art of marketing management is to steer a delicate line between the two conflicting factors (see Chapter 3 and Follow-up 1.2).

Exercises

1.1 Is marketing regarded as the means of generating profit in your organization? If not, is it because the marketing is wrong or because the perception of it is wrong? What needs to be done about it?

1.2 Are there some parts of your organization which appear to subscribe to the 'better mousetrap' philosophy? If so, what needs to be done about it?

1.3 Look at your company literature. Is the emphasis mainly on what your products or services *are*, or on what they will *do for the customer* (and see Exercise 9.1)?

1.4 If marketing is too important to be left to the marketing department, are the other parts of your organization playing their part sufficiently in the marketing task? Where are the main areas of weakness? What needs to be done about it?

1.5 Think of some ways in which the profitability of your organization could be improved by:
   ■ Increasing the size of the market.
   ■ Increasing profitability by *marketing* actions.

1.6 Is there a clear distinction in your organization between the roles of sales and marketing? Are both functions staffed by people of appropriate calibre and experience?

1.7 Consider the five 'myths' in Section 1.12. Ask yourself, honestly and critically, if any of them seem to prevail in your Company.

Follow-up

1.1 Is your organization likely to be recruiting any full-time marketing staff in the foreseeable future? If so, have those responsible for the recruitment prioritized the qualifications required as in Section 1.9?

1.2 Observe the key decisions which are made in your part of the organization during the next three months. Do you think these decisions exhibit the right balance between being market-driving and market-driven?

Why do people buy?

Value as perceived by the customer

Key business issues	Section
■ Every buying decision is different. We must determine the influencing factors before we start selling.	2.1
■ In some buying decisions, the product is not the major factor. In others, price does not dominate. 'Place', promotion, packaging, perception or other factors may play a crucial role.	
■ The relative ranking of these factors can change with time.	
■ A major task of marketing is to bring price lower down the ranking in the buying decision.	2.2
■ Customers do not simply buy a product or service but a whole bundle of attributes of which the product itself is only a part.	2.3
■ Intangible factors such as image, credibility and perceived track record can dominate a buying decision.	
■ Peripheral aspects of a product or service may have more influence than the core features on which it is based.	
■ Personal relationships, such as consultancy and partnership, can override everything else.	
■ These three factors, particularly the last, can actually eliminate all competition.	
■ People buy *benefits* not *features*, but the conventional 'features and benefits analysis' has some serious limitations.	2.4
■ Different people want different benefits from the same product. Benefits to some may be irrelevant to others and therefore dilute the message.	

■ A benefit to one person may actually be a disbenefit to another.

■ No single sales message can address all segments, but the cost of   2.5
targeting need not be high if simple principles are followed.

■ In a decision-making group, each member wants different   2.6
benefits. The message needs to be targeted.

■ In a distribution chain, each member wants different benefits.   2.7
The message needs to be targeted.

■ It is important to differentiate our product from the competition,   2.8
and present it as unique (or at least special) in a way which is
relevant to the customer.

■ By following these principles, our sales and marketing activities   2.9
can be given a sharper cutting edge.

■ Branding gives 'personality' to a product, and defines the   2.10
'stable' from which it comes.

■ The value of brand names may have a higher value than the
tangible assets on the balance sheet. This can cause trauma in
the boardroom in an acquisition situation.

■ The marketing of intangible services requires some special   2.11
attention, but it also has some special advantages.

■ Product companies might profitably add some services to their
portfolio.

■ Marketing, properly understood and applied, is entirely appropriate
to the development of professional practices and to virtually all
fields of consultancy.

2.1   The marketing mix

Before approaching a selling situation, we need to know the factors
which are in the mind of the buyer. Every buying event is different, and
generalizations are dangerous. To assume that they are the same will
reduce the chance of achieving the sale.

Let us consider a purchase which we ourselves have made, such as a
personal computer (PC). It is useful to analyse the various factors which
we may have considered.

- *Product*   Which particular computer did we buy and under what brand name? Was it at the top of the range with all the 'bells and whistles', or was it a more basic version? Did we buy it for word processing, for playing games, for serious programming, or for business use? Did other aspects of the product play an important role in the decision?

- *Price*   What price did we pay for the computer? Did we buy the cheapest model? Did we buy it from the cheapest supplier? Did we ask for a discount? Did we pay cash or buy on extended terms?

- *Place*   The 'place' in the marketing mix describes the means of contact between buyer and seller. Where did we buy our PC? Was it at a specialist computer shop, a department store, a catalogue showroom or a mail order house? Were we visited by a sales representative, or did we order it by telephone or fax? Did any of these aspects of 'place' affect our buying decision?

- *Promotion*   Promotion is any form of activity which surrounds the selling operation to increase the chance of a sale. In the case of our PC, how did we know about that particular model? Had we been influenced by advertising, brochures or other material during our search? Was there any special 'point of sale display' in the shop which led us to that particular shelf? Had we been influenced by an article in a journal or a presentation at a conference? Was there any particular inducement to buy, such as a discount or the offer of free hardware, software or some other benefit? Was there a period when free credit was offered?

- *Packaging*   For some products—a dispensing package such as an aerosol, for example—the pack plays a key role in the use of the product and may cost more than the contents. However, it is useful to broaden the concept of packaging. In a piece of equipment, it might represent the layout of the controls, keyboard, knobs, switches, etc., the user interface (MMI), the ergonomics of its use and so on. In the case of a consultancy proposal, the packaging might refer to the way in which the document is presented, laid out and bound. In some situations, because it is more visible, the packaging creates more impact than the product itself. Were we influenced in our PC purchase by the packaging as interpreted above?

- *Perception*   How did we perceive the product and the 'stable' from which it came? Was the brand name a strong influence in our buying decision? Did we consider whether the supplying company would still exist in a few years' time, so that there would be no problem in obtaining hardware and software support and subsequent upgrades? Did we believe that if a product came from that particular company it must be good, or reliable, or effective? Did we perceive that the product offered good value for money?

Perception describes what goes on in the potential buyer's mind concerning the product or service and the company from which it originates. The image may be accurate, but it may also be false or based on a situation which no longer pertains. A politician, reporting on a survey, stated that it was inaccurate, prejudiced and wrong. I am sorry, but if that's what people think, that is how they will vote! If our potential customers think that our product is the best or the worst in the world, or that we are expensive, slow to deliver, bad at after-sales service and so on, whether or not their opinion is correct, they will allow these factors to influence their buying decision just as much as the product itself.

The six factors above constitute what is generally described as the 'marketing mix'. It is normally presented in terms of the first four and is known as the '4 Ps' but the other two add a useful dimension to the technique.

There is nothing special about the six factors listed, and the reader is encouraged to substitute others as appropriate. They do not have to begin with 'P'! The key question to be considered is 'what are the main factors, ranked in order, seen from the perspective of the potential buyer, which are likely to influence this particular buying decision?'

The point about the use of the word 'mix' is that the buying decision consists of a number of ingredients which can be combined in an infinite variety of ways. Just as a Christmas cake has a different mix of ingredients from a light sponge, so it is with buying decisions. It is a mistake to imagine that they are all the same.

The marketing mix can also change over a period of time. For example, in the early stages of a new product or service, the determining factors may be promotion, by which people are made aware of the product's existence, and perception in terms of the image with which the customer views our product. Without either of these, the product and price may never be considered. Later in the life cycle, the task of creating perception has largely been achieved, and particular aspects of the product may assume first place. Later still, when a number of competing products all do virtually the same thing, product differentiation is hard to maintain and price may come to the top of the list. These crucial aspects of the life cycle are discussed in more detail in Section 13.2 (see Exercise 2.1, Follow-up 2.1).

2.2   The role of price in the buying decision

A major task of marketing is to bring price lower down the ranking in the marketing mix by pushing other factors upwards. A market leader may be able to justify a premium price by promoting the special attributes of the product and everything that goes with it. If we look at our own private and business purchases, we can easily find cases where we did not buy the cheapest product on the market.

One company bidding for a multi-million-pound tender came to the conclusion that there were ten factors likely to influence the award, of which price was number seven. It is not actually possible to rank the elements of the marketing mix as precisely as this, but the company is to be applauded for realizing that six factors might be more important than price in that particular situation.

In many cases, the most important factor is not the initial cost of purchase but the 'lifetime cost of ownership', i.e. the cost of ongoing support, consumables, service, maintenance and so on. A product which is initially more expensive might actually be the better buy; the cheapest purchase might be the worst possible investment. If this is so, the argument will need to be convincingly presented.

If someone comes to our home and tries to sell us a new kitchen or double-glazing, what happens if we ask the price early in the conversation? The request is refused, because the salesperson is wanting to build a stack of value in our mind—to bring other elements in the marketing mix higher up the ranking order—before quoting a price.

We are not advocating overpricing or exploiting the customer, but we are pointing out that price is only one of many factors influencing the buying decision. In some buying decisions the lowest price normally wins. In many other cases people are prepared to pay more than the lowest price—sometimes considerably more—because they are convinced that the benefits offered to them justify the premium being asked.

The danger is that people assume that all buying decisions are the same. This is a particular pitfall in industries which are diversifying from an environment dominated by lowest-price tenders into a free-market situation. People tend to extrapolate their thinking from the first scenario to the second. The simple fact is that much of the marketplace does not think in this way. By taking a market-based approach to pricing, it may be possible to increase prices in some cases and it may be necessary to reduce them in others. Most businesses have a mix of high volume/low margin and low volume/high margin sales; the objective is to maximize the total profit.

As we shall be discussing in Chapter 6, many companies overprice or underprice their products or services. This is because they have not clearly thought through the role of price in the buying decision.

2.3   Customers buy a whole bundle of attributes

Many people make the mistake of thinking that what they are selling is restricted to the product or service itself. Clearly the product is a crucial component of the marketing mix—without it we have nothing to sell! However, if we are honest, we have to admit that in many cases the product we are offering is not particularly different from the competition. If this is so, we are not likely to succeed by trying to prove that our product is the best, and yet this is the normal instinctive reaction of most people faced with a competitive situation. In these circumstances, the product cancels out in the buying decision and other factors take precedence. The company which is better at marketing gets the order. This is very frustrating for people who have spent years developing the product, but we have to face commercial reality.

There are three main areas of influence which can override the product itself, namely:

1. Intangible factors

2. Peripheral factors

3. Personal factors

We shall consider these in turn.

Intangible factors

Most people, such as the rational thinker, the scientist and the professional, tend to believe that customers buy what they can touch and see. They find it more comfortable to talk about the product; it is tangible, they understand it, they can measure it and they can make demonstrable claims about it. Unfortunately, what customers can't see is often more important than what they can. The fact that intangibles can't be described with the same degree of precision doesn't mean that they are any the less important.

Intangible factors, in both consumer and industrial buying decisions, may include perception and image, pride of ownership, or respect for being the first in the field to own a particular product. A car says something about our personality, taste and lifestyle. Possession of a certain brand may be more highly prized than the functionality of the product. Obviously something with a well-regarded brand image is often one of the best products, but this is not always the case.

Many products and particularly services are purchased because they bring peace of mind or because a problem is solved. The product or service is not the object of the purchase, but simply the vehicle by which the peace of mind or the solution is achieved. If this is so, it is the peace of mind or the problem solving which we should be promoting, not the product itself.

In consultancy and the professions, the product is, in effect, the person providing the service. 'Personal chemistry' between the service provider and the client, for better or worse, may rank much more highly than an objective analysis of the skills being offered. Confidence is paramount, but this may be misplaced and it is certainly unquantifiable.

The need to market these intangible factors is important when we are trying to create a positive image, but it is even more so when we are trying to overcome a negative perception. A good image may take years to create, but it can be lost in one simple statement or episode and take years to rebuild (see Exercise 2.2).

Peripheral factors

Many buying decisions are made not on the basis of the product or service itself but on side-issues which are relatively trivial. In a domestic product, the layout of the control knobs may be important to some and not to others. In a high-technology product, some aspects of much lower technology may be overriding.

An American company for which I was working received a telephone call on Christmas Day asking to speak to a service engineer. The call was put through to the engineer's home where he was playing with his children. The caller then rang off. Early in the New Year, we received an order for $100 000 for a piece of equipment. The buyer explained that he was the one who had telephoned on Christmas Day asking for a service engineer. Because we had one available, he bought the product. If we analyse that situation, we could say that the product we were selling obviously passed his buying criteria but so did the products from several rival companies. The overriding factor in his mind was the availability of service at critical periods, because a problem with our product could virtually bring his operation to a halt. The highly sophisticated product which had been developed over a period of years by PhD scientists was not the determining factor; it was the availability of a less qualified service engineer.

My wife drives a certain make of car because it has a front seat whose height can easily be adjusted. Although technically trivial, this was the clinching factor in the buying decision, rather than the compression ratio, the number of valves or any of the other features which cost millions of pounds to develop.

One of the most important factors may be to know that the company is likely to be in business in five years' time so that it can support the product and provide spares.

These and many other examples show that peripheral aspects of the product can be more important to the buyer than the core product itself. Knowing how customers value these peripherals might help us to achieve a more effective use of our R&D budget; some relatively minor amendments to the product might make it much more acceptable (see Exercise 2.3).

Personal factors

Personal factors may include the way in which a salesperson relates to a potential buyer, but there is much more to it than this. The goal which we are trying to achieve by promoting personal factors is a marketeer's dream—to eliminate all competition—not only from the immediate buying decision but also for an indefinite period thereafter.

I recently received a phone call from a manager in one of the UK's leading companies. He said 'Hello Colin—Dave here—how's your diary?' We looked at mutually convenient dates and arranged a seminar. There was no written invitation to submit a competitive tender which would be judged on a certain date by a panel—the only issue was when I was available. On that occasion at least, there was no competition. Obviously we have to earn such a position in the first place and we have to nurture our customers to maintain that privileged status but, as long as we can do so, there is a high probability that we shall continue to receive their business.

There are various ways in which this personal relationship can manifest itself. These are worth deliberately cultivating.

First, we might be seen as an expert to whom the buyers turn when they have problems. They want the difficulty to be removed so that they can get on with what they are really there to do. If we can quickly get to the heart of their apparently insoluble problem, we become an indispensable ally. An important step in the process may be to help them to realize that their problem is not what they thought; if we help people to identify their real problems, we may not always be guaranteed the business of solving them but we are surely in 'pole position'.

Second, buyers might regard us as the consultant to whom they turn for advice, quite outside the context of a particular consultancy project. They need our objective view and broader experience. One way of nurturing such a relationship may be to create occasional opportunities for free consultancy. The aim is to 'keep the door open' and to maintain a positive profile even when no immediate business is apparently being offered.

Third, we can be seen as a business partner. This comes about when we have a growing relationship with our client, so that we become involved in the longer term and often confidential strategic decisions which our client is facing. Our knowledge and our privileged position form an entry barrier to competitors, and the partnership strengthens as we become more closely involved with the client's business.

The aim of these three forms of relationship is to establish such a position that we are the first and, hopefully, the only person to whom the buyer refers when the need arises. The ultimate aim is that we are regarded as if we were part of the buyers' operation, so that they turn to us as naturally as they would make an internal telephone call to a colleague (see Exercise 2.4).

2.4   The features and benefits technique and its limitations

Almost every book and every course on marketing deals with features and benefits. However, many do the technique a disservice by presenting it in an inadequate manner. We shall present the argument, discuss its limitations, and then go on to show how, properly applied, a features and benefits analysis can be one of the most powerful tools in marketing.

Let us illustrate the technique by referring to a wristwatch. We can list the features as follows:

- reliable

- has a clear face

- has a stopwatch function

- fashionable

- expensive

and so on. The argument is that all these things are *features*. Features are *what the supplier puts into* the product or service; benefits are *what the customer gets out* of it. People don't buy features, they buy *benefits*.

A useful link between features and benefits is the phrase 'which means that'. So, in our watch example;

- it is reliable, which means that we won't miss the train

- it has a clear face, which means that we don't have to put on our glasses

- it has a stopwatch function, which means that we can time our child running a race

- it is fashionable, which means that people regard us as having good taste

- it is expensive, which means that we are seen as being successful

and so on.

Note that the last two benefits are intangible and unquantifiable, but they may actually weigh more heavily with some people than the less interesting tangible benefits.

What we are doing is to move away from the product itself to the issues which are of concern to the potential customers. They don't want a watch—they want what it will *do* for them.

This involves detaching our thinking from the product we are selling and taking the trouble to find out how the buyer actually thinks. For some people, such as high technologists, professionals or inventors, this is quite a difficult task. They can be so wrapped up in the world of technology, procedures, specifications, regulations and so on that they find it hard to think beyond these things to the concerns of the customer.

The technique is normally presented as part of the selling process. Salespeople are encouraged to sell the benefits rather than the features. However, it is much more than a sales aid, which is why it is included at this stage in the book. The right time to start thinking about features and benefits is at the concept stage in the design of a new product and the development of its marketing strategy. Customer benefits can often be built into the product at this stage much more easily and cheaply than later. They may not involve the highest technological aspects of the product, but they can give it a cutting edge in the marketplace.

Benefits ultimately provide value. The more value we can create for the customer, the more profit we are likely to generate for ourselves. (In most cases the value and profit are expressible in financial terms, but this is not necessarily so; the technique could equally be applied to a non-financial situation such as road safety.)

To make best use of the features and benefits technique we should take the analysis as far as we can in the customer's direction. For example, we have said that accuracy in a watch is a feature, and not missing a train is a benefit. We could say that not missing a train is actually a more refined feature, for which not missing an interview is the benefit, and we can take this some stages further:

Feature		Benefit
	which means that	
Accuracy		Don't miss train
Don't miss train		Don't miss interview
Don't miss interview		Get new job
Get new job		Earn more money

and so on

We do not have to use the word 'benefits' in our literature or our speech, and it is not always appropriate to show a double column listing the features and benefits. The important thing is that we use the language of the customers, refer to things which are important to them, and concentrate on the benefits which derive from using our product or service rather than on the product or service itself.

We now go on to show that, if used superficially, the technique can fail completely. The reason is very simple. We cannot make an automatic link between features and benefits—it depends on the buyer and on the situation in which the product is to be used.

First, different customers want different benefits from the same product, sometimes even from the same feature. The fact that a car can do 150 mph is of no benefit whatever to an old person who wants to use it in town for shopping.

Should we then list every conceivable benefit we can imagine, in the hope that the customer will be attracted by at least some of them? The problem with this approach is that the message is diluted. The buyer may be distracted by irrelevant claims, and fail to reach the very one which would have been convincing.

Second, and even more seriously, something which is a benefit to one person may actually be a disbenefit to someone else. Consider, for example, the control system on a domestic cooker. Some will want the benefit of automatic programming so that they can come home to a meal which is ready for them after a busy day's work. Others would see the technology as an insult to their culinary skills. The same applies to industrial equipment. In a routine manufacturing environment, the last thing a manager wants is the ability to change too many controls; a simple routine operation is required which can be carried out by relatively unskilled workers. In contrast, people working in a research environment might want every conceivable variable to be under their own control.

Benefits depend critically upon the presentation. Obviously they have to be based on fact, but we could produce two messages about the same product which portrayed entirely different benefits. When we come to consider market segmentation in Chapter 4, we shall see that this is precisely the approach that is recommended.

We are beginning to make the point, which we shall develop throughout the book, that successful marketing is not like firing a blunderbuss in all directions but is more like aiming a sniper's rifle at different targets in succession with different ammunition in each case.

We are not offering an easy life to marketing staff. It is much simpler to use a standard sales pitch or produce a standard brochure than to tailor our message to the situation. However, the more trouble we take to marshal the arguments, present the benefits and, particularly, target them to the needs of a particular reader or hearer, the more successful we are likely to be (see Exercise 2.5).

2.5   Different market segments want different benefits

Let us suppose that we are selling a car. We might list all the features and their corresponding benefits, prove their validity in terms of performance tests and so on, and illustrate them lavishly with pictures.

The problem is that people buy cars for very different reasons. For some, the image is the most important, with the benefit they that they will be regarded as people of taste, successful business executives, trendsetters and so on. Others want performance, measured in terms of acceleration and top speed. Others want economy, or roominess, or safety, or reliability, or a good resale value. Some will buy a car simply because the dealer offering the service is nearest to their home.

To meet these various needs, we need to break down the marketplace into segments, try to determine what will motivate each segment, and present the benefits accordingly. This targeting of benefits obviously increases the complexity of the marketing task, but we can group customers together so that we do not have to produce one brochure per customer! In Section 4.5 we suggest a way in which a family of brochures can be produced without incurring excessive cost and effort; the same is true of advertising, sales presentations and most forms of marketing communication.

In the course of my consultancy work I frequently see literature which tries to cover so many targets that it does not hit any of them effectively. This is not a good way of spending marketing budgets (see Exercise 2.6).

2.6   Each member of a decision-making group wants different benefits

It is a mistake to think that everyone who influences the buying decision comes from the same background as the seller. Technical people tend to think quite wrongly that the key message is always a technical one. Some professionals seem to assume that the general public understands and is interested in the jargon which they use in their profession. These attitudes create a barrier between buyer and seller.

In many buying situations, the decision is made not by one person but by a number of people who constitute what is known as the decision-making group (DMG) or decision-making unit (DMU). In a business situation, the DMG will be represented by various departments, functions and job titles—technical, financial, operations, budget holders, senior management, quality and so on. In a domestic purchase such as a holiday, the father, mother, teenage children and younger children will each want very different benefits.

As with the market segments, the task is to identify the individuals and departments involved in the buying decision, decide which benefits will motivate each of them, and present the message accordingly. In a large contract involving a long-drawn-out negotiation, this might involve separate presentations to different members of the DMG.

In other cases this approach is not practicable, and one brochure, letter, proposal or tender submission will have to serve all purposes. We need to find a means of presenting the benefits differentially, by having clearly identified sections covering the issues relevant to the different members of the DMG. We can't assume that anyone will read the whole document—indeed, we don't necessarily want them to. We want each of them to be motivated by the particular key points which are most relevant to them. The fact that the message is hidden in there somewhere is not good enough—the busy reader must be able to find it quickly.

In a face-to-face presentation where all members of the DMG are present at the same time, we must again have material available for each of them and present it in the right way at the right time.

The key point about a DMG is that, in principle, any one of its members can effectively veto the buying decision. To convince all but one may result in failure.

Apart from the formal DMG, there are usually some people who have no formal authority to sign a contract but who can have a strong positive or negative influence on the decision. Users are a typical example. If they don't like what we are offering, they will make their views known and thus effectively have the power of veto. If they like it, they will say so. Nurturing the interests of these people may be an essential part of the marketing process.

The make-or-break parts of a negotiation may be carried out at various levels of seniority within the two companies concerned. The better we are at marshalling all our resources and ensuring that they present an appropriate message to each member of the DMG, the greater will be our chance of success. This is a job for marketing and management, not just for salespeople (see Exercise 2.7).

2.7 Each member of a distribution chain wants different benefits

Let us suppose we are selling domestic central heating controllers. These are microprocessor-controlled devices, which can be used to control time, temperature, different zones in the house and so on. The distribution chain may be as shown in Figure 2.1.

The wholesaler probably deals with a whole range of products. The installer may be a very competent plumber, but is not necessarily familiar

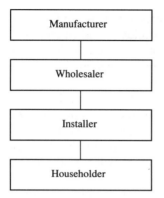

Fig. 2.1   The distribution chain

with electronics or microprocessors. The householder—the one who ultimately pays for and uses the device—is concerned with what it does rather than how it does it.

The benefits which are required will be quite different at each stage of the distribution chain. The wholesaler might be looking for quick delivery or a discount for quantity. The installer wants the benefit of a rapid trouble-free installation, and therefore needs very clear instructions and possibly a 'hot line' telephone link to sort out problems. The householder is looking for comfort, economy, the ability to preprogram the heating requirements and so on, and will want very clear 'user-friendly' instructions.

The distribution chain raises a key marketing issue. In what direction should we try to generate the movement? Should we try to 'push' our product, starting with the nearest part of the chain with whom we have the commercial contract, or should our efforts be directed to the far end in order to 'pull' the demand through? Most of the marketing effort in the fast-moving consumer goods (fmcg) area is directed at the ultimate consumer, creating a demand which comes back through the chain. There is not much point in persuading a supermarket to buy a million packets of washing powder if no-one is going to buy them.

Some readers may feel that this aspect of marketing is not relevant to them because they are not in the consumer business. They may be wrong! Consider a contractor/subcontractor relationship, or a consultant offering seminars to line managers through training departments! Are these not a form of distribution chain? What about a supplier whose components are incorporated into other equipment? This supplier may urge us to buy the products which have his or her particular brand of components inside, exactly following the principles of good classical marketing.

Wherever it is relevant, we have to find ways of targeting the benefits appropriately to each member of the distribution chain (see Exercise 2.8).

2.8 The unique selling proposition

The unique selling proposition—the 'USP'—sometimes known as the unique selling point or unique selling advantage, is both elusive and crucial. It asks 'what is unique about our product or service?' The philosophy is very simple. If we have correctly identified marketplace needs and if we uniquely meet those needs, the business will be ours. Unfortunately it is not usually as easy as this!

Grammatically speaking, a product either is unique or it is not. It cannot be fairly unique, very unique, nearly unique, or more unique than some other product. In the realities of business, however, very little is truly unique. What we are seeking to do is to differentiate our product or service from the competition. What is special about what we have to offer? Can we promote this 'USP' as a reason for buying? Can it enable us to justify a premium price?

It is important to recognize that it is a unique *selling* proposition. Uniqueness which is not valued by the purchaser is not a USP. We may have the only car in the world with square wheels; that is unique, but there is not likely to be much demand!

Some things which we regard as unique might actually have a negative connotation in the minds of customers. Claiming that we are the oldest-established company in our field might suggest that we are out of date in our technology compared with newcomers. Being the largest might imply that we are slow and bureaucratic compared with smaller operators.

It is very difficult to claim differentiation as a general practitioner (except, perhaps, on the basis of 'one-stop shopping'). If we have a broad-ranging expertise, we may need to present ourselves as offering multiple specialisms and marshalling an argument for meaningful differentiation in each.

As we have discussed in Section 2.3, differentiation can be based on intangible, peripheral and personal factors as well as on the product or service itself. Our product may be bigger, faster or more effective, but it may also make the buyer feel better, it might have a more attractive colour or it may be sold in a more friendly way than the competition.

The USP is, in a sense, the ultimate form of benefit. It needs to be targeted in the same way to different market segments, members of the DMG and links in the distribution chain. This form of differentiation is not rocket science, but it should not be despised on that account; it may make all the difference as to whether our product gets into orbit or not (see Exercise 2.9)!

2.9   The sharper cutting edge

Figure 2.2 summarizes the points made in the last five sections. It shows the way in which we can give our marketing efforts a 'sharper cutting edge'.

Marketing is about probabilities. There are no techniques which automatically give results, but thoughtful application of this approach will increase the probability of success.

The basis of the sharper cutting edge is, of course, features. Without features we have nothing to sell. They may be physical attributes as in the case of a piece of hardware, or they may be our skills and experience in the case of a service. Features are the foundation of our marketing efforts. However, used alone as they often are, they have a blunt cutting edge.

Moving up Figure 2.2, we come to 'benefits'. As we have said, these need to be targeted in three ways—to market segments, to members of the decision-making group and to members of the distribution chain. The peak of the figure, the sharpest cutting edge, is the unique selling proposition.

The more we can disentangle ourselves from the features, the better we can target our benefits to the needs of each particular customer. The better we can differentiate our offering by some form of uniqueness, the more effective will be our marketing (see Follow-up 2.2).

I am something of a rebel concerning some aspects of corporate identity programmes. The theory is that everything we do should reinforce the same identity. I used to have a colleague who said 'I have my principles, but if you don't like them I have others!' We may need to present a different identity to different market segments. For example, when it is beneficial to present ourselves as the largest international organization in the field, we should do so; in other cases, it might be much more appropriate to portray ourselves as fast-on-the-feet operators who can act independently without any bureaucracy or other constraints.

Fig. 2.2   The sharper cutting edge

2.10   Branding

If we heard that a particular car manufacturer was bringing out a new model, there are certain assumptions we would immediately make. These might concern the engineering quality, the performance, the reliability, the prestige, the price, the resale value and so on. This is because we associate certain qualities with the 'stable' from which a product comes. Marketing efforts are directed not so much at the product itself as in developing the 'personality' of the brand. This personality may be embodied in tangible factors such as 'outstanding performance' or in intangible factors such as 'makes you feel good'.

A key element of successful branding is that the particular product is positioned differently from all other products. This means that the product has come to occupy a certain position in our mind. The claim must be unique, simple to grasp and not easily confused with competitive claims, so that the product dominates that particular position.

The supplier engages in advertising and other marketing activities in order to build the personality and positioning of the brand. Branding can be embodied in the name of the product, in the name of a range of related products, or in the name of the company itself. In the case of fast-moving consumer goods or their industrial equivalent, the packaging may also be a means of communicating the brand identity, by means of its printing, its shape or both. Assuming that the claims are consistent with our experience, the message is cumulatively reinforced. It may be necessary over a period of time to modify the personality or move the positioning slightly, but this should build upon rather than conflict with the earlier claims.

A good brand image can be, literally, one of the greatest assets a company possesses. This is very relevant in an acquisition situation. If we are buying a company, the prime objective is not normally to acquire their factories, stock and other assets but to buy their market share, their customer base and their reputation which are part of their brand equity. One of the biggest mistakes an acquiring company can make is to change the name of the company! At a stroke, they may be destroying the very asset they have acquired. The value of the brand causes problems for accountants who complain that the tangible assets they are buying are worth less than the price they are being asked to pay, but this reflects reality. We can build new factories more quickly than we can build a brand identity, particularly in a worldwide marketplace. The premium which we have to pay is technically described as 'goodwill', but it encompasses far more than this rather vague accountancy term suggests (see 'Acquisition' in Section 10.2).

Market-led companies often develop a powerful brand name in one particular field and then extend its use into other quite different product areas. The common thread may be that they are appealing to the same socio-economic market segment. The fact that the new products have nothing to do with the original product is irrelevant. While the process may be a gradual one over a period of time, the ultimate result is a significant shift in the balance of the company's operation. Other companies may need to follow this example (see Exercise 2.10).

2.11   Marketing intangible services

It has been made clear from the start of this book that the basic principles of marketing apply equally to tangible hardware products and to intangible services. The reader has been encouraged to regard a service as a 'product'. Nevertheless, there are certain problems and tactics which are specifically associated with the marketing of services. There are also some advantages in marketing a service, and hardware companies might find an appropriate range of services a useful adjunct to their product portfolio.

If we are marketing a physical product, such as a video recorder or a car, we can demonstrate it, give the potential customer an opportunity to try it out, and, if appropriate, lend it for a period of time. With services such as consultancy, professional services, dedicated software and so on, none of these methods of convincing the customer is available. The 'product' doesn't even exist until we have performed the service. How do we overcome this? We shall consider several aspects.

Intangibility

The key point about a service is that it is intangible. Derived from the Latin, the word means 'cannot be touched'. In practice, the problem goes much further than this. The product cannot easily be judged or compared with other alternative offerings. Its performance cannot be measured. It cannot offer the comfort which a buyer can have if the product can be seen and tried out before purchase.

Somehow we have to generate a package of evidence which acts in the same way as the tangible aspects of a piece of hardware. The best way of doing this will depend upon the nature of the business, and confidentiality may have to be considered. Lists of current and former clients may be compiled, but it may not be appropriate to 'tout these around'.

Clients may be willing to write testimonial letters. In asking for these letters, we may have to promise some limitations on their use. A reasonable approach, which clients rarely reject, is to ask permission to show the letters to non-competing potential clients in a face-to-face situation, but to undertake not to use them for advertising or to send out copies unsolicited. It may be possible to describe a number of case studies of relevant past projects; we may or may not be able to use the name of the clients concerned.

It is very helpful if we can quote reference sites where a potential customer can contact a previous purchaser and, possibly, even visit the site in order to see the service at work. Some customers are very pleased, within reason, to show and talk about what they have; in other cases, confidentiality may preclude this. The privilege must not be abused, and reference sites should be used very selectively otherwise the goodwill may be destroyed.

Establishing a relevant track record is crucial to the marketing of intangible services. This aspect of marketing is developed in Section 4.8.

Uncertainty about the reputation of the service provider

Compared with fast-moving products, the number of customers and the frequency of purchase may be so low that a high profile in the marketplace is very difficult to establish. The potential client may not even have heard of the service provider, and finds it difficult to form a reliable and objective view of his or her calibre.

Effective ways of raising our profile include writing 'learned papers' in the appropriate journals, submitting interesting articles to the press, presenting papers at conferences, running educational seminars and so on. Although these activities are time consuming, they can be at least as effective as other ways of spending the marketing budget. To avoid undermining their authority and credibility, they should be deliberately divorced from a selling environment. We can, however, make use of them after the event, for example by sending out reprints of articles to a database of existing and potential clients.

Matching demands with resources

Any business has this problem, as customers do not place orders at a uniform rate exactly when we would like them to! The difference is that, with a physical product, we can build for stock if demand is low or offer delayed delivery times if demand is high.

A consultant cannot be in two places at once. An empty seat on a seminar cannot be occupied by two people next time. Specialist software cannot be written 'for stock'. The operation has to be performed with the resources which are available when the client wants it. One director of a major engineering consultancy firm lamented 'We always have fifty too many or fifty too few consultants'.

While it may never be possible to remove this problem completely, a helpful step might be to develop a portfolio of services, some large and some small. In general, the larger the project, the longer the lead time involved in negotiating for it. Conversely, it may be possible to obtain some small consultancy contracts relatively rapidly to fill in the 'profit gaps'. Although the value of these projects may not be large, the percentage margin may be much greater than in a large contract which generates intense competition as every supplier desperately tries to get the business, and they may represent a useful stepping-stone towards larger contracts later.

Pricing

With a tangible product, such as a piece of domestic or industrial equipment, we can have a reasonable idea of the price—within, say, 20 per cent—by looking at it and comparing it with competing products. With an intangible service, unless we have had considerable prior expertise in the particular area, we might be uncertain of the price by a very large percentage, possibly even a factor of two or three. Does the non-specialist have any idea what is the 'right' price to pay for legal advice, for registering a patent in Germany, for auditing accounts or for help with writing a business plan?

The absence of an obvious price reference for a service is not necessarily a disadvantage. We should not take advantage of the client's ignorance, but we do have the opportunity to create real perceived value and to price accordingly.

Rapid response, flexibility and low risk

Those who have worked with physical products are all too aware of the long lead times involved in the conception and development of new products. When the specification is finally agreed, we are faced with a long period of agony before we know whether or not the product is going to be commercially successful. There is a high risk and a high penalty for failure.

Intangible services gain in all of these respects. A 'new' product can be developed in a matter of days, amendments can be made at the touch of a keyboard, and the time from conception to launch can be a matter of weeks. It is important that those involved with the marketing of services exploit these enviable advantages to the full.

A profitable route for business development for companies in the tangible product field may be to add a range of services to the portfolio. For example, those who have developed expertise in modern manufacturing technologies could offer consultancy and training in these technologies (preferably to non-competing companies!). In this way they might generate gross and net margins which make their manufacturing operation seem rather unexciting by comparison (see Exercise 2.11).

Conclusion

To summarize, the principles of marketing, properly applied, are absolutely relevant to consultancy, professional and other services. In one sense they may be even more essential, because there is no tangible product which can draw attention to itself.

Exercises

2.1 Choose two different products or services sold by your company, and rank in order the three elements of the marketing mix which you think are most important in the purchasing decision. Note the ways in which the ranking differs in the two cases. How would you exploit the first on the list? (For example, if you think that perception is top of the list, what specific actions could you take to improve perception?)

2.2 Make a list of the intangible factors which influence the buying decision for your products or services. How could you make use of these?

2.3 Make a list of the peripheral factors which influence the buying decision for your products or services. How could you make use of these?

2.4 Make a list of the personal factors which influence the buying decision for your products or services. How could you make use of these?

2.5 Choose one of the company's products or services, and list the features and the corresponding benefits, using the link 'which means that. . .'. Ask yourself if some of the benefits you have listed could be described as more refined features, and apply the process again to take them as far as possible in the customer's direction.

2.6 List the market segments into which one of your products might be sold. How would you market differently to each segment (and see Exercises 4.2 to 4.5)?

2.7 Choose a sales situation and list the members of the decision-making group. Note the ways in which you would market differently to each member of the group. List the people who cannot make a purchasing decision but who could have a negative or positive influence.

2.8   Choose a sales situation and list the members of the distribution chain. Note the ways in which you would market differently to each member of the chain.

2.9   Sit down with a colleague, or a number of pairs of colleagues, and explain the concept of the unique selling proposition. Ask one member of each pair to try to convince the other that there is a USP in what they are selling in their business life; the other should do everything possible to destroy the claim. Reverse roles. Ask each person to say whether, when they were on the receiving end, they accept that their partner succeeded in demonstrating a USP.

2.10 What are the key components of the brand equity of your product or service? Are you exploiting the personality and positioning of the brands to full advantage? What further steps could you take? Could you use the brand as a vehicle for other activities?

2.11 If you currently market any services, what steps can you take to make the 'product' appear more tangible so that a potential client would be in a better position to assess its value? Are you sure that the services are being priced correctly (and see Exercises 6.7 and 6.8)? Think of some additional services which you could market to complement your present portfolio.

Follow-up

2.1   For the next three months, keep a record of typical buying decisions which you make in your business and private life (including those where you decided not to buy). Note the factors which most strongly influenced the decision. If you did not buy, was there anything the seller could have done which would have made a difference?

2.2   For the next three months, keep a record of selling situations in which you participate. Note against each where you think they ranked in Figure 2.2.

2.3   Read a book on competition, such as Porter, M. E. (1985) *Competitive Advantage*, The Free Press, New York.

What is involved in becoming market-led?

Setting our sights high

Key business issues	*Section*
■ A local, inward-looking, sales-led or financially led emphasis is a very inadequate substitute for being market-led.	3.1
■ We should be market-driving as well as market-driven.	
■ Becoming market-led involves significant culture changes.	3.2
■ We can be reactive and complacent, beginning to worry, limited by attitudes and systems, unwilling to make the commitment, panicking; or we can be truly market-led.	
■ A strong marketing function interfacing synergistically with other equally strong functions can transform a company and be a powerhouse for business development.	3.3
■ Those who have experienced this synergy would never settle for anything less; those who have not experienced it have never really understood marketing.	
■ Targets and resources need to be compatible.	3.4
■ Technical staff working to long time scales often have to interface with marketing and financial staff working to much shorter time scales. This can lead to confused decision making.	3.5

3.1 The development of the market-led philosophy

It is helpful to consider how modern marketing thinking has evolved. This will enable us to see where our company stands, and whether any changes need to be made. Deeply rooted attitude and cultural issues may be involved at the highest level. Middle managers cannot make progress if they are inhibited by the conservative attitudes of their senior managers.

A local operation

The simplest case is exemplified by a village bakery. They make things and people buy them. Customers come to them—they do not have to go out to the customers. Customers buy every day, and it is obvious if one of them has stopped buying. They talk face to face, and there is no need for all the complexity of modern marketing communications—literature, advertising, exhibitions, public relations and so on.

Innovation for our locally orientated bakery is simple, rapid and virtually risk-free. They make a few new cakes or loaves and display them on the counter. Within a few hours they know the level of the initial interest, and within a week or two they will have some idea of the potential for repeat sales. This contrasts with the intensely complicated process of new product development today, often involving massive investment and high risk.

With these enormous advantages, a local emphasis would appear to be very attractive. However, it also has corresponding problems which can be serious enough to kill a business.

First, locally-led marketeers are at the mercy of external forces which are outside their control. The population of the village may be declining, growing old, or moving away to the city. This problem is experienced by companies and even whole industries such as defence, nuclear and space, where demand is declining for reasons outside their context. Second, a new competitor may set up in opposition, so that the sales potential is reduced.

The problem of a local emphasis is well known to professionals such as solicitors and accountants. In the old days, they had their local client base which kept them busy and financially rewarded. Now, many of them are having to market their services proactively and even aggressively.

Another variant of a local emphasis is seen in operations which only sell in the UK. While this may offer enough potential for some companies, many are finding increasingly that they have to address at least part of the international market. The implications of this are considered in detail in Chapter 10.

An inward-looking operation

Looking inwards is particularly prevalent in areas where a high degree of expertise and experience is involved. The problem is that the expertise and experience dominate our thinking to such an extent that it becomes very difficult to give due weight to the needs of the external marketplace.

With increasing mechanization and the ability to manufacture in volume, a whole set of management skills has been built round the manufacturing operation. This can involve massive investment in capital equipment and systems, with the result that the factory tends to become the focus of senior management attention. The objective is to keep down unit costs by filling the factory's available production capacity. Telltale signs include the language which people use—describing the factory as a 'profit centre', for example. This is not in any way to denigrate the manufacturing process which is obviously essential when physical goods are being marketed, but to make the point that simply increasing the volume of output without establishing a market demand is a pointless and very costly exercise. An inward-looking emphasis on meeting our own needs is destined to fail if these do not coincide with the needs of the external market.

There is an exact parallel in cases where no physical product is involved. Management consultants, professionals of all types and many other practitioners can fall into the same trap. The instinct is to concentrate on 'what we do' rather than 'what they want'.

In both cases, the main emphasis of brochures, advertisements, tender submissions, proposals and other forms of communication is usually on telling the readers about ourselves, our resources and our past history. There is little identification with the customers' needs, and the readers find it difficult to relate the message to their own business.

These inward-looking attitudes can actually be encouraged by our education and training if they are not broadly based. The scientist is urged to search for technical excellence. The technologist grows up in a world of specifications and functionalities. The professional is taught to master the skills and procedures of the profession. In many cases, technical and professional education are only just beginning to put vocational skills into the broader business context. Whether we like it or not, the simple fact is that many orders go to suppliers who take the most trouble to identify with the customer, even if an objective analysis might show their product was in some way 'inferior'.

A sales-led operation

If we have a warehouse full of products, or a team of consultants without fee-earning projects, the instinct is to go out and sell. The battle-cry is 'sell, sell, sell'. What is wrong with that? Surely it is the right thing to do?

The problem with the sales orientation is that it assumes that we are selling the right product to the right people at the right price with the right claims, which may not be the case. I am reminded of the politician who, knowing that a forthcoming speech had a weak point, wrote in the margin 'argument weak—shout louder!'.

It is significant that the subject of selling is not addressed in detail until Chapter 8 of this book. The broader marketing and business issues which we are now considering are an essential prerequisite to a successful selling operation.

A sales-led environment can be very frustrating for managers who have a mature understanding of marketing. Harder selling and more aggressive negotiation are not the answer to every problem. Taking time to stop and think may make those selling and negotiating efforts much more productive.

A financially led operation

We have already stressed that marketing is a very financially oriented discipline. One of the key objectives of most operations is to remain financially sound—to make profit, to control costs, to increase the value of the company's equity and so on. These facts have important implications for the way in which business decisions are made. They will indicate the influence which financial management should have on strategic and tactical decisions.

Nevertheless, these financial objectives cannot be met if they are not consistent with marketing objectives. The customer does not owe us a living. We can control our costs down to a penny, and still fail utterly because we have not been able to generate income from the marketplace.

This is not to suggest that marketing departments should be free to violate budgetary control or to be casual about the way in which they spend company money. If anything, marketing managers should be *more* conscientious about financial matters than the financial departments themselves; in most organizations, marketing is spending the money while the financial departments are merely recording and commenting on where it is being spent. Marketing management needs to be intimately concerned with crucial issues such as investment, pricing, profit, cash flow and risk—they are central to the philosophy of marketing.

A market-led operation

This may also be referred to as being marketing-led, consumer-led or customer-led. The dominating emphasis is on the needs of the market-place. The first questions we ask are 'what are those needs?' and 'which of them are we going to meet?'. We then ask 'what are the implications for our organization?' Until we have answered these questions, we are not in a position to start manufacturing or building up expertise, or to start selling. We have to correlate the needs of the marketplace with the priority and the resources which we are willing to commit to meeting those needs.

Being market-led is really the subject of this whole book. It has far-reaching implications for our organization, attitudes, culture, salary scales, management style, recruitment—indeed for almost every aspect of our business. Ultimately it may be the biggest single factor affecting our profitability (see Exercise 3.1).

This leads us to a paradox. We should be market-led, and yet at the same time we should in some senses be market-leading or market-driving. Marketing is making the future happen. Although we depend crucially on our customers to enable us to do that, we cannot leave the initiatives to them. Considering the implications of this paradox for our particular operation can be very enlightening, and can help us to set the right balance for our attitudes and culture (see Follow-up 3.1).

3.2   Culture changes involved in becoming market-led

There are some common stages which companies may go through in the process of becoming market-led. The notes which follow are all based on my combined observation of a large number of companies; no reference to a particular organization is intended.

Reactive and complacent

Buyers come to the seller, and the seller's resources are completely utilized—they don't really need any more business. This is fine as long as the demand is sustained and the competitors do nothing to undermine the position. Unfortunately, with such a self-satisfied attitude, many operations have declined into an ongoing struggle for survival and some have failed altogether.

This reactive approach has been common in some professional practices. Accountants, solicitors, patent agents and others have histori-cally built their business through reputation and personal contacts. They have been brought up to feel (and the code of conduct of some professions actually encourages this feeling) that soliciting business conflicts with the dignity of their profession. The desire to avoid a situation where professionals spend all their time 'poaching' each other's clients is understandable, but these fears about marketing are based on a misconception. Some highly ethical and professional operations have to solicit all their business, but they would insist that they do so in an entirely professional and dignified manner. We would not market a management consultancy, for example, in the same way as double-glazing or time-share.

A similar situation arises with the privatization of nationalized industries or the move towards agency status of former government and ministry operations. It is also happening in the normal industrial world where, for example, a scientific research unit is being told that it can no longer rely on the parent company for all its work; the parent is free to go outside, and the research unit is required to generate new business in the competitive free market. In cases such as this, attitudes towards marketing are having to change; it is no longer sufficient to sit back and wait reactively for internal clients to approach them.

As we have said (Section 1.10), much of marketing is aimed at increasing the total size of the market. If a large number of people are not making wills, taking out patents, going to the dentist, seeking financial advice and so on, what is wrong with promoting the idea that they should? Those who assume that marketing only involves fighting our competitors reveal an inadequate view of marketing. If the total market size can be increased there is more for everyone—or rather for those who have the vision and initiative to create this new business.

Some people say that 'marketing does not work in our business'. Inadequate, inappropriate or inept marketing does not work in any business. We have to decide which particular form of marketing is right for us.

Reactive and beginning to worry

People in this group are becoming genuinely worried by the fact that demand for their product or service has dropped off. They tend to blame outside forces such as the economy, the government or legislation.

Rather than investing in marketing, the instinctive reaction of many people in this category is to cut costs. Of course there are times when cost cutting is appropriate, but there is a danger that we merely slow the downward spiral without addressing the real problem. Paradoxically, the better solution might be to spend *more* money, wisely and in acceptable quantities, to break the vicious spiral by *creating* new business opportunities.

Wanting to be proactive, but limited by attitudes and systems

There is a real conflict in the minds of people in this group. They want to expand their business and know that this will involve some extra effort and expenditure, but internal 'rules and attitudes' prevent them from doing so. We have already referred (Section 1.1) to the objection that 'marketing is a debit against profit'.

Companies in this category usually have no staff who are dedicated full-time to marketing activities. This is typical of consultancies offering management, engineering, design, scientific research, financial and other services. Virtually every member of the operation above a certain level is there to generate fees. Someone once asked me 'are you really suggesting that I should take people off fee-earning in order to do marketing?' as if I were crazy. Someone has to do it!

Managers with negative attitudes have a lot to answer for in these situations, as the following examples show:

1. Some companies, which are dominated by 'bean-counters', insist that any expenditure aimed at generating new business is booked against

an existing project. Who is trying to kid whom?! This exercise is not only pointless but also highly deceptive.

2. Statements are made such as 'we are not allowed to cross-subsidize different activities'. This really is the tail wagging the dog. The marketplace and the competition are not interested in how we do our accounting. While we are playing internal games, the competitors are laughing all the way to their order books.

3. Some companies insist that 'all contracts must make a profit, even the first in a new area'. At first sight this seems to be a very reasonable philosophy, but it represents a major trap for those trying to diversify from their traditional areas. A company might see opportunities for supplementing its defence business with the equivalent in the civil marketplace. However, the learning curve, the efforts needed to understand the requirements of this new marketplace, and the expense involved in making contact with potential customers will almost certainly cost more than the profit on the first few contracts achieved in this area, quite apart from any technical development expenditure involved. Once we have built this bridge the business may be highly profitable, but companies which are not prepared to take the long-term view will never find out!

It is pointless for managers to hide behind internal rules which they themselves have set. There are enough problems caused by the competition and the customers—we don't need further problems of our own making!

Another very understandable attitude is that staff joined the company in order to employ their particular skills, as scientists, professionals, specialists in manufacturing, finance, quality or whatever. They didn't expect to be involved in marketing and don't welcome the opportunity. The simple fact is that either they must do it or someone else must be brought in who will do it for them. Goods and services do not market themselves, particularly when times are difficult.

Wanting to be proactive but unwilling to make the commitment

People in this category know that proactive marketing efforts have to be made, but they try to do it without incurring the cost. One company decided that staff at a certain level should spend 20 per cent of their time doing marketing. The great merit of this decision was that the salaries were already accounted for. Somehow this one day a week was miraculously going to appear. On reviewing the situation six months later, however, it was clear that the actual time spent on marketing had fallen far short of this figure. No-one had made the difficult decision that certain activities had to be dropped or delegated or delayed, or that some means should be found of creating the time required for marketing. They had started very enthusiastically, but events rapidly overtook them. The art of management is the ability to control such situations!

Another problem in this category is that 'our salary scales will not allow us to recruit marketing heavyweights'. They either transfer staff without the necessary calibre and experience from other departments or they set their sights far too low when they recruit. The result is that their marketing is ineffective, and can even become a drain on profit instead of the means of creating profit. Again we have to ask 'who sets the salary scales and makes the rules? What are we trying to achieve?'

Marketing initiative sometimes comes from middle management but is not supported by senior management. The initiative is soon stifled. The essence of becoming a market-led organization is that change must start at the top. It is not reasonable to expect middle managers to do things which can change the whole strategic direction of the company without first agreeing with them the objectives, the strategy, the tactics, and the resources which will be made available (see Follow-up 3.2).

Proactive, panicking

Some senior managers, because they have read a book or been on a marketing course, suddenly go overboard. They allocate budgets, and recruit or appoint more marketing staff than their business can support at that time. Investment in marketing should be a planned, sustained and very carefully managed activity, appropriate to the marketplace and commensurate with the legitimate growth aspirations of the operation.

Market-led

Some industries, such as those in the fast-moving consumer goods area, have been market-led for a long time. The most senior managers are absolutely committed to the marketing philosophy, and they generate a climate within their company where marketing professionalism is encouraged and indeed demanded. They spend significant amounts of money on marketing, because they know that this is the only way they can generate profit and growth. They set their sights high when recruiting, appointing or promoting marketing staff, realizing that investing in mediocre staff is the worst of all worlds.

Successful companies realize that marketing is not something which takes place only in the marketing department. All senior and middle managers are trained in and committed to the marketing philosophy and are able to play their part in the overall marketing process.

Another characteristic of a market-led organization is that their forward business plans are coherent and consistent. They know that they have to make an investment before they can expect a return. They have done the arithmetic, described in Section 3.4, which shows how they will achieve a certain level of growth. If necessary, cultures and attitudes are changed and restrictive systems are abolished. Strategic business decisions are based on marketplace considerations rather than on the internal needs of the company.

As a result of professional marketing, such companies are often able to command premium prices and pay above-average salaries. They delegate profit responsibility to capable middle managers, demand results, and reward accordingly.

Such an environment is extremely stimulating and fulfilling. Of course there are problems and frustrations in any business, but at least the directors and managers in this group are doing the things which are most likely to lead to success, and are avoiding the self-imposed pitfalls of many of the other categories.

Culture change as a cause of stress

Changing the culture of a company can have far-reaching implications at all levels and in all disciplines. It can release creative energy, but it can also cause stress within the management team. Senior managers who lack marketing vision can stifle the efforts of middle managers and lead to immense frustration.

Readers are urged to consider the progression described above, see where they and their company stand in this respect, and decide what they need to do to become more market-led. In doing so, they must anticipate the disruption which is likely to be caused throughout the organization. They need to carry their colleagues and their staff with them, so that everyone understands what is happening and why, and what is required of each of them to make it work. The rapid growth in seminars on marketing is an indication of the need for non-marketing staff to be involved in the marketing process (see Exercise 3.2).

3.3   The benefits of a strong marketing function

Most senior managers are convinced that they need highly professional staff in functions such as manufacturing, research and development, finance, quality, personnel and so on. For some strange reason they do not seem to insist on the same calibre of staff in the marketing department! They transfer people from other parts of the business without any training, or they ask a relatively junior person to deal with brochures, and think that they have set up a marketing department! This low view of marketing professionalism affects not only the marketing function—it can have equally serious consequences in other parts of the

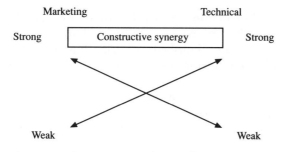

Fig. 3.1   The strong/weak interface

company. Let us assume for simplicity that everyone is either strong or weak, and that we are looking particularly at the interface between the technical and marketing functions. An example would be a new product development manager who needs a clear marketing specification—a 'user requirement'—before development of a product can commence. This can best be illustrated by a simple diagram as in Figure 3.1.

Four scenarios are possible:

1. *Weak marketing interfacing with weak technical*   This is obviously not worth considering.

2. *Weak marketing interfacing with strong technical*   This is a very common situation. It occurs in companies which have historically been technically successful but have not fully appreciated the role of marketing in the future development of their business. They have armies of highly qualified engineers, scientists, research workers, technicians and so on but have not had the vision to match these with marketing staff of comparable calibre. It is much easier in such a company to gain approval for the recruitment of a technical person than the marketing equivalent.

    The result is very frustrating. Mature technical staff know that their objective is to generate commercially successful projects rather than to design 'better mousetraps' which have the only merit that they are technically 'interesting'. They know that they should not start a new development project until marketing have given an authoritative user requirement specification on which they can base their own technical specification, but they fail to receive it. In its absence, they do their best to make up their own, but they do not have a sufficient understanding of marketplace needs. The only way to find out about customers is to live in their world, not in the R&D department.

3. *Weak technical interfacing with strong marketing*   This would be equally ineffective, but it rarely occurs. This would mean that the company knew what was wanted but could not deliver it.

4. *Strong marketing interfacing with strong technical*   This should be the aim of every company which is seeking to be market-led. A strong marketing function interfacing with other equally strong functions can transform a company and be a powerhouse for business development. Experience shows that this interface provides a very effective collaborative relationship, and is one of the prime characteristics of an organization which is good at market-based innovation. Good marketing and good technical staff have a lot in common—they are intelligent, articulate, and are not hidebound by bureaucratic attitudes—and they can work together very productively. This does not mean that it is 'all one happy family'—marketing and technical professionals may well have deep and protracted arguments—but the result is highly beneficial. The conflict is synergistic and creative, not destructive. Of course there should be an ongoing dialogue between the two functions, and I would expect technical staff to challenge marketing proposals very intelligently and vigorously, but that is not the same as doing their job for them.

The problem is that many senior managers have never met this situation. Those who have would never be satisfied with anything less. Those who have not experienced it have never really understood marketing (see Exercise 3.3).

3.4   Compatibility of targets and resources

One of the signs of marketing maturity is that the resources allocated to achieving the company's turnover and profit targets are compatible with those targets. The number and calibre of staff, and the budgets which they manage, are at the right level for achieving the desired results.

This sounds obvious, but in my experience as a consultant I often find situations where this is not the case. Managers put up proposals for a certain level of growth, but either do not provide or are not allowed to provide the corresponding marketing resources. This creates a 'time-bomb' situation and one has to ask 'who is trying to kid whom?' The following simple example, and the corresponding exercise at the end of the chapter, will enable readers to check this point for their own situation. We define:

T = target annual sales
A = average order value
X = conversion ratio orders/bids (%)
Y = conversion ratio bids/prospects (%)
V = value of possible business to be found
N = number of prospects to be found
$H1$ = person-hours to handle a prospect for which we do not bid
$H2$ = person-hours to handle a prospect for which we do bid

Let us suppose that we have:

Target annual sales	T =	£10 000 000
Average order value	A =	£500 000

We now ask what proportion of orders we expect to achieve from our bids. Let us assume that this is one in four:

conversion ratio orders/bids (%) X = 25%

Do we bid for every possible prospect we locate? Of course not. There are some we do not want or are not capable of fulfilling, and there are some where we feel that the competition is too intense. Assume that we bid for half of all the possible prospects:

conversion ratio bids/prospects (%) Y = 50%

This enables us to calculate the value of the possible business which we have to find:

$$V = T \times 100/X \times 100/Y$$

which in our example is

$$£10\,000\,000 \times 100/25 \times 100/50 = £80\,000\,000$$

In other words, we have to locate business to the value of £80 million, of which we will submit bids for £40 million and expect to be awarded the £10 million in our business plan.

Using the average order size, the number of prospects we have to find is

$$N = V/A$$

which in our example is 80 000 000/500 000 = 160.

Let us suppose that it takes an average of 24 person-hours to handle a prospect for which we do not bid and 120 when we do bid. The total time required is

$$H1 \times N \times (100 - Y)/100 \text{ for the no-bid cases}$$

which, in our example, is 1920 person-hours:

$$H2 \times N \times Y/100 \text{ for the bid cases}$$

which, in our example, is 9600 person-hours, giving a total of 11 520 person-hours.

Assuming 1600 person-hours per year per full-time equivalent person, we require 11 520/1600 = 7.2 full-time equivalent people to be devoted exclusively to this task. We have used the expression 'full-time equivalent people' because they may have other responsibilities. If they can only devote 60 per cent of their time to gaining business, we will require 7.2/ 0.6 = 12 people.

This is desperately simple arithmetic, but I have to say that a number of people I meet do not seem to have thought through the implications of their plans even in this basic way. Senior managers demand the results but will not allow the resources. I have also met the situation where managers are instructed 'from above' to increase their sales forecasts but are not allowed to increase their resources. In fact, if the targets and resources were compatible in the first place, a certain percentage increase in sales may require a disproportionately higher increase in resources— the incremental sales will presumably be harder to obtain. Obviously it is a good management discipline to impose stretching targets, but if they defy logic and are unachievable the result is demotivation not motivation. I repeat—'who is trying to kid whom?!'

Readers are urged in the strongest terms to see whether their targets and resources are compatible (see Exercise 3.4).

3.5 Time scales

A research scientist in one of the country's leading high-technology companies raised a very important issue on one of my seminars. She said 'The problem is that I am working to a ten-year time scale but I have to sell my ideas to accountants who are working to a one-year time scale.' This dilemma is perfectly understandable and is, ultimately, a failure of senior management.

Table 3.1, although not precise, indicates the time scales over which various members operate in three departments—technical, marketing and financial. The point which stands out from the table is that there is often no-one on the marketing or financial side working to the same time scale as long-term technical staff. Why not? Should there be? How can the right business decisions be made in their absence?

It will be argued by some that these roles are played by the board, and particularly the chief executive. While they undoubtedly have this role, it can only work if they have a good understanding of long-term market-place needs and trends. It is accepted that the market does not usually know what it wants over these time scales, but this does not absolve us from trying to get into their minds and discern what would be of value to them if we could provide it.

Table 3.1   Time scales

Time scale (years)	Technical	Marketing	Financial
0 to 1	Service support	Selling tactics	Accounting
1 to 3	Development	Product management strategy	Financial director
3 to 10	Research	?	?

We argue in Chapter 12 that the marketing cost of developing and launching a new product often exceeds the technical cost, and that more products fail for marketing than for technical reasons. If this is so, money spent on making better marketing decisions at the concept stage must be an essential investment.

If anyone needs convincing that there is an imbalance in their own company, it would be useful to write down the number of staff employed in each of the nine areas defined in Table 3.1. While not suggesting that the numbers should be equal across the functions for a particular time scale, we must ask whether is it right to have large numbers engaged in R&D with, sometimes, virtually no representation in marketing and the business development area of finance. Some people seem to think that people engaged in R&D are creating wealth while the others are dissipating it. This attitude is based on an unbalanced view of business, but unfortunately it is common (see Exercise 3.5).

Exercises

3.1   Which description in Section 3.1 most accurately describes your organization? If you were the chief executive, what steps would you take to move to a market-led operation?

3.2   Which description in Section 3.2 most accurately describes your organization? What culture changes need to be introduced? What would be the effect of these changes in terms of people, organization and investment? What training is required?

3.3   Consider the 'strong/weak' interface diagram (Figure 3.1). Which scenario most accurately describes your organization? Have you ever experienced the 'strong/strong' scenario? What steps need to be taken to move towards it?

3.4 Insert your own figures into the 'compatibility' calculation in Section 3.4. Are your targets and resources compatible? If not, what needs to be done about it?

3.5 Does your organization have the correct balance between a long- and a short-term focus? If not, do you need different attitudes, different people, more people, a different organization or what?

Follow-up

3.1 For the next three months, make a note of the main decisions which occupy your time. Against each, note the degree to which each of these decisions was considered on a market-led basis (e.g. by awarding marks out of 10).

3.2 For the next three months, keep a record of the amount of time you spend dealing with customer issues compared with company issues. Do you think you are spending enough time on customer issues? How can you release more time for the customer (e.g. by abolishing some tasks, meetings or reports, delegating some tasks to others, appointing more junior staff who can save time for senior people, etc.)?

To whom are we selling?

Market definition, segmentation and targeting

Key business issues   *Section*

- The definition of the business in which we are engaged is not a   4.1
  theoretical exercise but an essential basis for business strategy.

- Historic success does not guarantee that we have a future at all, let
  alone a profitable one.

- The business definition may have to change with time.

- Marketing is making the future happen.

- Customers are not all the same, but they are not all different   4.2
  either. Market segmentation defines the common factors which
  link customer groups within each particular segment.

- Segmentation is often defined by industry group, but this
  may not be the most useful basis.

- Multi-factor or sequential segmentation may be necessary.

- A number of different segmentation criteria may need to be used.   4.3

- Some key strategic decisions arise from market segmentation.   4.4

- Some key marketing actions arise from market segmentation.   4.5

- A key to business success is to target our marketing activities.   4.6

- Niche markets can have considerable strategic significance.   4.7

- Companies which are most successful at entering new markets   4.8
  are those which take the trouble to create credibility and track
  record.

4.1   What business are we in?

Definition of our business

Much time and paper is expended on internal documents defining business mission and related issues. However, these are often theoretical exercises performed mainly by specialists in staff functions, and they do not have the impact on line management decision making which they should.

The only point in engaging in such exercises, which take us away from the task of earning money for the company, is to assist the process of planning the strategic and tactical future of the business. An example of this type of exercise is the question 'what business are we in?' In marketing terms, the issue is absolutely crucial.

The 'right' and the 'wrong' definition

If we had said a few years ago that we were in the typewriter business, the prognosis would have been disastrous. If, on the other hand, we had said that we were in the word-processing business, we would have latched onto one of the fastest growth opportunities of the decade.

Similarly, mechanical watches have virtually disappeared whereas the sales of quartz and other versions have soared. Successful milkmen sell far more than milk. Petrol stations sell far more than petrol, and building societies deal with far more than buildings.

We only have to look at the companies involved in marketplaces undergoing similar changes to see how they have answered the question. Some have grasped the opportunity with enthusiasm. Others, for whatever reason, appear to have rejected it (although one wonders whether some of them have even addressed the issue).

This need for change is particularly relevant to high technology and fashion (interpreted broadly), where the rate of progress is so rapid and life cycles are becoming so much shorter that companies are constantly having to adjust their focus. The prizes go to those who recognize this fact and react accordingly. Failure comes to those who act as though it will not happen.

Historic success does not ensure that we have a future at all, let alone a profitable one. We might find ourselves appealing to a declining minority of customers. The world does not owe us a living.

The scope of our business

Apart from the actual definition of the business in which we are engaged, a clear statement about the *scope* of our business activities is also important. This is particularly so when we are faced with a changing business environment.

If we define our business too narrowly, we are restricting ourselves and excluding profitable growth opportunities as they arise. Our historic core business may decline, leaving us with an operation which is a shadow of its former self or which even collapses altogether. If we say we are in the cinema business, for example, we close the door to the exploding growth opportunities in the whole of the leisure industry. If we say we are only supplying the railway business, we exclude the other faster-growing forms of transportation. The relevance of this issue is discussed in Section 4.8.

Faced with changing circumstances, some companies go to the other extreme; they define their business mission so broadly that it does not help them to decide whether or not to engage in a certain activity. I regularly ask my seminar delegates what business they think they are in. I sometimes get an answer such as 'solving technical problems'. Do they really want to repair a car or a nuclear reactor, and do they have the appropriate resources?!

Reacting to change

In extreme examples of a changing business environment, the whole basis of our historic business may have virtually ceased to exist and drastic restructuring has to take place. Business development of this type is discussed in Chapter 13.

In more normal circumstances, when future trends have been identified well in advance, the art of ongoing business definition is to select areas adjacent to the existing business in such a way that they represent an evolution rather than a revolution. We can then proceed step by step, increasing our understanding of the related marketplaces, gradually building a track record, and using this new ground as a stepping-stone for yet further expansion. In this way the rate of growth is controlled, the attention of management is not diverted excessively away from the existing business, and any necessary changes in organization or in the quality and quantity of key skills can be managed. If the historic business ultimately disappears completely, the business is still viable and is in a position to exploit the new opportunities.

By taking this approach, management is able to remain in control of the situation. It is no use sitting back and bewailing a drop in orders as many companies do when confronted with changes in technology, market demand, political or economic factors and so on. The task is to make wise and timely decisions about the things which *are* within our control. As we have said, 'marketing is making the future happen' (see Exercise 4.1).

4.2 Market segmentation

The previous chapters of this book have emphasized the need to target our marketing efforts. The reader has been urged to think of marketing as using a sniper's rifle rather than a blunderbuss. The problem with this

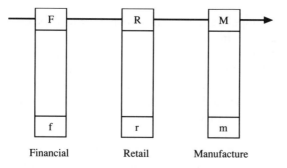

Fig. 4.1 Industry segmentation

approach is that, taken to extremes, it means that every customer is different. If this is so, what is the place of media such as brochures, advertisements, videos and so on which need a reasonably large audience for their financial justification?

The answer to this dilemma lies in market segmentation. Customers are not all the same, but they are not all different either. The need is to find a common factor or factors which link a particular group or segment. We can then have a marketing and sales approach which is uniform for that particular segment but which is different from that for the other segments.

Let us suppose that we are selling computer systems to industry. The obvious way of segmenting the market might be by industry classification, e.g. financial, retail, manufacturing and so on (see Figure 4.1). However, a little thought may show that the needs within a particular industry segment such as financial, measured by some factor such as size, sophistication or purchasing power, may vary widely. At the top end (F)—the headquarters of an international bank—the sale may require months of negotiation, detailed proposals, presentations, meetings, and so on, and the product will be an individually specified package. At the bottom end (f)—a small accountancy practice—the sale may be achieved in one hour by a visit from a sales representative, or even by responding to a catalogue or brochure, and the customer buys an 'off-the-shelf' product. If we then look at another industry segment such as retailing, exactly the same can be said. We begin to wonder whether the segmentation should, in fact, be at right-angles to the segmentation by industry, because there is much more in common *between* segments at a particular level than there is *within* each segment itself. In our example, there is much more in common between the computer system requirements of the international bank (F) and a large supermarket chain (R) which are in different industry segments than there is between the bank (F) and the accountant's office (f) even though they are both in the financial sector.

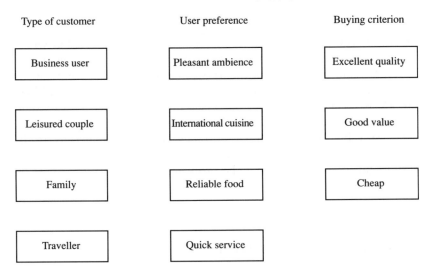

Type of customer	User preference	Buying criterion
Business user	Pleasant ambience	Excellent quality
Leisured couple	International cuisine	Good value
Family	Reliable food	Cheap
Traveller	Quick service	

Fig. 4.2   Sequential segmentation—eating in a restaurant

On the other hand, we do need to focus on industry segments as well, so that we can show that we understand their particular business and the ways in which it is different from every other business. In our example, we need to demonstrate that we are familiar with the language, culture and jargon of banking and finance, and that we can relate to their business environment, quite apart from any technical aspects of their specialization (see Exercise 4.2).

We are therefore driven to the conclusion that there is no single segmentation criterion which adequately serves all purposes. We may have to segment sequentially, using several different segmenting factors, in order to arrive ultimately at one or more segments which can be approached with relevant and targeted messages with a dedicated and specialized marketing programme.

An example of such sequential segmentation is shown in Figure 4.2 for eating in a restaurant. In this particular case, we have segmented in three sequential steps—by type of customer, by user preference and by buying criterion. These three segmentation criteria are discussed further in Section 4.3. We have then defined four, four and three segments respectively within each step. This gives 48 possible segments such as:

[Business user / International cuisine / Excellent quality]
[Traveller / Quick service / Good value]
[Family / Reliable food / Cheap]

Some combinations are unlikely to exist such as

[International cuisine / Cheap]!

There is nothing fixed about the number of steps or the number of segments within each step. The technique does not, of itself, tell us which if any of the segments we should approach. In this example, if we put all our resources into only one of the 48 segments so defined, we might be eliminating over 97 per cent of the target market! If we try to address them all, we will not appear to be expert in any. In practice, we would probably select some compatible combinations to give us a reasonable market size but a good degree of focus. It is as dangerous to be excessively focused as it is to dissipate our efforts in all directions. This is a serious business dilemma, but the problem does not get any easier by ignoring it (see Exercise 4.3).

4.3   Segmentation criteria

What are the possible criteria or factors which we might use to segment a marketplace? Three ways of approaching it are suggested (as used in the sequential segmentation exercise above):

1. *The type of customer*   The criterion might be the location of the customer. This is particularly true if we are a relatively small operation for which it is not economic to go beyond certain geographical boundaries. It might be the size of the organization—below a certain size they would not be interested in what we had to sell, or the level of business we might achieve would not justify the cost of selling to them. Conversely, above a certain size, the competition might be so intense that we would be better to focus our efforts lower down the scale. The segmentation criterion might be the profitability of the organization or the wealth of the individual, particularly if we are selling a high-priced or luxury product or service. It might be the management of the organization, in terms of style, expertise and so on; some companies will have their own in-house expertise, whereas others may need to go outside on a subcontract or consultancy basis. A further distinction might be made between existing and new customers, for which an entirely different marketing approach will be required.

2. *User needs and preferences*   Segmentation might be by intangible factors such as brand preference or by tangible factors such as quality, performance and ongoing support required.

3. *The way in which purchasing decisions are made*   The segmentation criteria might be related to the importance or frequency of the purchase, the importance of price, the volume in which it is bought, the distribution channel used, the purchasing procedure and so on.

These criteria will determine the way in which we sell the same product to different segments.

To summarize, market segmentation is not a theoretical exercise. There are only two reasons for doing it—so that we can make decisions (Section 4.4) and take actions (Section 4.5).

4.4   Strategic decisions arising from market segmentation

Possible decisions arising from market segmentation include the following:

Which segments should we address?

Some companies deliberately choose only one market segment and concentrate exclusively on that. Others may decide to address all possible segments. A good approach might be to focus on a small number of segments at first, and then move into others as our position becomes established in the first segments. There is no 'right answer' to this question, but whatever we do should be the result of a conscious decision after weighing up the alternatives, rather than allowing it to happen by default because no-one has taken the trouble to think through the implications. The issue of targeting is discussed in more detail in Section 4.6.

Do we need a different organization?

One of the possible segmentation criteria described in the previous section was the way in which purchasing decisions are made. These can vary so radically between different market segments that it may well be necessary for us to reflect this in the way we organize our sales and marketing efforts.

At the 'top' end of the market, we will need to employ senior skilled negotiators and, probably, proposal writers. At the 'bottom' end, a team of traditional sales representatives may be the most appropriate. People who are good at one may not necessarily be good at the other, and it may be necessary to recruit in order to buy in the necessary skills and experience.

Individual members of the senior management team may have a key role in selling. The chief executive, the financial director, the operations director and so on may be the best people to sell to their counterparts in the client company. If this is so, their workload must allow them to have time for customers. I was once asked to run a session on marketing for the board of a major subsidiary of one of the world's largest companies. I assumed that they wanted the latest theories on marketing from international gurus. I was then told that what they actually wanted was a session on 'selling techniques for directors', because they clearly recognized the point we have just made.

Are we prepared to make the investment?

Existing sellers will almost certainly have created barriers to entry. We may have to spend time and money before we can expect to make the first sale in a new segment. Such an investment may well be worth while, and establishing our place in the new segment may safeguard the future of our whole operation, but we should count the cost before taking the first step.

This approach contrasts strongly with the philosophy of dabbling in the whole market and responding reactively to opportunities which happen to come our way. This is not to say that we should reject opportunities which arise spontaneously, but relying on this approach does not constitute a professional and proactive business strategy.

Will different segments need a different product or variant?

Life is obviously easier for us if we can sell an identical product in all segments, but this is rarely possible. To attempt to do so is to limit our chances of success from the start. The customers in each segment need to feel that the product matches their particular requirements, while we want to incur the minimum of work and expense at our end. The customer should perceive maximum specificity, while we should achieve maximum commonality.

Can different segments bear a different price?

The normal approach to pricing in much of industry is to calculate the cost and add a percentage. The fallacy of doing this is argued in Chapter 6. The marketing approach to pricing is to judge what price the market will bear, based on the perceived value of what we are offering.

It is inconceivable that all market segments will value a product equally. The reasons for which a product is needed will vary between segments, as will the degree of competition and the cost of alternative solutions or of doing without the product, and these will all have an influence on price.

For these and other reasons, we will be most successful when we most accurately judge what price each market segment will bear for our products. The result will be the mix of high and low margins and volumes which gives us the maximum overall profit. The role of segmentation in decision making is yet another example of the need to target every part of our business activity to the particular needs of the marketplace (see Exercise 4.4).

4.5   Marketing actions arising from segmentation

Possible marketing actions arising from segmentation include the following:

Should we claim different benefits?

Different people want different benefits from the same product, and something which is a benefit to one person may be a disbenefit to another (see Chapter 2). We need to think through the implications of this for our whole marketing platform.

Should we produce different forms of communication?

Taken to its logical extreme, we will have to produce a different version of our literature and other forms of communication for each segment. Literature which tries to be all things to all people ends up not being very much to anybody.

Imagine a piece of equipment which could be used in a number of industrial situations, such as routine manufacturing, field service, research, avionics, and telecommunications. We might produce a series of five brochures. Much of the material, covering the details of the company and the general features of the product, would be common to the five versions. We could leave room for a photograph with which each individual target segment could identify, and a panel which highlighted the key benefits for that particular segment. By cleverly designing a family of brochures, we would be able to cover five very different targets for about the cost of two entirely separate brochures. Creative thinking of this sort can achieve both increased impact and reduced cost. Exactly the same thinking can be applied to the other forms of communication such as advertisements, overhead presentations, 'standard letters' or whatever else is appropriate.

Should we advertise in different media?

The most effective forms of marketing communication are normally those which use highly targeted media. Generalized advertising claims in non-specific media are only appropriate if we are selling to a very general readership.

The cost per subscriber of the advertisement will almost certainly be higher in the more specialist publications, and this has to be borne in mind when deciding media strategy. However, at the end of the day, the only effective measure is the cost of reaching a successful customer or, more correctly, the cost of achieving £1 of net profit as a result of the advertising.

If we decide to advertise in a number of different media to address different market segments, we need to target the message. We may only have to change a few key words or a picture, but it can make all the difference to the impact.

Should we offer different sales support?

This could include areas such as training, technical support, after-sales service, product enhancements, software upgrades and so on. The degree to which these areas of sales support are required will vary with the segment. Again, the more we can improve our interface with customers in each segment, the more credible will be our presence in the marketplace and the more successful we will be (see Exercise 4.5).

4.6   Targeting

Segmentation is an important marketing issue because none but the largest companies can profitably address all segments of a market. Targeting is the application of our marketing efforts specifically to the segments or subsegments which we have chosen.

It is important to recognize that our targets may be moving, otherwise we may be addressing the wrong target. This happens particularly in fast-moving scenarios such as high technology or fashion. Consider the computer market. Originally most of the turnover was in mainframes. Then came workstations and minicomputers. These markets then subdivided into portables, laptops, notebooks and so on. The companies which have been most successful in this fast-moving field are those which have pioneered the changes. Companies which have tried to live in the past have suffered the consequences. On the other hand, being too early can be as disastrous as being too late.

Marketing strategy must include an evolving targeting plan. We should not only be planning to target the existing segments but also thinking ahead to the next one or even two stages in the developing marketplace. A useful analogy is to think of a military commander setting out to invade a country, who establishes a beach-head, consolidates it, moves forward into a growing series of strongholds, and gradually plans to take over the whole territory. At each stage, everything is done to ensure that the enemy cannot take away the progress which has already been made (see Exercise 4.6).

Select, focus, target and commit

We need to select and focus on certain key market segments or subsegments, target our marketing efforts on the ones we have chosen, and commit appropriate resources in order to achieve our specific goals for these targets. This approach will give us a level of success which unfocused, untargeted and uncommitted marketing efforts can never achieve (see Follow-up 4.1).

4.7   The strategic significance of niche markets

We have spoken of segments and subsegments. A still further narrowing down of a subsegment can be described as a 'niche' market.

At first sight, a niche seems rather insignificant because of its small size. However, handled correctly, a niche can offer a highly profitable marketing opportunity to a particular company, and can permit the creation of such barriers to entry that competitors may decide to leave it alone. This is the ultimate objective of niche marketing—one company not only dominates the niche but also virtually 'owns' it.

As with segments and subsegments, niches may exist on an ongoing basis, or they may come and go in a rapidly changing situation. The skill lies in identifying, capturing and exploiting such niches and then, if necessary, moving on to others.

Figure 4.3 illustrates the point that what we think of as one market-place is actually made up a number of different markets and niches.

The markets and niches are defined by the variables along the two axes, based on customer segmentation and product segmentation. Customers might be segmented by factors such as needs, product preference, age or buying power; products might be segmented by the number of features they incorporate or some specific applications for which they are designed. As an example, customers for packaged food might be segmented into those who

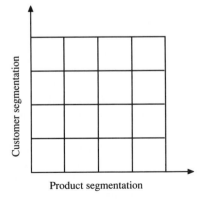

Fig. 4.3   Markets and niches

- like foreign food
- like interesting food
- like trying new things
- need convenience food because they are busy
- want to slim
- have dietary preferences
- have limited cooking facilities
- do not enjoy cooking

and so on. The products which such different customers might buy might include:

- oven-ready meals
- microwave meals
- ethnic meals
- diet foods
- slimming foods
- ranges of ingredients (e.g. sauce mixes)
- individual ingredients

and so on

Having defined the two axes, we obtain a number of 'boxes'. We then write the names of companies operating in each particular battlefield in the appropriate box. An indication of the turnover achieved by those companies would give added value to the exercise.

The probable outcome is that we shall find a cluster of companies selling in certain customer/product areas. The obvious inference is that the greatest potential is where the largest number of companies are operating. However, a little more thought shows that these are the very areas where competition is greatest. It may be possible to identify one or more smaller market opportunities which competitors have not begun to exploit. Although the overall potential is less, it may be much easier to gain a high share of one of these markets than 1 or 2 per cent of the busiest markets; the resulting turnover and margin may be higher, and the marketing costs lower.

For some companies, a well-chosen niche may be adequate to fulfil all their ambitions; it has the great advantage that the larger companies will not feel threatened and will probably not take any steps to retaliate. Other companies may not feel that a niche market offers sufficient potential to satisfy its long-term needs. However, it may represent an excellent 'stepping-stone'. This is particularly true if a company is venturing into a market which is outside its traditional core business, where it might not be appropriate to confront the existing market leaders head-on. A flanking attack, by which it can establish a foothold, test the acceptability of its product, assess its marketing tactics and confine any mistakes to a level where their impact is not serious, may be an excellent prelude to a stronger attack on the more substantial parts of the marketplace (see Exercise 4.7).

4.8   Credibility and track record

The importance of track record

Successful companies have created a track record in their core business areas. This is an immensely valuable asset which brings them continuing business. The problem comes when such companies need to move into new areas where they are relatively unknown. A delegate on one of my seminars said wryly 'we tried to start supplying the railway business, but unfortunately we didn't have a track record!'

Examples of this situation are companies whose historic core business has been in areas such as defence, nuclear and space. These markets will continue to provide business for the lifetime of the companies concerned, and it is right that their first priority should be to 'milk' the markets they know best. However, the demand has plateaued and begun to decline, while the number of companies hoping to get a living out of them has remained more or less constant. In these circumstances, companies wishing to continue to expand, or even to maintain their traditional profitability, will have to find new markets in which to ply their expertise.

This constitutes a fundamental marketing issue. On the face of it, there is no problem. The laws of nature are the same in the new and the old markets. An electron does not know whether it is a defence electron, a telecommunications electron or any other kind of electron! The principles of design, development, project management, standards conformance, safety and so on are identical. The main financial and business issues are generally similar. So what is the problem? We might think that all we have to do is to advertise, and the business from the new area will start coming in.

Unfortunately, this is not so, and companies which have tried it have had to learn the lesson the hard way. The failure is predictable, and it is a failure to appreciate the marketing issues involved. It arises from insufficient understanding of the mind of the customer.

Buyers consider a number of potential suppliers, perhaps starting with a 'long-list', moving to a 'short-list' and ultimately selecting one. A supplier who is not on the initial 'long-list' will never be considered. One of the most important determining factors is the perceived track record in that particular area of business.

Let us suppose that we are looking for project management skills for a major water-distribution project. Would we seriously consider suppliers to the defence, nuclear or space industries who know little about the water industry? Why should we take the risk of the unknown, when there are heavyweight suppliers who have already worked in our industry, who have established a good reputation and who can quote a long list of successful and relevant projects? The would-be supplier from another field has a low or even zero profile in the new area.

The position may actually be worse than having a zero profile—the 'outsider' may in effect have a negative profile. The technical criteria in the water industry may be somewhat different from those in the defence, nuclear or space industries. The prospect might hold the view, rightly or wrongly, that a contractor from one of these ultra-high-technology industries would be likely to offer overengineering, excessive time scales and a high price.

How can we create and demonstrate a track record?

One of the key hurdles to be overcome in moving into a new business area is to win the first contract. The problem is, of course, that we have no record of success on which to base our claim to credibility. It is much easier to get contract No. 5, 10 or 100, and yet the whole process cannot start until we have gained the first.

These early successes are so important that it is worth while going to great lengths and, if necessary, incurring substantial expense in order to do so. This does not necessarily mean offering a low price, although 'buying some business' may be an appropriate strategy. It might be better to 'overkill' the opportunity by bringing to bear considerably more technical, marketing and management attention than will be necessary once the track record has been established. Even if the early contracts are not particularly profitable in their own right, they form an essential stepping-stone towards the development of an ongoing business.

Customers often think, with some justification, that their business is special and different from all other businesses. There are matters such as language, jargon, culture, ways of doing business and other factors which we ignore at our peril. To move from where we have been to where they are may require a deliberate programme on our part.

How do we create the necessary credibility? We may have to recruit someone who has worked for many years in the new market segment, who can live, breathe, eat and speak the culture of that particular industry. We could use such a person first, to identify opportunities and problems in the new segment and second, to spearhead our marketing and selling approach in that market. If this were not appropriate, we might second a member of our existing staff to do nothing but concentrate on that segment for, say, six to twelve months. The brief would be to identify the opportunities and evaluate the implications of entering the new segment, leading to a business plan which would then be submitted for approval or modification. Once approval had been given, he or she would be the logical person to mastermind at least the initial entry into that market while additional resources were being assembled. As a side-benefit, a secondment of this type could be a very good way of developing the management skills of the person selected (see Exercise 4.8).

An imaginary case study

The 'case study' below is a composite picture based on the combined experience of a number of companies wanting to diversify out of their traditional areas. No reference to a particular company is intended.

The starting-point is that the companies concerned had all been commercially successful and had reached positions of leadership in their field. They expected to continue to make reasonable profits from their historic core business, but the demand was falling and was insufficient to meet the aspirations of all the suppliers. To generate real growth, they had to enter new markets of which they had previously had little experience. Their management and marketing resources which had been tailored to the earlier situation had to undergo a major restructuring.

The problems facing our imaginary company in the new situation were as follows:

CASE STUDY

1. Their management style was unduly conservative, bureaucratic and averse to taking risks.

2. Staff had the wrong business culture and attitudes.

3. The company had the wrong name and the wrong image.

4. The company had little orthodox marketing experience or expertise. Business had historically come to them from other companies with whom they co-operated, or had been gained as a result of ministry tendering procedures. The marketing department, inasmuch as it existed at all, was too small, was populated by low-calibre staff, and had little responsibility outside the areas of tender preparation and brochures. There were no sales staff, and managers had few contacts outside their core business area. They had a negligible marketing budget, and tried to 'hide' marketing expenditure within existing project codes. They had the wrong literature, and a corporate video which was entirely inappropriate outside their core area.

5. Pricing was based on cost and overheads, with no understanding of the price which the new markets were willing to bear. Their historic business had a much higher level of overheads than was appropriate to the new business areas they were seeking to enter.

6. In the new sectors, the company had poor credibility and no track record.

Faced with the above situation, the company took the following actions:

1. They made changes at senior and middle management level, filling some key posts with managers who had held responsible positions in highly competitive outside industries. They delegated responsibility to middle management, encouraged investment and risk taking, and then demanded results.

2. They changed the company name into one which did not solely reflect their former business area. They took specific steps to change their image as perceived by the outside world, presenting themselves as 'fast-on-the-feet' operators who could make decisions quickly.

3. They strengthened the marketing function by bringing in some key managers from heavyweight marketing environments, and undertook a major programme of marketing and business training for the existing key staff. They created and allocated marketing budgets. They set marketing objectives which were reviewed after six to twelve months. They appointed full-time sales staff and introduced sales incentives. They set up a proactive marketing programme which included mailshots and 'cold calling' into new areas.

4. They agreed a more flexible approach to pricing (which involved some tough battles with their corporate senior and financial management).

5. They separated some of the management responsibilities for the new areas from the traditional, to avoid culture clashes and to give due priority to the new areas.

6. They segmented the potential new marketplace, thought through the implications of addressing the various segments, and developed an 'invasion plan'. This involved prioritizing a small number of targets for initial marketing efforts, planning a second-phase expansion into further areas, but deliberately avoiding dissipating their efforts over too wide an area too soon. They appointed business managers for the main target market sectors. These were senior managers of calibre and experience, who were given responsibility for the profitability of the activities relating to the new areas (although they used common technical and other resources as appropriate, to avoid fragmentation and duplication). In particular, they were responsible for all sales and marketing activities in their own marketplace (see Section 13.1). They recruited some key staff from the main market sectors which they had selected. These recruits helped to develop a

Business Plan for the area and then assisted in achieving the agreed targets.

They then invested time, money and resources in creating a track record in the new market sectors. They recognized the key strategic importance of the first contracts in these new areas, and were prepared to go to great lengths to obtain them; profitability of these first contracts was not a high priority. They created new literature for each of the sectors, in a very flexible portfolio form which could be constantly updated as the track record developed. They avoided using the generic company literature and corporate video when they felt that they would give the wrong signals.

For some of the companies on which this composite picture is based, it is too early to judge the ultimate success of the programme but the initial results are encouraging. The management teams deserve credit for the seriousness with which they are building a new business and for their willingness to take a long term market-led approach. Their strategy is to be contrasted with that of other companies who sit back and feel that the world owes them a living (see Follow-ups 4.2 and 4.3).

Exercises

4.1 Define in not more than 20 words the business in which you think your organization is (ought to be) engaged. Are you satisfied that the definition sufficiently reflects future trends in the marketplace? Are you satisfied that the scope of the definition is not so narrow that it precludes growth or so broad that it does not help in diversification decisions?

4.2 Write down the way in which you normally segment your company's marketplace at present. In the light of Section 4.2 are you sure that this is the best way of doing it?

4.3 Carry out a sequential segmentation exercise for one of your main areas of activity. What issues does this raise that are not raised by a one-stage segmentation?

4.4 What strategic decisions do you need to make as a result of your increased understanding of market segmentation?

4.5 What marketing actions do you need to take as a result of your increased understanding of market segmentation?

4.6 Write an evolving targeting plan for your operation to cover at least the time span of the long-range strategic plan.

4.7 Fill in the grid shown in Figure 4.3 for your operation. What niche marketing opportunities does this suggest?

4.8 Choose a market which is new to your company which you are considering entering or taking more seriously than in the past. What specific steps should you take to create and demonstrate a credible track record? Should you appoint or second someone to 'champion' the opportunity?

Follow-up

4.1 Over the next six months, make a list of any marketing activities in which your company engages which are unfocused, untargeted or uncommitted. At the end of the period, share your findings with the relevant staff and decide what action needs to be taken to overcome these deficiencies.

4.2 Select a small group of colleagues, and make them familiar with the 'imaginary case study' in Section 4.8. Arrange to meet regularly, say every two weeks for a period of three months, perhaps over a sandwich lunch, to explore its relevance to your operation. At the end of the exercise, write a brief report to senior management with some clear and supported recommendations.

4.3 Read a book on strategic marketing, such as Kotler, P. (1994) *Marketing Management*, Prentice Hall Inc. 1994, Englewood Cliffs, New Jersey, or Johnson, G. and Scholes, K. (1993) *Exploring Corporate Strategy*, Prentice Hall International, Hemel Hempstead, UK.

Who are our competitors?
Competitive analysis and tactics

Key business issues   *Section*

■ Competition may come from a variety of sources, many of them   5.1
not the obvious ones.

■ Many companies wrongly act as if the only competition were
from other suppliers of an equivalent product or service.

■ Competition may come from other ways of doing the same thing,
an alternative product, other demands on budgets or from the
customers doing it themselves.

■ Failure to analyse the competitive situation may mean that
the wrong battle is being fought.

■ A detailed and ongoing analysis of the competition is a key part   5.2
of the marketing function, and may reveal unexploited
marketing opportunities.

■ There are many sources of information on the competition, some   5.3
of which are often underused.

■ Competitive tactics are a key part of the marketing function.   5.4

■ Attacking the industry leader carries particular risks but it can
be successful if certain principles are followed.

5.1 The nature of competition

A study of the competition is a fundamental part of the marketing task,
and most of this chapter is devoted to ways in which we can improve our
performance against other companies providing broadly equivalent
products or services. However, many people do not think sufficiently
laterally about the nature of competition. As a result, they employ the

wrong tactics in fighting the competitive battle. Most of their marketing effort is directed at showing why their product is better than the others on a like-for-like basis. As we shall show, competition can be very much wider than this and can come from entirely different sources. Failure to recognize this can mean that we win the argument but fail to get the order because we are arguing the wrong issues.

Let us illustrate the point by supposing that we are selling oil-fired central heating systems. There are five possible forms of competition:

1. *Other providers of the same product.*   These will be other suppliers of oil-fired central heating systems. Our task is to show why our system with its associated benefits is to be preferred to the other systems.

2. *Other ways of doing the same thing.*   This could be gas-fired central heating. Already the competitive ground has shifted. We are no longer trying to show why our oil-fired system is better than the other oil-fired systems. We have to sell the merits of oil rather than gas.

3. *Providers of an alternative product.*   This might be an electric fire in each room. We could be successful in proving that ours is the best oil-fired central heating system, and the family might say that, if they wanted oil-fired central heating, they would buy our system. Unfortunately, they prefer to have an electric fire in each room! In this case, the competitive battle we have to fight is first to show why central heating is to be preferred to individual fires, and only then to argue why our system is the one they ought to have.

4. *Other competitors for the customer's budget.*   Some people may think that the cost of central heating is beyond their means and they will have to put up with a cold house. In this case, we need to show why money is better spent on a heating system than on something entirely different, such as a loft extension or a new car. Put more generally, if a customer would like to have a number of things and can only afford a few, we must aim to make sure that our product is one of the few.

5. *The customer.*   It is important to realize the startling fact that the customer can be our biggest competitor. In our example, the householder may collect and chop wood and avoid buying any form of heating system. In this case, our task is to argue the benefits of the convenience and comfort of our product, which saves the trouble of providing and preparing the wood for heating the house.

These examples are trivial but they can easily be transferred to our own selling situation. The key point is to identify the actual competitive scenario which prevails in each case, so that we can bring to bear the relevant competitive tactics. If we ignore this, we can 'win the battle and lose the war'. We need to think laterally about the competition (see Exercise 5.1).

5.2   Analysis of competition

Having made the point that competition comes from a variety of sources, we now revert to considering the simplest form of competition—other suppliers offering broadly equivalent products or services. A knowledge of the competition is an absolutely essential part of the marketing function. The task is made harder by the fact that the situation can change rapidly and frequently. It is a hallmark of good marketing managers that they have an accurate and up-to-date understanding of the strategy and tactics of the key competitors. What sort of information do we require?

1. *Who are they?*   This should include an understanding of their ownership and organization.

2. *What is their financial situation?*   Are they fighting for survival? Do they have surplus funds to invest in new ventures? Are they able to increase their expenditure on marketing? Are their salary scales competitive—are they in a position to attract key staff from their competitors (including us)?

3. *What products or services are they selling?*   Competitive brochures and other key information should be available, kept up to date and in an accessible form.

4. *At what prices are they selling?*   Competitive price lists should be available. Even more importantly, there should be an understanding of the sort of discount they are prepared to give, and their approach to pricing tenders, if this information can be gained.

5. *What is their market share by segment?*   A broad idea of competitive market shares is essential to developing our competitive strategy. As will be discussed in Chapter 11, the cost of obtaining such information increases very rapidly with the accuracy which is required. The key question is 'if we knew the figures more accurately, would it influence any business decisions we might make?'

6. *What product features are they promoting?*   An analysis should be

made and kept up to date of all the key features, specifications and claims of each of the major competitive products compared with our own.

7. *What benefits are they claiming?*   Not only should we sell benefits rather than features, we should present our benefits as being more beneficial than those claimed by the competition.

8. *What are the strengths and weaknesses of the competition?*   It is a useful exercise to assess the relative strengths and weaknesses of our own company and the key competitors. This is normally done as a SWOT analysis—see Chapter 13. We are, as it were, playing a game of chess; we need to devote at least as much effort to the serious matter of business competition as chess enthusiasts would devote to what is, at least in theory, only a game!

9. *What is their retaliation potential?*   It is important to consider what actions key competitors would take if we were to do certain things. If we are the market leader, we may decide that we are relatively invulnerable; if we are not, we should be aware that a major competitor might take steps which could seriously embarrass us or even drive us completely out of the market.

To summarize, the marketing process does not relate simply to the buyer and the seller; the competition can be a major factor in the equation (see Exercise 5.2).

5.3   Sources of information about competition

How can we obtain a detailed and up-to-date knowledge of the competition? It is important to state that no form of industrial espionage is being advocated. We need to make an ongoing appraisal of the competition, rather like creating a jigsaw. Each piece of information may not be highly significant in its own right, but, over a period of time, a number of pieces combine to make a very useful picture:

1. *Published sources*   Key pieces of information are published from time to time, in business, financial and other journals, in the newspapers, on television and so on. We need to set up a system for capturing and accessing this information, and for maintaining it on a regular basis. It is worth devoting a considerable amount of expert effort to the system design, but the maintenance can be carried out by carefully briefed relatively junior staff. Data can be stored in paper filing systems with a

good method of reference, or it can be computerized with keyword access.

2. *Customers*   Customers are in frequent contact with our competitors. They receive early news of new products or services, price changes, changes in methods of distribution, special promotional and other activities and so on.

3. *Salesforce*   The salesforce is in daily contact with the marketplace and is constantly receiving snippets of information about the competition. The question is whether this information is reliable and statistically significant, and how it can be combined into an overall picture. The simplest starting point is for management to insist that every daily or weekly sales report and every overseas visit report should have a section on competitive activities. Also, sales staff should be encouraged to telephone 'hot news' to head office. The wise manager will not overreact to the first report of a certain competitive activity—it might simply be a representative trying to create a defence for having lost an order! However, when we begin to hear the same thing from several different sources, we can assume some measure of statistical significance.

4. *Buying competitive products or services*   This is not, of course, always possible, but where it is it should be a routine activity.
   In the case of hardware products, competitive products are often brought back to the engineering department and carefully dismantled and analysed. Some companies actually offer a repair service on other companies' products, which brings useful information as well as income. In the case of services, it may be possible for a member of staff to make use of some of them quite openly and to draw conclusions while doing so. Similarly, we may be able to learn something if we use competitors as subcontractors.

5. *Exhibitions*   Exhibitions are a major and instant source of information. When planning the staffing levels for an exhibition stand, it is worth allowing time for a detailed study of the competitors' stands. At the end of the exhibition the staff should be brought together to pool the knowledge they have gained. The latest competitive literature should be gathered and studied after an exhibition as an aid to developing our own literature (see Chapter 9).

6. *Independent market research*   Both qualitative and quantitative studies can be commissioned, on a one-off or regular basis (see Chapter 11). As with all market research, the criterion is whether the

information we gain is cost effective in terms of enabling us to make better business decisions.

7. *Interviews and recruitment*   In many industries, interchanges of personnel between competing companies are frequent and it is inevitable that they will bring facts and attitudes with them.

The better we are at harnessing the information from these various sources, the better equipped we will be to fight the competitive battle (see Follow-up 5.1).

5.4   Competitive tactics

Forms of competition

The competitive situation can vary from a monopoly at one end of the scale to a totally free market at the other. Most companies are operating somewhere between the two extremes, probably nearer to the free market.

In a monopoly there are no competitors; the monopolist controls the supply and, to a large extent, the price. Some monopolies exist because of legislation or because the industries are government-owned—public utilities, for example. Where such a monopoly is considered to be detrimental to the customer, a government sometimes steps in to create a free market. Other monopoly or near-monopoly situations come about because a major supplier establishes such a dominant hold on the marketplace that it is very difficult for others to enter.

As we move from a monopoly towards a free market, there is an increase in the number of competitors and the number of different products being sold, and a lowering of the barriers to entry. At its extreme, a free market would be described as offering 'perfect competition'; there would be a large number of sellers, none of whom could control the supply or the price.

The key issue, in whatever competitive situation we find ourselves, is 'what reasons can we create for customers to buy from us rather than from the competition? How can we differentiate ourselves in such a way that customers will put us at the top of their shopping list?' In a sense, the free marketeer is continually trying to create some of the advantages which the monopoly supplier naturally possesses, by attempting to 'own' the chosen segment.

Dominant companies will usually lead the marketplace and be first in the field with new products. Advantageous though this strategy may seem, there is an argument, particularly for smaller companies, to follow rather than to lead. This has the merit that the leaders can be allowed to spend the money to create the market and, sometimes, to make the mistakes; followers can then come in at a much lower level of effort, risk and expenditure. This has been described as being 'first in the field with a me-too product'; being tenth in the field with a me-too product is not such a good strategy!

Attacking the industry leader

What do we do if there is a clear industry leader who dominates a market segment in which we are already operating or which we are considering entering? It must be said that industry leadership is a very powerful position to be in. The knowledge, experience, product range and financial investment of the market leader can form a serious barrier to competitors. Does this mean that we should never contemplate attacking the industry leader? Certainly not, but the process carries high risk and we must carefully think out our tactics before embarking on such a venture.

Industry leaders can retaliate, possibly to the extent of completely driving away or even bankrupting a new entrant. Because of their strong position, they could cut prices temporarily and destroy the whole financial viability of the new entrant. They could, if appropriate, engage in a major advertising or promotional campaign which nullifies the more modest approach of the new entrant. They might be able to launch a new product which undermined the very basis on which the new competitor was hoping to build a platform.

What then are the tactics which we should use to attack an industry leader? First, we should realize that industry leaders may be vulnerable under certain circumstances, and take steps to exploit this vulnerability. They can become complacent and even arrogant, feeling that they have a right to leadership for evermore. They dismiss the early moves of competitors as insignificant. There was a world heavyweight in a particular field of specialist software who began to notice some competition from a distributor in the USA whom they dismissed as a 'cowboy' of no consequence. They allowed him to gain 5 per cent, 10 per cent and then 15 per cent of the market, realizing too late that he had become a major threat. Being a low-overhead company, the competitor had been able to buy market share at prices which the multinational could not match. Having established his position, he was then able to raise his prices and continue to run a very profitable business. The approach used successfully in this true case may well be open to others.

It is not only in the field of software that competitors can be relatively small and operate without the massive expenses, organizations, systems and other overheads of the larger operators. The same can be true of management consultants, trainers and professional experts in a wide variety of fields. If we are in this position, we have an enviable business advantage. We have tremendous freedom compared with the large operators, to price low and take the volume or to price high and take the margin.

Second, we should employ outflanking tactics rather than attacking head-on. We should choose the battlefield, rather than fighting on the leader's own ground. If it comes to major retaliation, the leader can always win. This might involve, for example, starting with a part of the marketplace or product range which has a lower profile than some of the more exciting areas.

Third, we must have a competitive advantage—some form of differentiation which is valued by the marketplace. We need to find some way in which we become a preferred supplier for at least part of the industry leader's business. Price is the differentiator which most readily comes to mind but, as we suggest in Chapter 6, we should consider other strategies first. By presenting the benefits rather than the features and by targeting those benefits (Sections 2.4 to 2.7), by creating uniqueness and differentiation (Section 2.8) and by creative use of segmenting, targeting and niche marketing (Chapter 4) we should be able to avoid the trap of the downward price spiral.

Fourth, we must be able to sustain the attack. It is worse than useless to start a battle which we are not able to continue.

Finally, the most successful strategy for attacking the industry leader, if the opportunity arises, is to choose a time when the leader has a serious problem. This can occur, for example, through a product recall, a failed development project, the loss of some key staff, or some other situation which diverts management's attention and temporarily lowers the barriers to entry. While we cannot create such an opportunity, it is worth having a strategy 'on the shelf' to bring into effect at the right moment.

Many readers will themselves be working for industry leaders. In this case they should interpret the above remarks in the sense of defending their leadership position; the tactics described are the ones which are likely to be adopted by their competitors! They should be on the lookout, and be prepared to repel serious-looking new entrants before they can make too much headway (see Follow-up 5.2).

Exercises

5.1 Write down an example from your own company of each of the five types of competition described in Section 5.1. What arguments would you use for getting an order in each situation?

5.2 Analyse your company's competitors using the nine headings in Section 5.2 (adding other headings if you can). What competitive problems or opportunities does this analysis reveal? Set up a system for maintaining this information on an ongoing basis.

Follow-up

5.1 Go round the organization asking the relevant staff what use they are making of the seven sources of information on competition listed in Section 5.3. In the light of this information, propose some specific ways in which this competitive information could be harnessed more effectively. Circulate a brief report on your findings to those involved, and arrange a meeting to decide what action should be taken as a result.

5.2 List the three to five most important tactics being used by the competition. Take extra time during the next six months to monitor these. What new strategies are your competitors adopting, and what countermeasures does your company need to take?

How do we set prices?

An underexploited management opportunity

Key business issues   *Section*

- Many companies underprice and some overprice. Pricing   6.1
  deserves far more management attention than it normally receives.

- Pricing is often too mechanistic, and financial departments have
  too much influence compared with marketing.

- Prices should be based wherever possible on what the market
  will bear rather than the cost of providing the product or service.

- New attitudes to pricing may be required, particularly when
  companies move outside their traditional field.

- In a free-market situation the customer does not know or care   6.2
  about our cost (with some exceptions).

- Different parts of the business have different profit potential.   6.3

- 'True cost' is impossible to calculate because it contains   6.4
  arbitrary allocations of indirect expenses.

- The price of a product rightly or wrongly implies something   6.5
  about its value.

- Marketing should do everything possible to avoid a commodity
  price situation, where all products are perceived as equivalent
  and people buy the cheapest.

- Although the price the market will bear is imprecise, there are   6.6
  several factors which can give an indication.

- Pricing should be used both strategically and tactically.   6.7

- In-company transfer pricing can kill business opportunities   6.8
  if it is not handled intelligently.

6.1   Price is what the market will bear

Pricing is a greatly underexploited management opportunity. Experience with a large number of companies shows that many of them set their prices too low while others set them too high. In the first case they are losing margin; in the second, they are losing volume. In both cases they are losing profit. The art is to use pricing in order to maximize total profitability.

In Section 1.10 we referred to three components of profit—market share, market size and percentage margin. We made the point that pricing is a fundamental part of the marketing function. It cannot be carried out in financial departments without reference to the marketplace or the competition.

What is the first thing we want to know when setting a price? Most people would say 'the cost of producing the product or service'. It is strongly suggested that this is not the best place to start. We should begin by asking 'what is the price which the market will bear?' Of course we need to know the cost, and ultimately we have to decide whether or not we want a particular piece of business, but the cost of providing a product or service is not the main factor determining what the customer will pay. The discipline of thinking first about the market and only then about our cost can lead to some very profitable conclusions.

In some buying situations, particularly when government tenders are involved, the cost of production is, of course, a major factor and, indeed, may have to be revealed. However, in the majority of normal free competitive market situations, the price which the market is willing to pay and the cost of production are much less closely linked than people think. This causes a particular problem when companies move from one sphere of activity to another, perhaps as a result of diversification from their historic core business. They make the mistake of assuming that pricing decisions are made in the new scenario in the same way as they were in the old, because the management team has never seen it working any other way. This is simply not true, and it leads to some very costly errors. We would go so far as to say that, if they do not learn to adapt their thinking, they may never succeed in the new marketplace.

This works both ways. High costs of production, which were (presumably) necessary in the former situation and which were passed on under the old cost-based pricing regime, are totally unacceptable in the new situation; the customer is simply not willing to fund unnecessary activities, whether in the form of overengineering, cumbersome bureaucracy or an inappropriate allocation of excessive overheads. In the other direction, managers may simply not be aware of the higher margins which are possible in the new free-market situation, because they are steeped in attitudes which were inculcated in an entirely different business environment.

Much of industry is wedded to the 'cost-based' pricing philosophy. (This is often referred to as 'cost-plus', but this phrase is used by some to describe a particular form of government contract which used to be common until it was realized that it was a 'licence to print money'.) The cost is worked out, often to several significant figures. A certain percentage is then added on, in order to achieve the desired percentage margin or return on investment. The work goes on in the accounts department, and is carried out by people who have little or no contact with the marketplace or with the competition. This mechanistic approach to pricing can be disastrous in a free-market situation.

It is impossible to achieve the optimum market-based price without considering the key marketing issues which we have discussed earlier, particularly the benefits offered to the purchaser and the differentiation and uniqueness of the product or service being sold. A true case which dramatically illustrates this point is of a software engineer who used to be charged out by his company at £800 a day. He then changed employers, and his new company charged him out at £400 a day! How could they both be right? Of course, they were not. The first company presented the value of this person and the excellence of the software skills he was providing in such a way that customers believed that they were getting a very good product. The second company set their sights so low in terms of image that they could not substantiate a higher price. The irony is that customers probably thought they were getting higher quality from the first company—'if it's that expensive, it must be good'—even though the individual providing the service was exactly the same.

How can we find out what price the market will bear? The answer is— 'with great difficulty!' Some pointers to this are given in Section 6.6. In spite of the uncertainty associated with market-based pricing, one thing is clear; if we don't even try to find out, we shall make less profit than we should.

I have even heard as a justification for cost-based pricing that people are comfortable with it because they can measure it accurately. Market-based pricing is imprecise, and therefore unacceptable to them. People who want nice neat answers to all business questions should keep away from marketing!

There is another key question which influences pricing decisions. How important to us is it that we win a particular contract? Do we need it desperately because otherwise our factory or our consultants will have insufficient work? Is it strategically important because it helps us to develop a track record in a new area? If so, we may choose to price at the lower end of the range of uncertainty in order to increase our chances. Alternatively, are we already so busy that further work will lead to capacity problems and excessive overtime, or to increased stress if we are a small consultancy operation? If so, we will probably price at the upper end of the range of uncertainty; if winning a contract is going to cause problems, we might at least make it worth while! With a cost-based approach to pricing, we would not reach these conclusions—we would probably not even consider the issues.

We are not suggesting that we should exploit customers by extorting an unreasonably high price from them. The discipline of basing price on value to the customer should actually prevent this, and we shall argue that some companies are overpricing. The point that is being made is that we should separate the issues of price and cost much more clearly than is often the case. If we can create good value for the customer at a low cost to ourselves, we deserve to make a good profit; if we can't, we shouldn't expect the customer to come to our rescue (see Exercise 6.1).

Three reasons are suggested for asking what price the market will bear before we think about the cost. They are discussed below.

6.2   Customers do not know or care about our cost

This is a 'black and white' statement designed to provoke! However, it is made because in normal free market situations it is true.

Consider a situation where there are two suppliers, Mr X and Miss Y, offering equivalent products. The costs and selling prices (in £, £000 or £million—whichever makes the reader feel more at home!) are:

	X	Y
Cost	70	60
Price	110	100

A customer asks the price from supplier X and is told '£110'. 'Ah, but I can get it down the road from Y for £100' is the reply.

At this point the customer is given the argument for paying £10 more. 'You see, my costs are high because I have a rather inefficient factory, I was forced into an unfavourable wage settlement, my raw materials buyer is incompetent, I have high wastage rates and high product failure rates, so I have to charge more!' This is obviously ludicrous, but is it really any more ludicrous than some of the reasons I have actually heard for charging a high price? These include:

1. The allocation of indirect expenses. I know of one company where two different parts of the organization can quote for the same project management task. One profit centre is allocated a corporate overhead, the other is not. This difference has traditionally been reflected in the prices quoted, in some cases to the same potential client! Not surprisingly, customers are not interested in the way in which bean-counters push artificial money round the accounts.

2. An internal royalty. Subsidiaries of some companies have to carry a

royalty charge if they use the company brand-name. The customer may well be prepared to pay a premium because of the enhanced value which the brand-name implies, but will not pay it simply because someone in corporate headquarters says so!

3. A move to a less demanding environment. Companies which have been offering a service where price was not the main issue (e.g. where safety criteria demanded an extremely high level of overheads) are now wanting to offer their under-utilized resources in the general commercial world. They have the necessary skills and equipment—the only problem is their historic cost. Before any progress can be made, the senior management have to agree that normal commercial rates can be charged. They would obviously like to be able to recover their overheads at the historic rate, but there is not much point in having a high percentage of nothing while plant and people lie idle.

There is no reason why customers should be expected to pay the premium in any of these cases, and yet in a cost-based pricing regime they are in effect being asked to do so.

Returning to our example, the sale naturally goes to supplier Y. Her volume goes up, and her unit costs go down. The reverse happens to supplier X:

	X	Y
Volume	Down	Up
Cost	Up from £70 to £80	Down from £60 to £55
Price	?	?

Supplier X is now faced with a problem. His unit cost is going up, and he is a cost-based pricer. He therefore increases his price from £110 to, say, £120. Clearly he is in a vicious spiral, and he will soon be out of business. The alternative is for him to remain in business by charging the market price in order to buy some time to achieve a healthier cost base. He may have to reduce his staff numbers, accept a lower dividend or profit share, move to a cheaper location or something; this may be unpalatable, but he has to find some way of breaking the vicious spiral.

Now consider supplier Y. Sales are going up, unit costs are coming down, and her only competitor has introduced a price increase. If Y is a cost-based pricer, she will bring her prices down—but why on earth should she? There is one possible reason for doing so—her only competitor is clearly in trouble and she may choose to accelerate the collapse. Apart from this, Y is in a virtuous spiral in which she is free to put her prices *up*, or to choose the part of the price–volume curve which maximizes profit. A cost-based approach to pricing would not have led her to that conclusion.

The above example is obviously trivial, and yet, in a more subtle form, these things do actually take place in well-known companies. It is not usually as overt as this. The time for a price review comes upon us. We suddenly remember that our overseas distributors have to be given 30 days' notice. A hurried meeting takes place, and the prices are amended. In these circumstances there is no time for a considered review of market-based pricing factors; all we can do is to see how the costs have changed, and reprice accordingly.

It must be said that there are two areas where customers may care about our cost. If they think we are making too much profit, they will not be willing to pay our price. At the other end of the scale, if we are a regular supplier, a major purchaser will not want to bargain so hard that they drive us out of business. However, this usually leaves a wide range of possible prices between the two extremes. With these provisos, the first fallacy of cost-based pricing is that the customer does not ultimately know or care about our cost (see Exercise 6.2).

6.3   Different parts of the business have different profit potential

The second fallacy of cost-based pricing is that it appears to assume that there is some rule of business which enables us to make the same percentage profit on everything we do. This leads to the adoption of certain norms which become built into the pricing decision-making process.

This assumption is totally without foundation. A balanced portfolio of high-margin/low-volume and low-margin/high-volume activities is perfectly normal. The aim is surely to maximize the total profit of our overall business activity, not the percentage margin of any particular subcomponent.

It is quite legitimate to say that there is a *minimum* percentage margin and a *minimum* return on investment which we are prepared to achieve. This is quite different from saying that we will use fixed percentages as the basis for pricing. Again, failure to realize this leads to overpricing in some situations and underpricing in others, with the inevitable loss of profit.

This is another case where extrapolating from one business environment to another is dangerous. I can recall being a member of a new management team which began to question the cost-based price structure of a key product range which we had inherited. We found, after spending some time considering the market price, that *we were underpricing by a factor of two*! How many other examples of incorrect pricing could be found if the necessary management time could be devoted to it (see Exercise 6.3).

This leads us to make the statement that many management teams should spend substantially more time on pricing. The resulting profit improvement could be surprising. Price increases which raised the average margin by as little as 1 per cent would have an enormous effect on return on investment in most companies. If one of the principal tasks of senior management is to increase return on investment, why do they not spend much more time wrestling with the issue of market-based pricing (see Follow-up 6.1)?

6.4   There is no such thing as 'true cost'

There is a third factor which makes cost-based pricing not only inappropriate but actually impossible! It is that there is no such thing as 'true cost' anyway.

This statement may come as a surprise to people who live in a world of computer printouts giving minutely detailed costs. It is certainly possible to attribute the cost of materials and direct labour quite precisely to different products, and the allocation may even be reasonably realistic when applied to production overheads.

However, when we come to the true indirect expenses, such as strategic marketing, general and administration expenses, senior management expenses, site costs and so on, the allocation is inevitably going to be arbitrary. The normal method is to allocate them as a percentage of turnover, but is this necessarily 'real'? Why not allocate them on the basis of the added value which each activity generates, or the amount of time the managers spend thinking about it?

When discussing this issue, one managing director claimed that the allocation of overheads was 'very difficult but we do it very precisely'. Surely the truth is the opposite—it is relatively easy, but the result has a high degree of arbitrariness.

This is not to say that there is no value in 'activity-based costing'. It is important to know where expense is being incurred. The problem is that we can only allocate a proportion of the total cost. To use this method for determining prices is therefore flawed, quite apart from the fact that it is the wrong way of doing it (see Exercise 6.4).

6.5   The danger of a commodity price orientation

The word 'commodity' in this context implies that there are a number of products or services which, although not necessarily identical, are broadly equivalent or substitutable. Typical commodities, listed in the financial sections of the daily papers, are items such as coffee or nickel.

The price follows the well-known principle of supply and demand; when supply exceeds demand, prices fall and vice versa.

In these circumstances buyers will hunt around until they find the cheapest. In other words, in a commodity price situation, price is the most important factor in the buying decision. It is top of the list in the marketing mix, and the other factors hardly play any part as long as the specification is met.

There is nothing wrong with commodity trading—it has its rightful place in the commercial world—but it does not follow the normal rules of marketing. The danger is that people assume that they are in a commodity market when they are not. It is simply not true that people always use the cheapest accountant, lawyer or dentist, or always buy the cheapest package holiday, restaurant meal, computer or television set.

The commodity approach is the opposite of the marketing philosophy which relates price to value. Part of the job of marketing is to bring price lower down the list of priorities in the mind of the buyer. By pushing the benefits to the top of the list, we attempt to reduce the significance of price.

Markets tend to move towards a commodity position as they mature. When a product is new, it is relatively easy to give it a meaningful differentiation. In a mature market, many products exist and they tend to be very similar; differentiation and the price premium which this can bring are much more difficult to achieve. The rate at which this takes place is accelerating in many fields as life cycles become shorter. Today's unique selling proposition is tomorrow's commodity.

A commodity orientation is death to professional marketing. If we cannot prevent such a situation, we might as well get rid of the marketing department, set up in a low-overhead shack in a development area, and try to play the commodity game by its own rules. One of the tasks of marketing is to keep taking steps to lift the product out of the commodity orientation, by introducing new benefits and enhanced value in the mind of the customer. We might argue that this is one way in which the marketing function can help to justify the cost of its existence. Beware the commodity price orientation (see Exercise 6.5).

6.6   How do we determine the market price?

We have said that determining the price the market will bear is not always easy. Nor, to be fair, is there one single price. We can and should take steps to find out the general price range which the market is willing to pay, but, at the end of the day, it comes down to the price which an individual customer is willing to pay on that occasion.

The general situation is described by what is known as 'price elasticity of demand'. This attempts to quantify the amount by which sales will increase if we reduce the price by a certain amount and vice versa, and is typically used in a high-volume selling situation (see Section 6.7).

For businesses where the unit sales volumes are much lower, the statistical approach is not practicable and other means have to be adopted. These can include:

■ *Finding out the available budget* An innocent question such as 'is there a budget for this?' or a more direct one 'how much is in the budget for this?' may well elicit a response (obviously we have to judge whether the response is true, or is simply a negotiating tactic). If the budget is £50 000, there is no point in quoting £51 000 unless we are prepared for what may be long-drawn-out negotiations at a more senior level.

■ *Suggesting a 'guide price'* We could try to test the situation without doing anything irretrievable. We might quote 'a figure for budget purposes' and see what reaction we get. If it becomes clear that we have pitched the price wrongly, we may be able to modify it, perhaps using a changed specification as the justification.

■ *Finding out authority levels* In most organizations, individuals and committees have certain levels of authority within which they can spend their budget without reference to more senior management. This is perhaps a more sensitive issue than the budget level and it should be approached with care, but a question such as 'if it were less than £10 000 would you be able to approve it?' might elicit a response.

■ *Posing alternative situations* If we are able to offer alternative specifications, such as the basic or enhanced version, we may discover how much the buyer is prepared to spend.

■ *A direct question* This might take the form 'how much are you prepared to pay?' I have taken the rather unusual approach of asking a group of seminar delegates how many of them would not have come if the price had been higher by £50, £100 or £150. While not pretending that this was an accurate measure of price elasticity, it certainly gave some useful information!

The above approaches should not be used in an underhand way, and we will only be successful in the long run if we are offering good value to the marketplace. Persuading customers to pay too high a price is not a basis for a good business, quite apart from its moral implications.

The effect of discounts

The price elasticity curve shows the frightening effect of giving a discount which salespeople are all too ready to do in order to achieve their sales quota. Let us suppose that our management plan requires us to sell 1000 units at an average price of £1000 to achieve a turnover of £1 million, and that the gross margin at list price is 30 per cent, i.e. the cost of the product before indirect expenses is £700. Times are tough, and we find that sales are dropping behind target. We decide to offer a discount to boost sales.

We start with a modest 5 per cent discount, and sales do indeed increase. However, we do a little arithmetic and find that we need to sell 20 per cent more to achieve our budget gross margin. At a 10 per cent discount, we have to sell 50 per cent more, and at a 15 per cent discount 100 per cent more! Perhaps we should put more marketing effort into justifying the higher price, because the consequence of the discounting approach is disastrous. Note that these figures are not strictly correct, because we have not allowed for the effect of volume on cost, but they illustrate the point (see Exercise 6.6).

Faced with this vicious circle situation, what normally happens is that we fail to achieve either the volume or the margin figures. In the example quoted, a discount of 10 per cent and a volume shortfall of 25 per cent would give a gross profit shortfall of 50 per cent, which is disastrous.

Like democracy, trying to find out market prices has its limitations but any alternative is far worse. The better we are at doing it, the higher our profitability is likely to be (see Exercise 6.7).

6.7   Pricing should be used both strategically and tactically

So far, we have argued that price is a key part of the marketing operation. We have urged that the benefits of the product or service should be presented in such a way that price is not the main factor in the buying decision. This philosophy should be built into our pricing strategy.

Nevertheless, there are times when tactical use of pricing is absolutely appropriate. When launching a new product, or embarking on a new marketplace such as a different market segment or geographical region, the first few sales are absolutely crucial. If we or our product are unknown, the lack of profile actually constitutes a barrier to purchasing. It would almost be worth giving the product away in order to begin to establish a track record! More seriously, special offers or discounts may be worth while, but we must be careful not to undermine the perceived value of what we are selling. It might be better to announce the full price to establish the product's positioning, but offer concessions to get the initial orders.

The price/volume relationship

An orthodox shape of the price/volume curve is shown in Figure 6.1. It is a theoretical model used by economists, and makes certain assumptions about the marketplace and the competition which do not always apply in a real situation. Nevertheless, it is a useful starting-point in our thinking about pricing strategy and tactics.

The essence is that our turnover and therefore our profitability vary at different points along the price/volume curve. We have an infinite choice of options between high margin/low volume and low margin/high volume. The profitability calculation is, of course, affected by the fact that there is almost certainly a cost/volume curve as well; higher volumes gained as a result of lower prices can reduce our unit costs and thereby generate a further contribution to profit.

The curve in Figure 6.1 is referred to as 'price elasticity of demand'. Numerically, this is defined as:

$$\text{Price elasticity of demand} = \frac{\%\ \text{change in demand}}{\%\ \text{change in price}}$$

For example, if reducing the price by 1 per cent causes the demand to increase by 2 per cent, the elasticity is 2. If we have to reduce the price by 4 per cent to achieve a 2 per cent increase in demand, the elasticity is 0.5. When the figure is more than 1, the demand is said to be elastic; below 1, it is inelastic. (Strictly speaking, the figure is a negative quantity, but this is usually ignored.)

For fast-moving consumer goods, such as soap powder or baked beans, where tens or hundreds of millions of units are sold each year, the suppliers will test one price against another, perhaps in separate but comparable locations. Their aim is to determine the slope of the tangent of the curve at the price level chosen—i.e. how many more or fewer units they could expect to sell if the price were decreased or increased by 1p, 2p, 5p and so on.

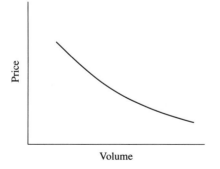

Fig. 6.1   The price/volume relationship

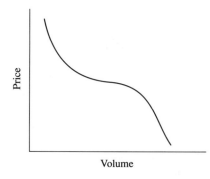

Fig. 6.2   A saturated market

There is a problem, of course, in that the buying decision is a multi-factor operation. The rather simplistic curve assumes that all other things are equal—which they never are. Competitors and customers have a habit of doing unpredictable things! Nevertheless, this approach can help us to clear our thinking and force us to ask questions which we might not otherwise ask.

However, we must give a word of warning. The curve may actually take a quite different form. A second possibility is shown in Figure 6.2.

The left-hand part of the curve, representing the higher price region, is reasonably orthodox; however, something strange happens as prices come down. At the lower end, however much we reduce prices, the volume does not appreciably increase. This is because the market is saturated. In this situation, reducing our price still further is the worst possible thing we could do—we would lose margin but not create extra demand. Somehow we have to find a way of getting up to the orthodox part of the curve where we can maximize profit in a more healthy price/volume relationship.

A similar situation arises when new suppliers try to enter an existing market which is already crowded. Prices are already depressed, and coming in at a lower price still is unlikely to be profitable. Somehow they have to justify a higher price by meaningful differentiation.

A third possible price/volume relationship occurs when price represents a strong segmentation criterion. Figure 6.3 is a diagrammatic representation of three market segments, each of which follows a reasonably orthodox pattern.

An example might be foreign holidays. At the top of the market, tailor-made holiday packages are offered for several thousand pounds to discerning buyers who wish to escape from the masses. The second section might represent the good value family holiday sought by many holidaymakers. The third and lowest part of the curve is the real cut-throat area where a cheap price overrides all other considerations.

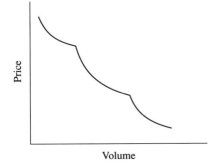

Fig. 6.3   A segmented market

An interesting strategic question is whether a company can operate credibly in more than one segment. There is a danger of confused brand image, so that the more expensive (and more profitable) offerings are undermined by the cheaper. It might be better to use different brand-names or even different companies for addressing the different segments.

A rather surprising but very important price/volume relationship is shown in Figure 6.4. At the top of the curve the volume increases as the price falls, but lower down the curve the volume actually *decreases* with a further drop in price. This illustrates the important point that price gives a signal about the value of the product or service we are selling. If something is too cheap, the perception is that it cannot be any good. This applies to hardware products, but it applies even more to intangible services where it is harder to attribute a 'correct' price. If consultants, lawyers or financial advisers are much cheaper than average, we might think very carefully before entrusting the future of our business or our personal wealth to their care.

It is not suggested that most companies will be able to draw scientific graphs of these curves, but the principles behind them are absolutely crucial and deserve a great deal of management attention.

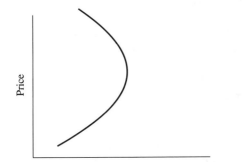

Fig. 6.4   The effect of price on perceived value

Strategic and tactical pricing

Several options are open to us on strategic and tactical pricing.

1. *'Skimming'* This is when we price at the top of the market, as we might skim cream off a jug of milk. We are not attempting to go for the mass market—we make our profit from a high-margin/low-volume approach, leaving competitors to do the opposite. We have to convince the customer of the value of what we are selling. Curiously, in the skimming situation, the high price may actually constitute part of the perceived value—people want to be seen to be driving the most prestigious car or wearing the most expensive suit.

2. *High pricing* This approach would be adopted where people are prepared to pay for excellent quality, increased reliability, sophisticated functions and so on. The suppliers use the price/volume curve to their advantage. This presupposes that they are sufficiently in tune with the marketplace to be able to predict, at least broadly, what the effect of the chosen price will be.

3. *Normal competitive situation* This occurs when a number of companies are selling broadly equivalent products in the same marketplace. As has been explained throughout this book, the key issue is to differentiate our product from the competition and to do everything possible to bring price down the ranking of criteria determining the buying decision.

4. *Low price* This approach would be used when we want to maximize the volume in order to achieve low unit costs. The advantage is that it makes it almost impossible for competitors with lower volumes to compete at a profit. The problem is, of course, that the margin available to us may not be sufficient, in spite of the high volume, to meet our targets for profit and return on capital employed (see the discussion on discounts in Section 6.6).

5. *Rock-bottom pricing* This tactic would be used when the overriding consideration is to achieve volume. This situation might arise when we have a very underutilized manufacturing resource where the fixed costs are having to be paid anyway. The argument is that it is better for us to sell products at a price which makes at least some contribution to fixed costs than to have no contribution at all.

   Rock-bottom pricing might also be used as a temporary measure in order to damage a competitor. This is possible when companies have large financial resources; they use the profit from another part of the enterprise, with a view to raising prices and increasing profitability once they have successfully reduced the competition. This approach might also be seen in the case of a very high-value tender. In these circumstances, there will almost certainly be a number of suppliers who are willing to offer rock-bottom prices because they desperately need the volume.

While rock-bottom pricing may have a role in a multi-product situation where other products are making good margins, it can be highly dangerous if our whole operation is based upon it. We have to find some way of moving up the price scale, by convincing the buyer that the value of what we are offering is greater than the others and therefore justifies a premium price.

This discussion again confirms the point that a great deal of senior management attention needs to be devoted to pricing. Obviously the various tactics are meaningless if we start with a cost-plus approach to the pricing operation (see Exercise 6.8 and Follow-up 6.2).

6.8 In-company transfer pricing is often handled badly

The situation described below is a composite picture based on real-life situations in a number of companies. No reference to a particular company is intended. It raises some key issues on in-company transfer prices, i.e. the prices at which goods are transferred in the books from one part of the company to another for onward sale to the third-party marketplace. It applies to both international situations and to those where two different parts of the company are involved in the same country—one making and one selling.

There are some legal constraints on the way in which money is moved around the world. There may also be sound financial reasons, such as a tax loss carryforward, why the corporation would like to make profit in one location rather than another. Within these constraints, however, there is considerable freedom to manoeuvre. In any case, the argument is not actually dependent upon where the profit is made—it is based on the assumption that the corporation's prime objective is to maximize total profit irrespective of where it is earned.

In this fictional illustration, Andrew Smith ('A'), the manager of the UK-based profit centre Alpha, is trying to sell his products into the USA, the largest market in the world. Corporate policy dictates that he should sell through profit centre Beta, another subsidiary of the same US-based corporation, managed by Barbara Wilson ('B').

B is interested in a certain product manufactured by Alpha, for which the published in-company transfer price is $75 (for simplicity, freight, duty and inflation are ignored at this stage). She feels that the product could be sold for about $100, as similar products are being sold by the competition in the range $85 to $115. This would give a margin of only 25 per cent, but it is incremental business and it is worth trying. She sells 1000 units in year 1, making a gross margin of $25 000 at 25 per cent.

At her budget review meeting, B is told that a 25 per cent margin is too low. She decides to increase her selling price to $110, because the product is good and the corporate name could command a premium. She sells 800 units in year 2, making a gross margin of $28 000 at nearly 32 per cent. At the next budget review, she is congratulated for increasing both her percentage margin and her dollar contribution.

However, at the same budget review of profit centre Alpha, A is criticized for losing volume, from 1000 to 800 units. Is he not pricing himself out of the market by charging $75? He checks his standard cost and finds that it has increased from $50 to $55 because of the drop in volume. There is not much room for manoeuvre, but he decides to talk to B.

He explains that the drop in sales is having a bad effect on his unit costs. B replies that she could sell more if the transfer price were lower. A explains that he could not give a lower price unless B could take a larger volume so that the unit production costs could be reduced. B thinks that by dropping her selling price she could sell 1300 units at $90 or 2000 at $80. However, to keep the percentage margin at a volume of 2000 units, she would need a transfer price of less than $55.

A knows that this is impossible. He estimates that his unit production costs would drop to $48 at 1300 per annum, or $45 at 2000 per annum, but he would be worse off. He had been making $25 000 on 1000 units; at a transfer price of $55 he would only be making $20 000 on a volume of 2000 units even with the lower production cost.

The problem is that both A and B are judged on the profit they make out of their part of the operation. A and B decide to look at various price/volume options to see which gives the best profit, with the following results:

Market price ($)	80	90	100	105	110
Volume (units p.a.)	2000	1300	1000	900	800
In-company transfer price ($)	75	75	75	75	75
Value of sales to Beta ($000)	160	117	100	94.5	88
Value of sales to Alpha ($000)	150	97.5	75	67.5	60
Unit cost to Alpha ($)	45	48	50	52.5	55
Cost of sales to Alpha ($000)	90	62.4	50	47.2	44
Gross profit to Alpha ($000)	60	35.1	25	20.3	16
Cost of sales to Beta ($000)	150	97.5	75	67.5	60
Gross profit to Beta ($000)	10	19.5	25	27	28

B needs the profit. She thinks that she should perhaps increase her price to $112 or $115. She even considers buying from a third party.

This seems wrong to A. Customers are willing to pay $110 or more for a product which could be made for as little as $45, and yet his colleague B is considering sourcing outside. He examines the options in more detail to calculate the effect of different transfer prices:

Market price ($)	80	90	100	105	110
Volume (units p.a.)	2000	1300	1000	900	800
Unit cost ($)	45	48	50	52.5	55
In-company transfer price $80	$K %	$K %	$K %	$K %	$K %
GM to Beta	0 0	13 11	20 20	22 24	24 27
GM to Alpha	70 44	42 40	30 37	25 34	20 31
In-company transfer price $75					
GM to Beta	10 6	20 17	25 25	27 29	28 32
GM to Alpha	60 40	35 36	25 33	20 30	16 27
In-company transfer price $70					
GM to Beta	20 12	26 22	30 30	31 33	32 36
GM to Alpha	50 36	29 31	20 29	16 25	12 21
In-company transfer price $65					
GM to Beta	30 19	33 28	35 35	36 38	36 41
GM to Alpha	40 31	22 26	15 23	11 19	8 15
In-company transfer price $60					
GM to Beta	40 25	39 33	40 40	40 43	40 45
GM to Alpha	30 25	16 20	10 17	7 12	4 8

In every case, the figures show that B needs to sell a lower volume at the higher price to increase profit, whereas A needs the higher volume at a lower price. These two are in direct conflict. There is no transfer price which is 'right' for both of them.

After a while, they realize that they have been trying to answer the wrong questions. They are each paid to maximize their own profit, but the figures show that their interests are diametrically opposed. They are each being asked to maximize *local* $ or *local* %. However, if they had both been asked to maximize *total corporate* $, the picture would have been very different:

Volume (units p.a.)	2000	1300	1000	900	800
Total corporate GM ($000)	70	55	50	47	44
Total corporate GM %	44	47	50	50	50

In this particular case, maximizing total corporate profit would mean selling to the marketplace at the lower price and getting the extra volume. (In other cases, the reverse might be true.) With this approach they would also be able to bid for some very large tenders which they had previously ignored because there had been insufficient margin for both parts of the organization to make a 'normal' level of profit.

The business reality is that the only thing that matters to the corporation is what it costs to make and what some third-party customer will pay for it. The in-company transfer price has no bearing on this whatever.

The problem can be overcome if each profit centre is judged against its approved *budget*. It doesn't really matter *where* the 'profit' is made. The treasurer will need to decide what is legal and what gives the best tax advantage, but that's no problem—the in-company transfer price doesn't affect the total profit.

Conclusions

1. Our real aim is surely to maximize the total corporate $ profit rather than local $ or percentage profit.

2. Where this can be done by two profit centres each achieving their own individual objectives, that's fine. Unfortunately there are cases where individual interests are in conflict, where the two profit centre managers will never be able to reach agreement if they look only to the interests of their own profit centre. In this particular case, it is in the interest of A *and the corporation* to sell the higher volume at the lower margin. The interest of B is diametrically opposed to both of these, and yet it is B who is the one who is charged with making the decision about whether or not to sell the product and at what price. She is judged on the basis of her local profit, irrespective of the effect this has on other profit centres or on the corporation as a whole. She is even given the option to source outside if that improves her own local profit!

3. The best approach is for the two profit centre managers to see what will generate the maximum profit for the corporation, decide whether the business is worth having, and then and only then negotiate on how the profit is to be split up. In other words, the effort should be to make bigger cakes and not just fight over the crumbs.

4. As long as we are judged against budget rather than in absolute terms, and everyone understands what we are doing and why, it is perfectly

possible to transfer at the price which gives the best combination of post-tax profit and motivation while keeping within the law.

5. There are large potential areas of business (especially tenders) where a competitor who takes a single slice of profit can offer a price which is too low to enable us to take two slices of profit in different parts of our operation, with the result that we don't get the business.

6. A profit centre usually makes less profit when it sells to another internal profit centre than when it sells to a third-party customer. The accounts are extremely confusing if the two sources of profit are combined. The more successful we are at generating in-company business, the worse we seem to be doing! It would be much easier to judge performance if the accounts showed in-company transfer profit separately from third-party profit.

These conclusions require a rational analysis of the total company situation by people who are mature enough to look outside their own immediate areas of responsibility. The issues will not even be discussed in this way in a sales-oriented environment where the culture assumes that all problems can be solved by tougher negotiation. For this reason, many large corporations fail to gain large amounts of profitable business which could be theirs for the taking. Exactly the same situation pertains within the manufacturer's own country, if there is a requirement to sell through company channels whose performance is judged on their part of the operation only.

There are great merits in profit centre management and devolved responsibility, but this is one of the disadvantages. The above argument indicates a way of getting the best of both worlds, but only if the situation is clearly understood and intelligently managed (see Exercise 6.9).

Exercises

6.1 Examine some recent pricing decisions made by your organization. To what extent were they based on 'what the market would bear' rather than 'cost-plus'?

6.2 Do you think your customers know about your costs? Do they care? What can you do to promote the *value* of your product or service, in order to reduce the linkage between price and cost?

6.3 What range of percentage margins do your products or services have? Is this range based on a good assessment of what the market will pay for the different products, or have the prices been influenced by some internal 'norms'? What opportunities for profit improvement does this offer?

6.4 By what percentage could you reasonably change the 'cost' of one of your main products by reallocating some fixed expenses? Would this make any difference to your pricing decisions?

6.5 Are any of your products 'commodities', or are any moving in that direction? What can be done to lift them out of the commodity environment or to reverse the trend?

6.6 Check the arithmetic in the discount calculations in Section 6.6.

6.7 What further steps can you take to find out the price the market will bear?

6.8 How accurately do you know the effect on volume of increasing or decreasing your prices by 1 per cent, 5 per cent, 10 per cent, 25 per cent? Are you sure that you are pricing correctly? Is there one product for which you could do some experimenting with different pricing without too much risk in order to test the elasticity? If not, could you do some market research into the same area?

6.9 If you sell through another part of the same company, familiarize your counterpart with the content of Section 6.8 and then examine the six conclusions at the end of it. What opportunities for increasing total profit does this exercise reveal? How will you split the extra profit between the two parts of the business?

Follow-up

6.1 Over the next six months (or other suitable period, depending upon whether you have an annual or other cyclical pricing regime) record the time you spend on preparing for and making pricing decisions. *Exclude any time spent on costs!* If at all possible, get your colleagues up to and including chief executive level to do the same. At the end of the period, ask yourself what would have been the cost of spending twice this amount of time. Do you think this would have been a profitable use of senior management time? (Do some arithmetic on the likely results.)

6.2 Read a book on pricing, such as Winkler, J. (1993) *Pricing for Results*, Butterworth Heinemann, Oxford.

Part II
THE ROLE OF
COMMUNICATIONS

How do we communicate?
Principles of communication

Key business issues	*Section*
■ Many different means of communication are available to us. Each has a different purpose and should be used accordingly.	7.1
■ A considerable amount of money is wasted because people do not ask 'What are we trying to say?' 'To whom?' 'With what objective?' 'Through what medium?'	
■ Communication is a progressive process, starting from zero and leading to placing an order. The purpose of each element of the communication is not to sell the product but to sell the next step.	
■ The key to cost effective communication is qualification of leads. We want quality of leads not quantity.	
■ Generalizations such as 'marketing does not work in our business' are often very superficial judgements based on an inadequate understanding of marketing.	7.2
■ Extrapolation from one selling situation to another can be highly dangerous. Methods which work in one case may be totally inappropriate in another.	
■ The size of the target audience is a key determinant of the forms of communication to be used.	
■ Impersonal means of communication should be used in the early stages of the communications process to generate qualified leads. Expensive personal selling should then be used to follow up.	
■ External agencies are experts in communications. We still have to take responsibility for the message.	7.3
■ Product launches are often handled inadequately. A professional launch brings together almost all aspects of marketing.	7.4

7.1   The progressive communications process

In our daily experience, both business and personal, we are bombarded with a vast amount of marketing communication. It takes a variety of forms—advertisements, brochures, letters, telephone calls, faxes, visits and so on, and we may understandably wonder how effective it all is. A large proportion of this communication is ineffective because some very basic questions have not been addressed:

What are we trying to say?
To whom?
With what objective?
Through what medium?

What are we trying to say?

When asked to engage in some form of marketing communication, the instinctive reaction of most people who have not been trained in marketing is to tell people about their product or service. They support their presentation with lists of specifications, equipment, functionalities, skills, past achievements and so on, the whole emphasis being 'this is what we do'. At first sight this seems perfectly reasonable but it is, in fact, quite the wrong way of going about it, as we shall explain in Section 7.2.

To whom?

Communication is a two-way process—communicating *with* people rather than *at* them. It starts with finding out something about the potential customer and his or her needs. Then, and only then, can we go on to say what we have to offer because, by this stage, we have learned at least something about what they might need and we can target our message accordingly. This important aspect of the communication process is discussed in Section 8.2.

We are often having to 'sell' to a number of different people, each of them coming from different perspectives and having different needs (see DMG in Section 2.6). Until we are clear about the target at which a message is aimed, we can't possibly compose the message itself.

With what objective?

This is where the biggest mistake is made. The objective is to sell, of course. Wrong! This is only true when the sale is made during a very simple encounter such as, for example, in a shop. The objective is more often to 'sell the next step' (see Section 7.2).

Through what medium?

The word 'media' normally refers to different forms of advertising—press, television, magazines, posters and so on. However, it is useful to broaden this to include every form of marketing communication. We have a wide variety of media at our disposal—personal contact, literature, proposals, advertising, presentations, letters, telephone calls, exhibitions, public relations and so on—with literally an infinite number of ways of combining them. In each case we need to ask 'is this the most appropriate medium' (see Exercise 7.1)?

'Selling the next step'

In most of the cases in which readers are involved, the selling process is much more complex than a single encounter. It involves a number of stages and the whole process may take days, weeks, months or even years. The objective of any form of marketing communication should therefore be to 'sell the next step' in the process. If the 'next step' is to complete the deal, well and good, but there may have to be several intermediate steps before this is possible.

Where a sale takes place over an extended period of time, the number of people involved in the purchasing decision may also increase. Similarly, a number of people from the selling company may become involved—seller to buyer, quality manager to quality manager, engineer to engineer, financial manager to financial manager, chief executive to chief executive and so on.

The important point to realize is that a sale is usually a process leading up to an event rather than a single event on its own. If the extended process is not managed properly, the event—the point at which the buyer actually commits to purchasing—may never be reached.

What are the stages in this process? Let us start by assuming the most difficult case. The buying company has never heard of us. They do not know that they need our product or service, and even if they did, they would not take the initiative in coming to us. They would not put our company on their long-list, let alone their short-list. This is a particular problem when we are diversifying from our historic core business into areas where we have no track record, as discussed in Section 4.8. Unless we take the initiative, nothing will happen; the selling process has stopped before it has started! (Actually, this might not be the most difficult case. We might start not from a low profile but from a negative profile—for some reason the buyer is actually predisposed against us. This might come about, for example, because of some perceived problem with our product or company, justifiable or otherwise.)

Another situation might be that the buyers know in a general sort of way that we are in the right field, but do not have enough information to decide whether or not to approach us. Again, we have to approach them.

This is why the whole culture of 'reactive selling' discussed in Chapter 1 completely fails. Unless we are proactive, i.e. we take the initiative to go out and make the first contact, nothing at all will happen.

The next stage, after the customer has actually realized that we may have something to offer, is a growing understanding of what we have to sell; this is accompanied by a growing understanding by us of what the customer might need. The needs which a customer initially expresses may not actually be the real needs, and certainly not the total needs. Part of the job of the seller is to help the buyer to understand what is really needed. If we succeed in doing this, we may not be guaranteed the sale but we are almost certainly in 'pole position'.

The next stage is serious negotiation. In a simple case this will involve presenting our solution, answering questions, overcoming objections and generally progressing towards the close. In a more complex case, such as a tender for a major capital project, the process may involve proposals, presentations, meetings, visits and so on.

This last stage is 'commitment to buy'. This takes place when the buyer has decided to proceed. In a major purchase, the decision may be 'subject to contract' (as when we buy a house). There may have to be important discussions over contractual, legal, logistical and other aspects; these are a crucial part of the selling process—the sale can be lost at this stage.

The point about recognizing the progressive nature of the selling process is that, in many cases, only one of these stages can be achieved at a time. The art of effective selling is therefore to focus on the issues involved at each particular stage—selling the idea of a meeting, for example. The ultimate goal of achieving the order will, of course, be in the back of our mind, but it will not dominate our actions in the earlier stages (see Follow-up 7.1). This approach contrasts radically with most forms of marketing communication, which can be summarized as 'this is who we are, and this is what we do'.

'Qualified leads'

If we send out a leaflet or put an advertisement in a journal, the initial probability of a sale might be one in a thousand. If we speak on the telephone to someone who has received this first communication, the probability might increase to one in twenty. If we meet the person face to face, it might increase to one in two. The probability reaches 100 per cent when an order is signed.

The point is that we are progressively 'qualifying' the lead. It is very important to recognize that the objective is to obtain quality of leads and not quantity. It costs a great deal of money to process leads; contacts who are unlikely to buy should be eliminated, or relegated to a lower priority, as early as possible in the process, so that attention can be concentrated on those who might.

The progressive nature of marketing communication can be illustrated by a true case study in which the author was involved. The objective was to sell the research and development services of a technical institution. They had had links with industry over at least twenty years, and had some useful ongoing customers. The objective, however, was to do some pioneering and to gain business from companies with whom they had had no prior contact.

Various options were open to them. They might run a series of 'open days', to which invitations were widely issued. Alternatively, a number of technical experts might make forays into various parts of industry where they thought there might be an opportunity. What we actually did was neither of these, but it resulted from a careful analysis of the selling process as outlined above.

We started by making a list of potential targets by consulting appropriate directories. (An alternative, which would have saved time but which would have cost more money, would have been to purchase lists of companies in certain categories.) Targets were selected as being companies above a certain size within a hundred miles and operating in technology areas where they had expertise.

A 'cold mailshot' was then carefully written. A key part of the strategy was to understand that the objective of this mailshot was *to sell an interview*, not to sell the services of the institution. A single-page leaflet was included to establish relevance and credibility, but the whole emphasis of the letter was that I should visit a senior person in the target company. The letter described the benefits of the interview as a means of linking the company with a wide range of skills, without involving any commitment and without taking more than an hour of their time.

An important part of this approach was the 'reply form'. This is described further in Section 9.3. Sixty per cent of the letters received a reply, and 50 per cent of these (30 per cent of the total) resulted in an interview on the customer's site, a very high percentage by most standards.

The second stage was to identify the potential needs of the client. In some cases they had an existing problem which outside assistance might help to solve. In many cases, with judicious probing, they were able to come up with a number of areas where some assistance could be valuable. At this stage very little was said about the actual technology being sold. The whole emphasis was on providing business solutions, within agreed costs and time scales. The objective was to achieve the third stage, a meeting on our site. The conversion ratio of visits to the client into structured meetings on our premises was about 75 per cent (22 per cent of the total), again a very high figure by most standards.

At these meetings, an agenda had been agreed as a result of the initial visit, and the right technical staff were present. They probed the needs more deeply and then described how they would address the particular problems which had been identified. Where appropriate, they demonstrated the facilities to the potential client and described past successes in similar areas. The objective of the meeting was to see whether it would be worth submitting a proposal.

Thereafter, the process went in the normal manner of invitations to tender with a contract ultimately being awarded or not. The crucial point is the process which led up to this invitation to tender. After all, the client had not come to us.

We had gone out to the client, assuming that there might be some business but with no actual demand expressed (see Exercise 7.2).

Having established that the marketing communication process involves a number of very different stages, and readers will no doubt be able to amplify these, we can now examine the role of the various elements which we are able to use. The important point is that each one is there to achieve a different objective during the progressive communications process. The way in which each is used will depend on a variety of factors—the size of the target market, the value of a potential order, the number of people involved in the decision, the length of time likely to be taken for the whole process from start to finish, and so on.

7.2   The role of different methods of communication

A qualified professional person once said to me 'We tried marketing—it doesn't work in our business'. Such a generalization simply showed that the speaker had not thought through the marketing process. What she meant was that they had written a brochure which was lying in the basement gathering dust! Inappropriate and inept marketing does not work in any business, but we cannot dismiss the whole multi-billion-pound communications industry on such a superficial basis.

Another person, a highly qualified scientist, said 'When I get a journal, I open it over the wastepaper bin and tip all the inserts away; therefore inserts are a waste of money'. Let us suppose for a moment that he is right (although, interestingly, he was attending my seminar as a result of one of my inserts!). To extrapolate to the world from a sample of one shows a scientific inconsistency which would have caused him to fail his school exams, let alone his university degree! We are dealing with statistical probabilities in this sort of marketing. We may all be nauseated at times by the 'junk mail' that arrives through the post, and obviously some of it is more effective than others, but the simple fact is that the advertisers do it because it works. They know that most of it will be ineffective, but they have done their arithmetic and they know that, provided they reach a certain number of replies, the campaign will not only have been successful but will also have been more cost effective than other ways of achieving the same level of response.

Figure 7.1 indicates the relative effectiveness of impersonal and personal forms of marketing communication at different stages in the selling process. The philosophy has been described in the previous section as 'selling the next step' and obtaining 'qualified leads'. The vertical axis is an unquantified measure of the relative effectiveness of each form of

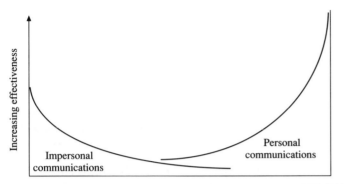

> > > Increasing awareness of need for our product > > > PURCHASE

Fig. 7.1   The role of personal and impersonal communications

communication as the customer proceeds towards a purchase. The horizontal axis indicates the increasing awareness of the customer to the need for our product or service; the time scale could be 2 minutes in a shop or 2 years in a contract negotiation—the principle is the same.

The effectiveness of *impersonal* media such as brochures and advertising declines as the communications process proceeds. Their role is to take the potential customer, at a relatively low unit cost, to the position where it begins to be worth employing *personal* selling efforts.

Quite apart from the cost of using personal selling early in the cycle, there is another very good reason why this should not normally be done. Sales staff are trained to close deals. They are highly motivated to get orders. In these circumstances, they are not going to be very excited if they are asked to give a lecture or travel around simply trying to generate interest or 'fly the flag'.

We must be aware of making generalizations. The precise way in which impersonal and personal communications should be used depends critically upon the potential size of the target market. Table 7.1 distinguishes four situations.

Direct approach to small defined customer base

If we are selling components to car manufacturers, it would be ludicrous to send out a brochure and then decide that the manufacturer of millions of cars was not interested in our product simply because the brochure did not result in an order! The size of the target market is so small numerically that we can and must approach each one individually. The role of impersonal means of communication, such as brochures, videos, case studies and so on, might be to create a general background image within which to carry out our marketing strategies and support our personal activities.

Table 7.1 Size and diversity of target market

Customer base	Route to market	Example of customers	Communications strategy
A **Small defined**	Direct to customer	Car manufacturers	*Personal* with whole market
			Impersonal (e.g. brochures, videos, case studies) to create image and support personal activities
B **Large defined**	Direct to customer	All major manufacturers	*Impersonal* narrowly targeted (e.g. direct mail) to qualify leads
			Personal with qualified leads
C **Effectively infinite**	Direct to customer	PC users	*Impersonal* broadly targeted (e.g. inserts, adverts) to qualify leads
			Personal with qualified leads
D **Effectively infinite**	Through sales channels	PC users	*Personal* with channels
			Impersonal (e.g. inserts, adverts, point-of-sale display) to create pull-through and support channels

Direct approach to large defined customer base

Let us suppose we are selling a service which could apply to all major manufacturers. Examples might be computer integrated manufacture, quality management, standards conformance, training, safety, or other forms of manufacturing expertise. The size of the target market is too large for the initial approach to be made personally in every case, even though we could 'pre-qualify' it by only including manufacturers above a certain size. The strategy would probably be to use narrowly targeted impersonal communications, such as direct mail with a letter and brochure, in order to qualify the leads. Personal contact would then be made with those who had shown some response.

Direct approach to effectively infinite customer base

By 'effectively infinite' we mean that the group is so large that there is no way in which we could contact the whole group. This is an important statement to make, because we may go on to conclude that a potential customer who has rejected our first approach may not be worth any further effort—we feel that we would be better to go on to new targets which have not already rejected us. (Against this it could be argued that a second and third approach may reinforce the earlier approach, so that we are more likely to achieve a response in due course. We have to make this judgement in the light of the particular situation.)

An example of an effectively infinite market approached directly would be all users of personal computers. We might use an advertisement or an insert in appropriate journals. The aim is to qualify the leads to determine which ones should receive our personal marketing efforts. We might follow up the leads from the advertisement with a personal letter as stage 2, and then try to 'sell a demonstration' to those who have responded to the letter as stage 3.

Approach through sales channels to effectively infinite customer base

Again the customers might be users of personal computers, but the difference is that we are selling through wholesalers, retailers or some other form of sales channel. Our efforts would obviously be personal with each sales channel in terms of selecting, appointing, training and motivating them, but we would not have direct contact with the ultimate purchasers. Our impersonal marketing efforts would probably be aimed at creating 'pull-through' (see Section 2.7). This could involve providing the channels with some way of reinforcing their own sales efforts such as point-of-sale display material for their outlets and also, possibly, advertisements, inserts, and so on. This expenditure would also encourage the management of the channels to make a corresponding effort on their part.

By studying the four examples above, and relating our own business to one or other of them, we can see that the use of impersonal and personal means of communication has to be very clearly thought out. An enormous amount of money is wasted on untargeted impersonal communications, and our aim should be to increase the percentage response progressively as we learn from experience. Equally, the productivity of our much more expensive personal efforts can be increased significantly if we first qualify the leads and target our efforts accordingly (see Exercise 7.3 and Follow-up 7.2).

7.3   The role of external agencies

When asked about their marketing communications, some people reply 'Oh, our advertising agency does that for us'. An in-house publicity department might play a similar role.

It is very important to understand the different roles of the client and the agency or publicity department in the communications process. The reason we use expensive outside resources is that they are experts in *communication*, which most of us are not. However, the client has to take responsibility for most (if not all) of the *message*.

If a client has a very large budget for advertising, literature and so on, a good agency will dedicate people to serve that particular client. They will invest time learning to understand the marketplace, the products, the customers and the competition. They will then be in a position to assist the client in developing marketing strategy and in articulating the message to be communicated, even though ultimate responsibility still rests with the client.

If a client has a smaller budget, it is a matter of commercial common sense that an agency is not willing to devote such resources to the account. The responsibility for defining the message is almost entirely the client's.

Failure to understand the distinction between the message and the communication vehicle is a cause of an incredible amount of wasted money. It leads to companies producing very expensive glossy brochures which say very little (see Exercise 7.4).

7.4   A product launch

One of the indicators of marketing professionalism is the attention which a company gives to a product launch. This is too often a low-key affair, with staff being ill-prepared and without the whole range of back-up material which is necessary to ensure its full success. In a marketing-led company, the launch is a major logistical exercise involving almost every department in the company.

If the 'product' is an intangible service rather than a piece of hardware, the launch programme is obviously less complex but the same degree of professionalism is required. Key aspects of a launch programme for a hardware product are as follows.

The product

Although this might seem a novel approach in some companies, the product will actually be available at the time of the launch! Appropriate stocks will be on the shelf, and the ongoing production programme with all its ramifications (materials procurement, production planning, etc.) will have been put into place. Spares will be available in appropriate quantities.

Salesforce

The salesforce will have been thoroughly trained in both the technical aspects of the products and the agreed approach to marketing them.

They will have been given individual targets and a specific programme of incentives. Launch meetings will have been held around the country and overseas as appropriate, not only to communicate the facts but also to build up enthusiasm and commitment.

Sales manuals will have been prepared to assist the personal selling efforts. The ideal sales manual is a structured document which enables the salesperson to take the prospect through the benefits of the product in a relevant manner, but allows for individuality in presentation and accommodates flexibility in the sales situation. Some companies have an absolutely pre-programmed sales 'spiel', but most of us would feel that a more intelligent and flexible approach is actually more effective.

Launch publicity

Suitable literature will have been prepared, translated into key languages as appropriate, and distributed in adequate quantities to all members of the salesforce. Advertising will break at the time of the launch in appropriate media.

A launch is often planned to coincide with a major international exhibition, and a correct balance will have been struck in the design and layout of the stand between the launch of the new product and the ongoing promotion of the existing product range. Public relations activities will have been coordinated, press releases will have been distributed and, possibly, a press launch meeting will have been held.

Sales channels

Distributors, agents, wholesalers or retailers will have been involved in the launch as appropriate. The salesforces of the distribution channels will have been trained and equipped in the same way as the company's own sales teams. The sales channels will have agreed targets to which they are expected to perform. If the product is an 'off-the-shelf' item, they will hold demonstration units and agreed stocks which they have purchased (perhaps being given a special initial incentive to do so). They will have made time for their sales and servicing staff to be trained by the supplier. Other aspects of the responsibilities of distributors are discussed in the appendix to Chapter 10.

This list is not complete, and the relevance of each item will depend very much upon the situation. However, although the points seem desperately obvious, it is my experience that many launches fail simply because no one took the trouble to coordinate the whole programme. The entire motivational impact of a launch sales meeting can be lost if the sales staff are told that some item such as brochures will not be available for two weeks. Why should they be expected to perform professionally if 'head office' can't do the same (see Exercise 7.5)?

Exercises

7.1 Select a piece of promotional literature used by your company, and a piece which you have received as a potential customer, and assess them against the four questions in Section 7.1.

7.2 Consider the case study in Section 7.1, and see whether a similar process could be used for promoting your organization into a new area.

7.3 Apply the framework of Table 7.1 to your own situation. What ideas does it give you for improving your own use of impersonal and personal communications?

7.4 Consider the relationship between your company and external communications agencies. Is it working well? Should you be doing more to create the message rather than leaving it to them?

7.5 Using Section 7.4 as a guide, assess the effectiveness of your last product launch. What steps will you take to ensure that the next launch is more successful?

Follow-up

7.1 Every time you are involved in a selling situation, ask yourself 'what is the next step?'. Concentrate on this rather than on the ultimate sale, until it becomes second nature to you.

7.2 Read a book on marketing communication such as Smith, P. R. (1994) *Marketing Communications: An Integrated Approach*, Kogan Page, London.

How do we sell?

Personal communication

Key business issues   *Section*

- Selling can be learned. It is a fallacy to assume that salespeople   8.1
  are born.

- Personality in a salesperson may be important, but far less than is
  commonly thought. Selling in most businesses is an extremely
  rational process.

- Selling starts with listening rather than speaking. We should   8.2
  prepare open-ended questions which will progressively lead
  customers to reveal their real needs.

- Presentations should be specifically prepared for each occasion   8.3
  and targeted to the particular customer. Standard presentations
  do not sufficiently exploit the opportunities.

- It may be worth attending a 'presentations skills' course, but
  attention to the message is even more important.

- Objections should be anticipated in advance and a reasoned   8.4
  answer prepared.

- There are many techniques for closing the sale. The sale should   8.5
  not be left to close itself.

- Selling can be carried out by full-time sales staff or by others   8.6
  (e.g. technical or professional) as part of their normal work.
  There are advantages and disadvantages to both.

- A combination of sales and other staff can be the most effective,
  with generalists bringing in specialists at the appropriate time.

- Existing customers should be nurtured and used.   8.7

- A complaint which is well handled can actually increase loyalty.

8.1   Selling can be learned

We often hear the statement that 'salespeople are born and not made'. This view is usually based on the caricature of a salesperson as a rather slick operator with the 'gift of the gab' who earns high commission payments at the expense of the unfortunate victims.

Readers will quite rightly reject this view as being totally out of character for their own business. Selling is an extremely rational process which can be taught and learned. Self-assurance and the ability to present and persuade are not enough and do not make up for the benefits which can be derived from a professional sales training programme.

In a book which covers the whole of the sales and marketing function, it is possible to describe only some of the main techniques of selling. If the reader is stimulated by this overall introduction, it would be worth seeking out a specialist training course, book or video.

8.2   Selling starts with listening rather than speaking

> 'I keep six honest serving men
> (They taught me all I knew);
> Their names are What and Why and When
> And How and Where and Who.
> RUDYARD KIPLING

The instinct of many salespeople is to bombard the hearer with a mass of facts and arguments which are supposed to lead to the placing of an order. Through ignorance or enthusiasm, or because the seller wants to keep control of the conversation, the whole direction of communication is one-way—it is communicating *at* rather than communicating *with* the customer.

We need to create a situation where customers start to talk about their business or personal situation, their problems and their needs. Then and only then can we apply the solution. If this sequence is not followed, we may be advocating a remedy for the wrong disease or even a remedy for which there is no known disease!

Suitable questions should be posed at an early stage in the conversation, in a very unthreatening manner, in order to get the prospect talking. An over-aggressive approach will have the reverse effect.

When approaching a sales interview, it is worth preparing some questions in advance which will begin to generate this two-way communication. Clearly we not going to interview the buyer with an intrusive clipboard listing a number of questions to which we demand answers, but this does not excuse us from taking a professional approach to preparation. A useful hint is to write down two or three questions on the second page of a pad of paper. The mere act of writing them down will probably register them in our memory, but, if not, they can probably be seen through page one or the pad can be casually flipped open as a reminder. Obviously we must be prepared to depart completely from our prepared opening questions, but if we try to plan the interview there is at least a chance that it will go the way we had hoped.

These questions should be open-ended and not capable of being answered 'yes' or 'no'. (Obviously there may be some diagnostic questions which need to be asked first, but these should not be confused with the open-ended type of question designed to delve into the buyer's real needs.)

A useful approach is to ask the buyer what problems are being experienced, and then ask about the effect of these problems on the business. This problem-and-effect approach encourages the buyer to realize the extent of the need.

Even with this method, there will be times when the question does not lead to the desired response. It may be necessary to probe ('that's interesting—what exactly did you mean by that?'), to rephrase the question, or to approach the subject from a slightly different direction: the objective is to get the customer talking.

When we have begun to form a view as to the buyer's needs and motivations, and the 'hot buttons' which are likely to lead to a favourable response, then and only then can we begin to apply our solution (see Exercise 8.1 and Follow-up 8.1).

8.3   Presentations should be prepared and targeted

People rightly think that presentations should be carried out as professionally as possible. They prepare handouts, overhead transparencies, slides, videos and other media which are aimed at presenting their products and company in the best possible light. Laudable though this is, it can actually have a negative effect. The danger is that the mechanics of the presentation can take precedence over the message being presented.

The problem is that some presentation media are inflexible. If we have invested a great deal of time and money in a corporate video, for example, the instinct is to show it on every possible occasion. This is fine as long as we are presenting to homogeneous audiences whose needs are all the same. The problem is that they are not. One of my clients was good enough to confess that he had fallen into this trap. 'As I watched their reaction to the video,' he said 'I could see their eyes glazing over— we were giving the wrong signals.'

The other extreme—not preparing anything—is equally ineffective. Experienced people feel that they have been doing presentations for many years and that 'it will be all right on the day'. They do not anticipate the questions and problems which concern that particular client, and therefore do not have the right material available. They give the impression that if the company can't even prepare a presentation properly, their product or service can't be much good either.

The art is to achieve a balance between these two extremes—preparing thoroughly but not allowing the mechanics to get in the way of the message. Some suggested guidelines are given below:

1. *Find out as much as possible about the client's needs in advance.*
   Selling starts with listening rather than speaking. If the presenter has already met the client, this should not be a problem. However, if we arrange a 'presentation at head office' which is given by others, it is essential that a clear brief is given on the background of the client, the objective of the presentation and the desired outcome of the whole process. Too often visitors are given a standard tour and presentation, and the seller is left wondering why so few of the efforts appear to bear fruit.

2. *Decide the specific objective of the presentation.*   Thinking back to Section 7.1, we have to decide what is the 'next step' in the communications process. What sort of commitment we are aiming to get from the client and how we are going to get it? It might be an agreement to submit a proposal, a further visit, a meeting, a discussion, a demonstration, or a visit to a reference site. Whatever the objective is, it should be clearly understood by everyone involved in the presentation. It is more important to sell this next step than to do a hard sell on the product or service at too early a stage in the process.

3. *Be clear about the message.*   Before doing the presentation, the person or team involved should write down in a few words the key points which they want to communicate. They should ensure that these points come across clearly and unequivocally throughout the presentation, in a way which can be remembered by the hearers.

4. *Concentrate on their needs not your skills.*   This point is often particularly badly handled in presentations. It is much easier to talk about ourselves than about the client's needs. Success goes to those who realize this and take the trouble to overcome it.

5. *Be flexible.*   In spite of everything which has been said above, we still need to be flexible on the day. Unforeseen questions and problems may arise, and it is no use sticking to our planned format if the client

is temporarily concerned about something different. One way of overcoming this in a professional way is to have alternative presentation material available in a readily indexed and accessible form. As an example, I prepare my seminars to meet the client's brief as closely as I can. However, I always have with me twenty copies of about fifty different handout pages which can be passed round immediately if an unforeseen point arises. This balance between being very well prepared and being flexible is the key to success (see Follow-up 8.2).

6. *Attend a 'presentation skills' course if necessary.* Such courses are obviously worth while but are not a substitute for the recommendations above. A client once said to me 'I attended a presentation skills course. At my next presentation, I avoided all the errors such as jangling keys in my pocket, and I felt that I had done a really good job. I told the audience that we were wonderful and had been in business for fifty years; unfortunately it achieved nothing!' It would be better to present a really clearly targeted message in a slightly unprofessional way than to have a very smooth presentation of the wrong material. However, it is better to be right on both counts!

8.4   Overcoming objections

Objections are points raised by the potential buyer, true or false, relevant or irrelevant, which stand in the way of a positive buying decision. Until we have dealt with a particular objection it may be impossible to make any further progress.

We will sometimes encounter objections we have not heard before, so that we have to think very quickly and give the best answer we can. However, some of the same objections come up time and time again, and it is well worth preparing an answer in advance. These may include the following.

Price

This is perhaps the most common objection. We could even argue that, if price is never an objection, we are underpricing! As we said in Chapter 2, our aim must be to bring price down the ranking in the buying decision by emphasizing the benefits which are most likely to be relevant.

The 'lifetime cost of ownership' is often more important than the initial price. The cheapest software package may be the worst possible purchase if the supplier cannot give the necessary support, upgrades and so on. A product which is cheap to buy but very inefficient and expensive to run may be a very bad investment. The seller must present these arguments, even to the extent of carrying out an investment appraisal on behalf of the customer. This is particularly true if the idea has to be 'sold' internally to people who may look at the initial price and disregard the other financial implications.

If we are selling to intermediaries such as wholesalers or retailers, who are going to sell the product onwards to their own customers, they will want to buy as cheaply as possible. It may be possible, however, to persuade them to work with us to create a higher perceived value and price for our product in the marketplace. This helps to lift the product out of the commodity situation (see Section 6.5), and creates more profit for both parties.

Features

The buyer may say that our product lacks certain features possessed by the competition. Overcoming this objection will depend upon whether the feature is essential, optional or just of passing interest. Every buying decision is a compromise, and we have to convince the buyer that our total package is better than the other total packages. By concentrating on the benefits (Section 2.4), we may be able to overcome the lack of a particular feature. If the feature really is essential, we either have to add it to the product or withdraw from the contest, but we should not concede a costly change in specification too readily.

Complication

Many products which are technically very sophisticated, such as word processors, are used by people who do not need to understand the technicalities. We should provide user-friendly manuals, with a really good index and reference system. They should be written in language the user can understand and not in the inventor's jargon. I once wasted an hour trying to execute a certain function on my word processor because I did not realize that I had to look for 'snaking columns' in the index.

Fear of the unknown can be overcome by explaining that we have a very thorough training programme, or a 'hot line' for instant advice when a problem arises. We should not deny that our product is complex—we might even present it as a virtue, describing it as 'sophisticated' rather than complicated—but we need to realize that the prime need of the customer is usually for simplicity and peace of mind.

Lack of authority

Our contact may seem to be happy but does not give the go-ahead. This may be because authority has to be sought from a more senior person or a committee.

What do we do if the buyer says 'I'm happy with what you have said but the decision will be made at the board meeting next Thursday week'? The answer is not 'ring on Friday week'! We should first ask whether we could take part in the presentation. Without this, we disappear from the scene and have to rely on the buyer to do our selling for us, and it is unlikely that the presentation will be as convincing as the one we would give. The buyer is not an expert in our product and may have been talking to competitors, and so the loyalty may not be as strong as we had believed.

If this is not acceptable, the next best plan would probably be for us to help the buyer to do a good presentation. We might provide additional handouts, overhead foils or other visual aids. We might help to work out the financial implications of the purchase in terms of return on investment for the company. After all, the buyer wants to do a professional presentation to senior management, and will welcome anything we can do to help.

Loyalty to another supplier

The potential buyer may seem to accept what we say but explains that they are using another supplier. We should not criticize the other supplier, because that would imply that the buyer had been exercising bad judgement. We might try to get part of the business at first. Multiple sourcing has many advantages, particularly in terms of reducing risk. We might just drop the hint, in a low-key and uncritical way, that their present supplier may be taking them for granted. We could explain how we would provide all sorts of additional support and services which the present supplier is not giving.

Hidden

There are times when everything seems to have gone well and we can't understand why the buyer will not reach a decision. The problem may well be a 'hidden objection' which, somehow, we have to bring to the surface. The open-ended questions described earlier can often reveal the hidden objection. If this fails, the next stage in the selling process—attempting to close the sale—may be the best approach (see Exercise 8.2).

8.5 Closing the sale

There are literally dozens of techniques for closing the sale. They range from the low-key rational approach to those which virtually border on tricking the customer into agreement. We concentrate in this book on those methods of closing a sale which can be used legitimately and honourably.

The objective is to get the buyer to commit to going ahead with the deal (perhaps subject to contract). The most widely applicable techniques for closing a sale are as follows.

The trial close

This is not offering the prospective customer an opportunity to try out the product, although this can be a useful tactic in some cases. The trial close is 'testing the water' in an unthreatening manner to see whether sufficient progress has been made.

A 'throw-away' expression might be used such as 'are we ready to go ahead, then?' This approach may succeed. If not, the buyer may indicate areas which need more discussion, thereby revealing a hidden objection.

It is important that we do not give the impression that 'I must have an answer now'. In such circumstances, the buyer is likely to say that the answer is 'No'!

The summary close

This involves summarizing the progress made to date, orally, on paper or on a whiteboard. We note the various points which we think have been agreed. At each one we carefully observe the reaction of the buyer, to detect positive or negative buying signals. The probability is that, faced with a written summary, the buyer will give the go-ahead. Alternatively, a hidden objection may be revealed which needs to be dealt with. The same or another method of closing can then be adopted.

The assumptive close

The objective is to lead the buyer increasingly to think ahead as if the purchase had already been agreed. We would ask questions relating to the post-purchase situation such as 'where will you be installing this equipment?' 'How do you want us to train the operators?' 'When do you want us to start?' and so on. Thinking about these issues may encourage the idea of having our product or service.

The alternative close

This is one of the most common methods of closing and is used frequently in our personal and business life. In a shop it would take the form 'would you like the red one or the blue one?' 'Will you take it or shall we deliver it?' 'Cash or credit?' and so on. In an industrial situation there is considerably more scope for offering alternatives, not only in the product itself (the basic or the enhanced model) but also in payment terms, delivery schedules, ongoing support and so on.

The objective is to encourage the buyer to weigh up the relative merits of two alternatives, either of which is acceptable to us. The debate is 'yes versus yes' rather than 'yes versus no'.

The concession close

This is where some concession is offered in order to secure the sale. It might be better to offer free product or service rather than a straight financial discount, because it costs us less. Also, the perceived value of what we are selling may be diminished if we are too ready to reduce the price.

There are two important points about the concession close. First, we should not go as far in the first instance as we might be prepared to do. If we are prepared to offer 10 per cent discount, we might offer 5 per cent and allow ourselves to be talked up to 6 per cent or 7 per cent; the buyer has won a victory, and we have saved some money. Second, and even more importantly, we should trade the concession for something, preferably the order. We might use an expression such as 'if I were to give you a 5 per cent discount, would you give me the order now?'

Keeping control

Whatever method is used for closing the sale, it is essential that the seller keeps control of the situation. We can't wait for the sale to close itself. How often do we fail to make a purchase when an intelligent and sensitive use of an appropriate closing technique might have been successful? By the way, the sale has not been completed until we have received the money (see Exercise 8.3 and Follow-up 8.3).

8.6 The selling role of non-sales staff

Many companies have clearly defined departments which are responsible for the selling function. Others, such as small companies, technical or professional consultancies, accountants, lawyers, patent agents, universities, local authorities and other organizations wishing to market their services, may not have a single member of staff whose prime role is selling. The only people available for selling are those who are employed primarily to do something else.

Some operations fall somewhere between these two descriptions. They have a small sales resource which they know is inadequate, but they are not sure whether to expand this or to ask non-sales staff to do some selling on a part-time basis.

There are advantages and disadvantages to both approaches. Some of the factors are listed below:

Non-sales staff: advantages
1. They can make the product or service more tangible. They live in the world of the product and are able to speak about it with authority.

2. The needs can be thoroughly investigated. They realize the finer points of detail about the product and its application, and should be in a position to ask careful probing questions.

3. They can establish a more detailed rapport with the client. This is particularly true when they are speaking to people who understand the jargon and ways of thinking which are common to them both.

4. Quality is more easily demonstrated—the seller is the 'maker'. This is particularly important in the case of consultancy, where people are the product.

Non-sales staff: disadvantages
1. The selling effort is limited to the availability of people who are actually employed to do something else.

2. Non-sales staff can waste a lot of time in their enthusiasm for the technical aspects of the product.

3. Most non-sales staff are product orientated rather than customer orientated, and live in a world of features rather than benefits.

4. Particularly in intangible services such as consultancy or research, the 'seller' may be so enthusiastic as to reveal key parts of the solution to the buyer during the selling process. The buyer goes away highly delighted, solves the problem and is never seen again!

Full time sales staff: advantages
1. More sales effort is available. Staff are employed full-time for this task, and are motivated and usually given incentives to do nothing but gain orders.

2. They have better control over customers. They live in their world and understand how they make decisions.

3. They should have a market orientation rather than a product orientation.

Full time sales staff: disadvantages
1. There may be a high cost per customer because they quickly find that they need to call in a specialist to back up their own efforts.

2. Sales people *may* have an unnecessary tendency to price cutting. If their commission depends on turnover rather than profit, and they are authorized to give discounts, why would they not do so?! This is a failure of management, but it certainly occurs.

3. Sales staff may come up with unnecessarily customized solutions. They are so anxious to get the sale that they concede points on the specification which have more far-reaching technical and cost implications than they had realized.

There are clear advantages and disadvantages of using full- and part-time staff in the selling operation. The answer may lie in a combination of both, along the following lines:

1. Use impersonal communications early in the sales cycle to identify qualified leads.

2. Use full-time generalist sales staff to follow up those leads to achieve further qualification.

3. Bring in specialist resources (e.g. technical or professional) in those cases where a sale is most likely.

In this way we can have the advantages of both options without the disadvantages (see Exercise 8.4).

8.7   Nurturing existing customers

Nurturing existing customers may not seem to bring incremental short-term rewards, but it is an essential part of our task. We cannot take anyone's loyalty for granted, and competitors are out there attempting to win our customers for themselves. In any case, there are other reasons for looking after them. They may speak spontaneously on our behalf, or they may be willing, for example, to open their facilities as a 'reference site' to which we can invite potential customers. Such privileges should not be abused or used too often, but they can be an invaluable method of reinforcing our own marketing efforts. After all, we are paid to say that we are good; customers are not, and their testimony is therefore much more credible.

An interesting situation arises with a dissatisfied customer. It has been said that a satisfied customer can bring us five more, and a dissatisfied customer can lose us ten. We should deal with the cause of dissatisfaction if at all possible, because it can influence other potential buyers. This is just as true if the fault is not actually ours; hearers will react as if it were. However, and this is the key point, a dissatisfied customer whose cause of dissatisfaction has been removed may actually become more loyal than someone who has never had cause to complain. A vaguely satisfied customer may, in fact, not be particularly loyal; a customer who has had a problem which the supplier went to great lengths to solve may become one of the supplier's most positive allies in the future. We need to strike a careful balance in our selling efforts between existing and new customers (see Exercise 8.5).

Exercises

8.1 Think of a sales situation for your company. What do you want to know about the customer? What open-ended questions could you ask in order to elicit this information?

8.2 Make a list of the main objections which you encounter in selling your company's products or services. Against each, write the key points in your argument for overcoming the objection.

8.3 How would you use the assumptive close, the alternative close and the concession close in your business?

8.4 Consider the advantages and disadvantages of using non-sales staff and full-time sales staff in your business. Do you think you have the right balance?

8.5 Are you paying enough attention to existing customers? Consider some customers who have recently been dissatisfied with your company. Do you think the dissatisfaction was handled in the best way? How could it have been improved?

Follow-up

8.1 Make a habit of writing down two or three questions in advance of each meeting with a potential customer.

8.2 Make a habit of considering items 1 to 5 in Section 8.3 in advance of each presentation.

8.3 If appropriate, read a book on selling techniques such as Prus, R. C. (1989) *Making Sales*, Sage Publications Inc., Newbury Park, California.

How do we use impersonal communications?

Literature, proposals, letters, telephone, exhibitions, advertising, PR

Key business issues   *Section*

- Much promotional literature is ineffective because it relates more   9.1
  to the supplier than to the customer.

- Promotional literature can often be significantly improved
  in a relatively short time if it is judged against certain
  guidelines by an in-house panel.

- Proposals and responses to invitations to tender often fail to   9.2
  differentiate the supplier from other competitors. It is essential
  to identify and emphasize the 'win themes'.

- A proposal can often be significantly improved in a relatively
  short time if it is judged against certain guidelines by an
  in-house panel.

- Sales letters are often not read because insufficient thought   9.3
  has been given to the message and the response expected.

- A well-designed reply form can increase the effectiveness of letters.

- Use of the telephone for marketing can be made much more   9.4
  effective by following simple principles.

- Much of the money spent on exhibitions is wasted. Properly   9.5
  planned and used, exhibitions can be one of the most cost-
  effective tools of marketing communication.

- Qualification of leads is the key to exhibition follow-up.

- Much of the money spent on advertising is wasted because its   9.6
  role is not clearly understood.

9.1   Promotional literature

The situation in which literature is received

Imagine the scene. Someone is expecting to receive a piece of our literature through the post that morning. He wakes up and says to his wife, 'I'm looking forward to today—XYZ are sending me their new brochure'. He gets to the office and enquires eagerly whether the post has arrived. He asks his secretary to cancel his appointments and take his telephone calls so that he won't be disturbed, clears his desk and spends two hours reading the brochure from cover to cover.

If only that were so! In reality, the document first has to get past the secretary, who is trained to protect the manager from junk mail and other time-wasting intrusions. It then arrives in the in-tray, where it quickly becomes covered with other documents. It sits there for several days until the recipient has a blitz on the pile, after which it will end up in the bin, in the filing tray or—and this is probably the best we can hope for—in the briefcase to be read at home at the week-end or on the train. In other words, we have about two seconds to capture the recipient's interest, and to create a greater impact than all the other documents which constantly flood in.

One of my favourite photographs is of my young son lying on a beach in France devouring a model railway catalogue—which he did for a whole fortnight. If only our literature could command the same degree of attention!

How are we to do this? We make no apology for repeating the first three simple questions posed in Section 7.1:

1. *What are we trying to say?*   Is our message concerned with establishing an image, giving information, creating warm feelings, generating a demand or is there some other message?

2. *To whom?*   Will it be read by specialists or by generalists or both? Will it be read by people whose interest is primarily technical, financial, operational or what?

3. *With what objective?*   Is the document merely intended to supplement other marketing efforts, or is it aimed at getting a response in its own right such as a request for further information, a telephone discussion, a visit, a demonstration or even an order?

Some suggested guidelines for effective promotional literature are given below. It is a useful exercise to take a piece of our existing literature and, very objectively, to award marks against these criteria. I do this exercise on most of my in-company seminars, and it is surprising how often the marks turn out to be low, even for a piece of literature with which the client was previously quite happy.

Promotional literature guidelines

Suggested guidelines are as follows:

1. *Overall impact on first sight*   What is the immediate impression on seeing the front cover of the document (within a maximum of two seconds)? Is it going to create sufficient impact to ensure that it will at least be kept for later reading?

2. *Initial interest*   Does it capture the recipient's initial interest compared with all the other documents, so that it will be read further when there is time (e.g. put into the briefcase). In the meantime, will it leave some sort of positive feeling in the mind?

3. *Customer orientation*   Does the document relate to the needs of the reader, does it present benefits, and are these benefits targeted to the needs of the particular recipient, or does the document just talk about the supplier and the products?

4. *Uniqueness*   Does it establish a unique selling proposition? Does it present the company as offering something unique, or at least special, to differentiate it from the large number of other companies offering apparently similar products or services?

5. *Logical structure*   Does it take readers logically through a progressive argument leading to a conclusion and action, and can they easily find the parts they might want to study?

6. *Ongoing interest*   Is it sufficiently interesting to sustain attention, so that the reader will be willing to devote some time to studying it in detail?

7. *Market segmentation*   Which market segments is it aimed at? Does it do this adequately, or does it 'fall between several stools'?

8. *Decision-making group*   Is it addressing members from several different disciplines (technical, financial, general management, operations, quality, etc.)? If so, is there at least something for all of them (even if there are some parts which are more relevant than others)? Can they find the part which they might want to read, or is it hidden in a mass of detail which, to them, is irrelevant?

9. *Comparison with competitive literature*   Will our proposed document compete favourably when laid alongside current copies of the competitive literature? We often have to win the 'battle of the literature' before we can win the 'battle of the product'.

10. *Novelty*   Does the document have something to lift it out of the ordinary, perhaps by really creative use of photography, diagrams, pictures of computer screens and so on? Most companies have buildings with windows and cars parked outside, and most boxes have knobs on—we have to do better than that! A promotional brochure is not a catalogue—it is a document fighting for attention.

11. *Style and image*   Is the style appropriate to the marketplace, the reader's operation, the supplier's operation, and the product? Quite apart from the actual content, what does the reader perceive about the supplying company from the quality of the document and the intangible image which it conveys. One client admitted that their literature very accurately portrayed their company's image—of being conservative, out of date and boring!

12. *End of the document*   Does it reach a conclusion and invite a response, or does it simply stop because there is no more space?! Does it contain some sort of offer, possibly for further information or for a visit or demonstration? For example, the brochure promoting my own seminars invites readers to telephone for an informal exploratory discussion; in this way, they are able to consider the relevance of the seminars without any commitment or high-pressure selling. Should the name of the contact be printed? If it is, the person usually leaves the next week! If it is not, it is impersonal. A slot for a visiting card is a useful way of overcoming these problems.

Examining a document against these twelve criteria will often reveal some specific steps which can be taken to improve its effectiveness next time it is printed. While it is not suggested that documents can be written by a committee, frequent use of these criteria on workshops has shown that a small group of non-marketing managers who have spent a few hours learning the basics of marketing can come up with very sensible proposals for improving the effectiveness of a piece of literature in a surprisingly short time (see Exercise 9.1).

The problem of multi-purpose literature

Many documents fail to be effective because they attempt to be 'multi-purpose'. They try to address too many targets, and therefore do not address any targets adequately. This often comes about because the whole budget is spent on one rather lengthy document, whereas it might be far better to produce a number of one-page leaflets each of which has a specific and quite different purpose.

Even then, the instinct is for companies to write product-oriented literature and to use it for all market segments. It might be better to have market-oriented literature, each piece covering a number of products which are relevant to that particular market.

A cost-effective strategy might be to have a good glossy general piece of literature designed to establish credibility, reputation, image and so on, and then to have a number of different short leaflets each targeted at a particular market segment. It might be acceptable for these short leaflets to be produced internally by desktop publishing; this has the great advantage that they can be updated frequently as the track record develops, and even modified to meet particular situations. With a little ingenuity, the general brochure can be printed in the form of a wallet which can contain an appropriate selection of the individual market segment leaflets. By doing this, the literature budget can be used to best effect, and individual customers can be given the documents which will be most effective in identifying with their particular needs (see Exercise 9.2).

9.2 Proposals and invitations to tender

Many companies are accustomed to a culture in which they produce 'estimates' or 'quotations' in response to 'enquiries'. These documents do not attempt to make claims about what they are selling, to differentiate themselves from the competition, or to persuade in any way. They are typical of a 'reactive' marketing approach. These companies have to learn instead to produce 'business proposals' in response to 'marketplace opportunities'.

Two different situations may be distinguished. In the first case, we are completely free to decide the format, length, content and emphasis of the proposal which we are preparing for a potential customer. In the second case, we are given a prescribed format, sometimes extremely lengthy and complex in its structure, which we are required to complete; failure to comply with the required format may automatically invalidate our tender submission. In either of these cases it is strongly recommended that, before beginning to draft the sections and 'fill in the boxes', we write down on a single sheet of paper the key points which we judge will constitute the 'winning bid themes'.

This is an important discipline for two reasons. First, if we cannot briefly encapsulate the message we are wishing to convey, it is doubtful whether we have thought it through sufficiently. Second, the more the client is wanting to push our submission into their format, the more effort we will have to make to ensure that we emphasize the points that *we* want to communicate. There is the story of the preacher who said 'First I tell them what I am going to say, then I say it, then I tell them what I have said'. This is good advice for the submission of proposals or, indeed, for most forms of marketing communication, because it clarifies and reinforces the key message to be communicated.

Before we begin to write a single word, we need to know who will read the document. Will the award be adjudicated by an individual or by a board or committee? In the latter case, which business disciplines will the group represent (see decision-making group in Section 2.6).

We should be very clear as to the specific objective of the proposal. Is it intended to achieve the award of the contract in its own right, or is there a preliminary objective such as a demonstration, a feasibility study, a visit or qualification for the short-list? It is important to put all our effort into achieving the specific objective of the document and not to do a half-hearted job of trying to obtain the order if this is not the likely outcome of this stage in the negotiating process.

We then need to identify the competitive scenario within which this particular award will be considered (see Section 5.1). If we have not correctly understood this, we may 'win the battle and lose the war', i.e. convince the reader that our product is the best but lose the contract to some other competitive force (such as an alternative way of solving the problem).

We are now in a position to start writing the document! The one-page summary of the 'win themes' should be prominently displayed (perhaps on a whiteboard or flip-chart) the whole time we or our colleagues are writing the text.

Some suggested criteria against which the proposal can be assessed are shown below. Some of them are similar to the criteria for assessing promotional literature, because many of the needs are the same.

1. *Summary*   Are the key issues and main selling points clearly set out? Many of the recipients will be too busy to read the whole submission, and will form their judgement on the basis of the summary and a selected inspection of parts of the main proposal. Our aim should be to get agreement from the summary alone!

2. *Overall impact on first sight*   Most proposals and tender submissions are likely to receive at least a cursory glance. However, we have to bear in mind the psychology of the situation and the fact that those who award tenders are still human beings with all the normal motivations and prejudices. If a proposal looks professional and well presented, it is more likely to be read in a favourable light than one which looks boring.

3. *Ongoing interest*   Does it look interesting and worth reading at length? Does it contain pictures, diagrams and arresting statements at strategic points in the document so that, if the reader glances ahead, the appetite will be whetted?

4. *Competitive situation*   What form of competition is the proposal designed to address? Does it do this effectively?

5. *Customer orientation*   Does the document relate to the reader's needs by highlighting relevant benefits, or does it just talk about the supplier's products, skills and resources?

6. *Decision-making group*   If the document is addressing members from several different disciplines (technical, financial, general management, operations, etc.), is there at least something which is designed to attract each and every member of the decision-making group? We can lose a tender by failing to convince only one member of the DMG.

7. *Uniqueness*   Does the proposal present the company as offering something unique, or at least special, to distinguish it from the competition? As we explained in Chapter 2, the differentiation may be in the form of intangible, peripheral or personal attributes and not necessarily in the product itself.

8. *Curricula vitae* (if appropriate)   Have CVs been specifically targeted to this project and the needs of this particular client? Obviously we cannot alter the basic content of a CV, but the emphasis and method of presentation can make a great deal of difference. It is much easier to pull a standard CV off a word processor, but it is worth spending a few moments targeting it. This is particularly true in a consultancy situation, where the skills and experience of the consultants are paramount. It might be possible, for example, to highlight a panel showing 'experience of Dr X which is particularly relevant to this project'.

9. *Financial issues*   Has a soundly based financial argument been presented? This may involve issues such as investment and return, lifetime cost of ownership, risk and sensitivity (Section 12.7) and cash flow, in order to assist the financially orientated reader to reach a decision.

10. *Structure and layout*   Has full use been made of the freedom which the client permits to present the argument in the most persuasive manner, or have the 'mechanics' got in the way? Does the document

take the reader logically through a progressive argument leading to conclusion and action? Does it have a good index (if appropriate)? Can the sections be found easily? Again we are recognizing the fact that people are busy (or even lazy!), and we want to make it as easy as possible for them to receive our message.

11. *Style and image which it conveys*   Is the style appropriate both to the buyer and to the seller? Has good use been made of graphics, diagrams, charts, graphs, etc. in a way which conveys the appropriate degree of professionalism? Quite apart from the actual content, what does the reader perceive about the company from the quality and style of the document? The unwritten message can sometimes be more powerful than the written one, and images which the recipient receives from 'reading between the lines' can speak more powerfully than the words themselves.

12. *Key points*   Are the 'win themes' clearly developed throughout the text, and are they emphasized and progressively supported? Is there a recapitulation at the end which leaves the key points in the reader's mind? Remember the preacher! (See Exercise 9.3 and Follow-up 9.1.)

9.3   Sales letters and 'mailshots'

In this section we are referring to any written communication with a potential or existing customer which is designed to further the communications process and qualify the lead as described in Section 7.1. These might include letters to individuals with whom we have had prior contact, or a programme of 'cold-mailshots' to people whose names and addresses we have obtained in some way.

A number of the points below have already been made in connection with other forms of communication. This is quite deliberate, and the reader is encouraged to take a common approach to the whole subject of marketing communication.

The following guidelines can be used for judging a letter which has already been written. This might be one which we have sent to a client or one which we have received from someone attempting to sell to us. Two points are paramount:

■ We must be clear about the objective of writing, and emphasize this in the opening and closing paragraphs. The whole letter must be worded in a way which is most likely to achieve that objective. For example, if the specific objective is to 'sell' a meeting, the emphasis should be on the reasons for having a meeting; generalized messages about the company or the product should be used only as a means of reinforcing the main aim.

■ We have to find some way of getting past the secretary who is paid to protect the manager from 'junk mail'. The letter should always be addressed to the reader by the correct name (which has been checked by telephone if necessary)—never 'The Managing Director: Dear Sir or Madam'. The opening sentence should refer to some specific event such as a meeting or project, or describe financial or technical issues in such a way that the secretary does not feel authorized to reject it.

Guidelines for a sales letter

1. *Objective*
   Why are we writing? (overall objective)
   What should the letter achieve? (specific objective, e.g. next step)

2. *Structure*
   Opening
   Commands attention
   States the objective
   Establishes link with previous contact or event

   Middle
   Develops the theme(s)
   Presents facts
   Offers benefits
   Creates a link to the close

   End
   Summarizes
   Clearly states the next actions

3. *Layout*
   The letter should have good visual appeal
   The eye should travel smoothly down the page
   It should be easy to see which parts refer to what

4. *Language*
   Avoid trite and overused phrases
   Avoid pomposity
   Avoid both coldness and inappropriate familiarity
   Ensure perfect punctuation, spelling, use of tenses

5. *General impression*   The whole letter must be attractive, readable, credible and persuasive and must represent our company as a worthy partner (see Exercise 9.4).

Reply form, used mainly for mailshots

One of our objectives is to make it as easy as possible for the recipient to respond. It may be worth including a reply form. The example given below was used in the 'case study' described in Section 7.1; the reader might like to reread that section in order to understand the situation in which the reply form was used.

Reply Form

To: *(ourself)*

(please tick as appropriate)

[   ]   Please contact my secretary to arrange to visit me for an exploratory discussion
[   ]   Please telephone me to discuss the possibilities in more detail
[   ]   Please send me more general information
[   ]   Please send me specific information in the areas shown below
[   ]   Please contact me again in . . . . . . months' time
[   ]   Please delete me from your mailing list
Other comments, or areas of interest *(leave more space)*

Name . . . .*(filled in beforehand by ourselves if possible)*
Company . . . .
Position . . . .

Some important points need to be made in relation to this reply form. The first option 'Please contact my secretary to arrange to visit me . . .' is based on an absolutely crucial point. Why do we want to arrange the meeting through the secretary and not the manager himself or herself? The obvious answer—that the manager is busy—completely misses the point. What is the objective of the letter? It is to gain an interview. At what point have we achieved our objective? When the manager has *ticked the first box*. Once we have achieved this objective, we must not allow a change of mind. We don't want to start discussions over the telephone, because our aim is to meet the buyer face to face. Once the first box has been ticked, the secretary will not feel able to question the decision. The manager has asked for an appointment, and all that has to be done is to arrange a mutually convenient date.

If I were a purist, there would only be the one box to tick, and there would be no other options. However, I am also a realist, and so some alternative options have been offered.

The last option, 'Please delete me from your mailing list', is controversial and should only be used where the target market is effectively infinite. It is based on the assumption that an initial rejection is actually a useful piece of information and that our efforts would be better directed to other potential clients on the list. In any case, there is nothing to stop us going back after a few months anyway!

The response can be increased if we enclose an envelope addressed to ourself with an actual stamp on it—not a business reply envelope. This is based on the assumption that people will not throw stamps into the bin in the way that they would a reply-paid envelope; the easiest way of dealing with it is to tick a box and put it in the out-tray!

It is not suggested that this particular approach is a stereotype for all business situations, but I have used it very successfully myself and it may give food for thought to other readers (see Follow-up 9.2).

9.4   The telephone

The telephone is increasingly becoming a vehicle for marketing communication. Its use is extended by the use of fax and video conferencing, and, no doubt, we shall soon be communicating by virtual reality!

The telephone involves much lower cost and management time than most other forms of communication. If used properly, as one step in the communication process (see Section 7.1), it can be very effective.

However, the telephone can also be extremely frustrating and even counterproductive if certain tactics are not followed. It can easily be ignored, or a message can be rejected without any embarrassment on the part of the recipient. It is much harder to gauge the reaction of the customer over the telephone than in a face-to-face situation where body language and behaviour can be very significant.

We can distinguish two situations. When the caller is known, the conversation is relatively straightforward. When the caller is unknown, there is an added complication and a higher risk that the call will go wrong. We will therefore consider the more difficult situation—the 'cold call'.

As with all forms of marketing communication, it is essential to decide in advance what is the objective of the call. For most readers it is quite unrealistic to expect to gain an order over the telephone; the purpose of the call is to try to diagnose the potential for doing business and, if this is favourable, to move on to the next stage of the communications progress—arranging a visit, for example.

The first step is to get past the switchboard without discussing the reason for the call. In a large company this is not normally a problem, but if we are trying to contact someone in a small company or in the home, the person who answers may say 'X is not here at the moment—can I help you, or would you like to leave a message?' That is the last thing we should do. The call may not be returned, but that is not the point. If it is, it can place us at a serious disadvantage. We should spend at least a few moments preparing for the call, recalling its objective and refreshing our memory on the background by referring to previous documents if necessary. If we receive a call out of the blue, we may be in a meeting, we may forget why we wanted to speak to this person, or, at very least, perform less well than if we had made the call ourselves after suitable preparation. In other words, we want to take and keep the initiative in the selling situation.

Let us suppose that we have got through the switchboard to the target's secretary. Part of the secretary's job is to save the manager's time by filtering out unwanted callers. We must somehow make the secretary feel unable to reject the call or to make any decision about the subject matter. We might refer to important financial issues or to specialist or technical details which the secretary does not feel authorized to comment upon.

What do we do when we have overcome the first two hurdles and are now speaking to the right person? Let us suppose that we are trying to arrange a visit. The purpose of that visit will be to diagnose the potential, start to unearth the customer's problems and begin to propose a solution. It is essential that these key steps are left to the meeting and not dealt with inadequately over the phone. If we are going to fail, as we sometimes will, we would rather fail after a face-to-face meeting. Marketing a meeting is no different from marketing a product—we have to sell the benefits of the meeting.

This means that we will deliberately resist requests to 'tell me a bit more about what you are selling'. We are trying to sell the interview, not the product. We therefore have to try to persuade the hearer to give us ten minutes or two hours or whatever is appropriate.

They may try to reject the idea of a meeting by asking 'could you send me some literature?' Again this should be resisted, possibly along the lines 'I could send you some general literature, but if I can just visit you briefly I can give you the literature which will be most helpful to you'.

Properly used, and bearing in mind the multi-stage approach to communication, the telephone can be a tremendously useful and cost-effective means of marketing communication. Badly used, it can be an expensive way of losing business (see Follow-up 9.3).

9.5 Exhibitions

The role of exhibitions in the selling process

Experience of running exhibitions of all sizes in all parts of the world has led to one clear conclusion. Exhibitions can be the best and the worst way of spending marketing money!

They can cost tens or hundreds of thousands of pounds. On the other hand, as a management consultant, I have taken a few square metres at a major exhibition for less than £2000, and at a more specialized exhibition in a hotel for a few hundred pounds. Those who have dismissed exhibitions as being beyond their reach should perhaps think again.

An exhibition can take a potential buyer a long way along the selling process—sometimes from beginning to end—all on the one occasion. The stand and its display panels, the literature, and our mere presence at the exhibition are forms of impersonal communication aimed at creating awareness and generating interest. A visitor who has shown some interest in the 'impersonal' material can then be addressed by 'personal' communication.

An exhibition is a classic case of 'selling the next step' (see Section 7.1). This step may be a written proposal, a visit to the client, a visit to the seller and so on. We need to qualify leads by follow-up category—we do not want quantity of leads but quality. An unqualified list of names and addresses is useless because there is no option but to treat them all in the same way, putting them on a standard mailing list.

Training for manning a stand

Everyone manning the stand should be trained in the basic principles of marketing, most simply encapsulated in Figure 2.2 (the 'sharper cutting edge'). The instinct of many people, faced with a visitor to the stand, is immediately to talk about the products on display and to explain what the company does. Staff must be trained to present benefits rather than features, to target those benefits to the needs of each individual visitor, and to present the company's unique selling proposition. Similarly, the exhibition panels should concentrate on the needs of the buyer and not only on the products of the seller, as they usually do.

Advantages of exhibitions

Those who are unsure about the cost effectiveness of exhibitions should compare them with alternative ways of spending the same amount of marketing budget—more literature, more visits by sales staff, more advertising and so on. If we do this, we shall probably conclude that there are some distinct advantages afforded by exhibitions.

1. *Potential customers come to the seller.*   This saves us time and money, particularly at an international exhibition.

2. *Many customers can be seen in a short time.*   We can hold several useful business conversations per hour, compared with one or two per day if we were to visit buyers at their own locations.

3. *Responsible decision makers attend and are accessible.*   This includes people who are not normally available to be seen during the selling process, such as senior managers. At an exhibition they are available, relaxed, more willing to talk and even to open their diaries.

4. *New potential customers attend.*   People who would never have been on our long-list let alone our short-list of potential customers may be contacted at no incremental cost.

5. *Contact is face to face.*   More can be achieved in an hour at an exhibition than in many days of patient plodding by other means.

6. *Exhibitions offer good visual impact.*   People who would never respond to an advertisement or a piece of literature may be attracted by a stand and its display.

7. *An exhibition can be a good vehicle for a 'mini test market' of a new product.*   Nowhere else can we encounter such a large group of potential buyers in such a short time. We must beware of the problem of an unrepresentative sample (see Chapter 11), but that is true of any market research situation.

8. *An exhibition is an excellent vehicle for evaluating a new market segment.*   Many companies are having to diversify into new areas, and an exhibition can act as a very good first filter. We might decide to go no further because competition is intense, or we might judge that the potential is sufficiently great to justify further investigation; alternative ways of reaching these conclusions might take much longer.

9. *A large number of leads can be generated and qualified for follow-up.*   The work starts when the exhibition is over!

Disadvantages of exhibitions

Compared with other forms of marketing communication, exhibitions have some potentially serious disadvantages:

1. *They are expensive.*   The stand space, in the form of a 'shell scheme' to which one has to add panels and possibly a whole internal display structure, can cost more than £200 per square metre. On top of this there is the cost of fitting and providing services. The cost of staff is more than their salaries, travel, accommodation and related expenses—it is their 'opportunity cost'. While they are attending the exhibition, they cannot be earning fees or generating profit in other ways.

2. *Much of the effort is wasted.*   It is very difficult to avoid spending time with people who do not buy. However, a large proportion of any marketing effort is wasted, and an exhibition can actually be very productive.

3. *The environment is very competitive.*   A buyer whom we visit may or may not see some of our competitors before making a decision. A buyer visiting our stand can evaluate the whole of the competition the same day.

4. *Instant judgement is required.*   Unfortunately, the people who express most interest in the products—students or R&D staff who are trying to keep up with the latest technology—may be the ones who are in the least position to place an order. We need to decide how best to allocate our precious time.

5. *Exhibitions can be extremely useful to competitors.*   They will visit our stand (having conveniently mislaid or changed their badges!) in order to find out the latest technical and commercial information.

Objectives of taking an exhibition stand

These will vary widely, and it is essential that they are well thought out, agreed and understood by all concerned before the exhibition takes place. In many exhibitions, in the USA for example, visitors come prepared to buy. They expect special exhibition offers. In other countries such as Germany, the whole environment may be much more restrained and little business may actually be concluded at the exhibition itself. Some possible objectives of taking a stand are:

1. *To get orders.*   If it is the sort of exhibition where this is possible, it is essential that the right staff and information are available!

2. *To get leads.*   This is the most common and most worthwhile objective of an exhibition. The essential point is to ensure that the leads are qualified and prioritized.

3. *To create, enhance and maintain the company's image.*   From a negative viewpoint, our absence might be regarded as a bad sign. However, we should take a much more positive approach and use the exhibition to develop our image, reassure existing customers and attract new customers.

4. *To get editorial comment.*   Exhibitions are surrounded by a vast press machine, and editors are hungry for good material. This should be carefully written so that it will claim both the editor's and the readers' attention in the midst of a mass of conflicting messages.

5. *To carry out market research*   This is discussed in 'advantages' above.

6. *To assess the competition.*   At most exhibitions, all the major competitors will be present. It is important to take the opportunity of observing what the competition is saying and displaying (or not displaying!).

7. *To support and find agents or distributors.*   It is common for a distributorship agreement to require both parties to participate jointly in key exhibitions, on a combined or adjacent stand. Exhibitors may also be able to find new partners at an exhibition. Whether they like it or not, they will be approached by various people promising them the earth! Agreements signed up in the euphoria of an exhibition can prove to be disastrous, and thorough checking is essential (see Chapter 10).

Targets

Having established the overall company objective, it is important that individuals are clear about what is expected from them. In many cases, a special incentive should be given for business generated at the exhibition.

Targets might be based on the codes listed under 'follow-up' below. There are three main purposes for having these targets:

1. To motivate and to judge the performance of individuals and the whole team.

2. To assess the progress of an exhibition and take corrective action if necessary. We might decide after the first day that we need more staff or a different type of staff, or that we should rearrange the stand in some way.

3. To help us to decide whether the exhibition was worth while and whether it is worth taking a stand next time. If no criteria for success were established in the first place, we cannot judge whether they were met.

Invitations to exhibitions

Exhibitors should not rely solely on the invitations sent out by the exhibition organizers. They should have their own detailed lists of actual and potential customers. Names, titles, etc. must be carefully checked. Possible groups include:

1. Existing clients invited centrally, by marketing or senior management

2. Existing clients invited by individuals, for example by senior management or by technical specialists

3. Potential clients known by someone in the company

4. Potential clients not known by anyone in the company

5. Existing clients of other parts of the organization who might be potential clients for the company which is exhibiting

6. Potential clients known to be buying from the competition

7. Others

Very differently worded invitations should be sent to the various groups listed above (but they rarely are!).

The right opening question

'Can I help you?' This is about the worst opening question! It invites the answer 'no thanks—I'm just looking', or 'yes please—I'd like to hear about your product in detail'. This can close the door on some potentially key prospects who do not want to reveal their interest. Conversely, it can open the way to time-wasting conversations with people who have no genuine intention or authority to buy.

Non-threatening questions such as 'What use do you make of ...?' 'What sort of problems do you have with ...?' 'Would you like to be able to save money on ...?' 'What are you hoping to find at the exhibition?' are much more likely to get the prospect talking in the way we want.

Follow-up

It is essential that there is some simple means of recording details of visitors, and that all staff manning the stand use the same system so that follow-up can be arranged on a consistent basis. The name, title, address and job title can most easily be recorded by stapling a visiting card to the enquiry form. The most important information is then the follow-up action. We must decide and record who is going to do what by when, before we speak to the next visitor. A simple code can be used to define categories for follow-up such as:

A. A visit arranged on the spot
B. Visitor to be telephoned within one week to arrange a visit
C. Specific information to be sent on ... and then followed up
D. Contacts to be made after ... weeks to arrange ...
E. No immediate interest but keep on mailing list

There is other information which would be useful but is not always obtainable. The enquiry form might have a checklist to be used as appropriate. Examples are:

What is the contact's role in the buying decision?
Who else is likely to be involved?
Has there been any other contact between the two companies?
Is there a budget?
When is a purchasing decision likely to be made?
What is the visitor's specific interest?
What details of the current operation are relevant?

Making the exhibit more successful at attracting visitors

We need to find a way of differentiating our stand from all the others in order to attract visitors. Exhibits increasingly tend to look the same. Some equipment is not particularly attractive, and computer displays are often unintelligible. We need to make imaginative use of layout, equipment, demonstrations, sound, light, display panels and staff. The biggest draw at a zoo is the feeding time for the penguins, and a little ingenuity may suggest some relevant and regular attraction which we can announce in advance and which will draw people to the stand. As an example, a company involved in industrial safety arranged to have a dust explosion every fifteen minutes.

We finish where we began. Exhibitions can be the best and the worst way of spending marketing money. Some people who have never considered taking a stand might be pleasantly surprised by the results if they followed the above guidelines (see Follow-up 9.4).

9.6   Advertising

As we know from our daily experience, there is a very large and high-profile industry dedicated to the business of advertising. Two parties are involved when we advertise apart from ourselves and the target audience.

First, there are the communications experts such as agencies, designers, media specialists, copywriters, and many others. Their role is to create the campaign and the message, and to implement it after agreement with the client. Second there are the media, the vehicles for the message, which include television, radio, cinemas, newspapers, journals, magazines, posters and point-of-sale material, as well as the more exotic examples such as racing cars, lasers, sky-writing, balloons, taxis, supermarket trolleys, toilet doors and—who knows what next?!

There are two distinct aspects of advertising—the *message* and the means by which the message is *communicated* (see Section 7.3). The creative and logistic sides of communication are specialist functions for which it may well be worth employing an expert. Readers who wish to study advertising in more detail are recommended to read a book on the subject. This will give advice on matters such as the choice of an agency, developing an advertising campaign, selecting the media and assessing the results of the campaign.

As advertisers, the following points are important for us:

1. We cannot assume that people will spend time reading our advertisements. The consumer marketing purist would argue that we can say only one thing in an advertisement, and that this must be said very succinctly and with high impact. In a high-technology or professional situation the message can be more complex than this, but it is healthy to bear the principle in mind. The instinct of many people is to try to say far too much, with the result that very little actually gets through.

2. We should bear in mind the progressive communications process described in Section 7.1. What is the purpose of the advertisement? If it is not to sell, what *is* it there to do? Is it to sell the next step? What is the next step? How quantified are the objectives? How do we judge its success?

3. We probably have between one and three seconds to capture the initial attention of the reader or viewer. Advertisers with large budgets would submit their advertisements to a panel, perhaps using modern psychological and other techniques to judge the potential effectiveness of the advertising. The cost of 'space', whether in a journal, a newspaper, on television or some other medium, can be considerably higher than the cost of originating the advertisement. It obviously makes sense to test the advertisement, probably in several different versions, before irretrievably committing the money to the media. If our budget does not justify this, we might test an advertisement on a panel which we have set up ourselves. The panel should preferably be composed of potential customers who have not bought from us in the

past, rather than loyal customers or members of our own company who will have a biased reaction.

An alternative to print advertising, i.e. space on a page of an appropriate journal, is a loose insert. This has three advantages. First, it is more likely to be seen—at least the recipient has to take the trouble to throw it into the bin! Second, even if it is not read straight away, it may be kept in a pocket, file or drawer from which it can emerge at a later date. Third, it can easily be passed to a colleague for whom it is more appropriate. Admittedly, the insert is following most of the other ways of advertising into disrepute through over-use, but the better journals limit the number of inserts in any one issue. A careful comparison of the relative cost of inserts and print advertisements needs to be made, together with an assessment of their response rate; the rest is simple arithmetic!

It is useful to apply to advertising the test with which this book opened. If marketing is not the means of generating profit, there is something wrong. My own seminar business has been built up by means of hundreds of thousands of inserts over a six-year period, almost all of which has been in a recession. The advertising from the earlier years is still bearing fruit today, and the whole campaign has yielded an excellent profit (see Exercise 9.5)

9.7   Public relations

General

To some people, public relations (PR) and marketing are almost synonymous. This view reveals a very limited understanding of marketing; it also undervalues the specialized role which PR has to play in the whole marketing communication process.

PR is one of the means by which the 'personality' of a company or product is created and communicated. In terms of Figure 7.1, PR is an important but relatively low-key activity which starts long before the buying process commences and continues for an indefinite period afterwards. Its purpose is not primarily to sell or even to communicate detailed messages about the products. It is concerned more with enhancing the reputation of the organization. If, when the name of a company is mentioned, our mind spontaneously turns to thoughts such as reputability, quality, reliability or high standing in the marketplace, it is probably because we have been influenced by an effective public relations process, perhaps over a period of many years.

As with all forms of marketing communication, PR can be carried out by internal staff, external consultants or a combination of both. The role of the external consultant is to advise, create, challenge and, if required, to manage the PR process and key events in the programme.

PR activities

The type of PR events which are most appropriate varies enormously with the industry. In a high-technology or professional field, activities such as publications, educational aids, conferences, panels, open days or the sponsorship of a university chair might be most appropriate. For a product appealing to the general public, television, radio, visits and the sponsorship of sporting, cultural and other events might be used. For a company with a local marketplace, some newsworthy charitable gift might be cost-effective. For all of them, activities such as influencing VIPs, politicians and City opinion formers, press releases, press conferences and newsletters might play a role.

Press releases

These are considered separately because many companies produce press releases without drawing upon external expertise. The following guidelines may be helpful.

- Have something which will capture people's attention. This may be a good headline, an interesting human story, or a really creative use of photography or graphics. People do not read every word, and boring technical details do not grab the casual reader's interest.

- Realize that editors are hungry for good copy. If we are known to provide good material which requires the minimum of amendment, they are more likely to be receptive to our offerings in the future.

- Assume that the editor has a pair of scissors! *We* want to have as much space as possible; the *editor* has a certain number of column centimetres to fill. It is very annoying if the heart of our message is cut out for lack of space. The key points should appear at the start, and we should assume that our submission will not be printed in its entirety.

- Take advantage of the fact that an article may have more credibility than an advertisement because it is seen as being more objective and independent. Furthermore, it costs nothing.

- Accept that, unless we have a very strong hold over the media, a lot of luck is involved. A brilliant article might be rejected because that particular issue is already full. We may need to submit many times to get the coverage we want.

■ Finally, remember the key questions—'what are we trying to say, to whom, with what objective?' This applies as much to PR as to other forms of communication.

Corporate identity

We have discussed the fact that the image of a product can be a key factor in the buying decision (Section 2.3). The image of the company which supplies the product, or the 'corporate identity', may have an equally strong influence. Rightly or wrongly, people will make assumptions about the product on the basis of the 'stable' from which it comes (Section 2.10).

A corporate identity programme aims to exploit this fact. It develops, communicates and reinforces the identity, reputation and personality which the company wants the market to recognize. An important aspect of such a programme is that the same image is presented across the whole range of communication media—not only the more direct forms of marketing communication such as advertisements and brochures but also items such as letterheads, envelopes, signs on buildings, vehicles, ties and anything else which can aid recognition.

Broader issues for PR

PR can be effective for objectives which are less direct than the promotion of the company or its products to the customers. We may wish to appeal to the community by showing that we are good citizens or good employers. We might want to show that we care for future generations. We might want to be philanthropic by sponsoring worthwhile activities such as health or education. It is very difficult to attribute a specific sales volume to such actions, but they can reinforce and give credibility to our more direct forms of marketing (see Exercise 9.6).

Exercises

9.1 Evaluate a piece of your company's promotional literature against the twelve guidelines in Section 9.1, awarding marks out of 5 for each factor. What would you do to improve the literature next time it is printed?

9.2 Do you have a problem with multi-purpose literature or with product-oriented literature? How could you create a cost-effective hierarchy of market-oriented literature which would serve different market segments more specifically?

9.3 Select a recently submitted proposal for a contract which you might have expected to win but which was *not* awarded to you. Evaluate it against the twelve guidelines in Section 9.2. How could you improve the proposal if you had the opportunity of resubmitting it?

9.4 Take from your filing cabinet or hard disk a letter which you have recently sent to a potential customer but which did not achieve the desired response. Evaluate it against the guidelines in Section 9.3. How could you improve the letter if you had the opportunity of resending it?

9.5 Ask a colleague to select an advertisement from a company in a field similar to your own. Look at it for two seconds and then write down what you can remember about it. If you were a potential customer, would you read any further? Having read it, would you take any action? Repeat with other examples. Apply the same approach to your own advertising. How could you improve its effectiveness?

9.6 Consider the PR activities used by your organization at present. Which of them are not as effective as they should be? Are you missing some opportunities?

Follow-up

9.1 Cultivate the habit of writing down the key 'win themes' before beginning to write a proposal. Evaluate it critically against these themes before submitting it.

9.2 Consider whether a reply form of the type discussed in Section 9.3 could be appropriate to any part of your business. If so, design a form, test it on a sample of potential customers and evaluate the results.

9.3 Make a summary of the points on using the telephone in Section 9.4 which are relevant to your business. Have this on display by your telephone to use as a checklist for the next three months. Modify the list in the light of your experience.

9.4 Before manning your next exhibition stand, acquaint all the staff involved with the content of Section 9.5. If possible, hire a training video or arrange an exhibition workshop with a suitably experienced consultant.

What about overseas?
International marketing

Key business issues	Section
■ The rest of the world is not an extension of our own country.	10.1
■ This has major implications in terms of national, business and financial culture, and language.	
■ The concept of 'global marketing' has some advantages but also some limitations.	
■ Various levels of commitment to international marketing are possible, each with a corresponding degree of risk and reward.	10.2
■ Routes to market include home-based, agent or distributor, strategic alliance, setting up a subsidiary and acquisition.	
■ A credible presence in an overseas market often requires a substantial investment. It may be better to focus on a few key markets at first, and then move on to others.	10.3
■ Overseas customers need virtually the same access to product support as those in the home country.	
■ A distributorship agreement is not only a legal document but also a major aid to negotiating.	Appendix
■ Partners such as agents or distributors should need us at least as much as we need them, so that they are hungry for business on our behalf.	

10.1   The rest of the world is not an extension of our own country

We are all influenced by the culture in which we live, and expect others to think the way we do. With some notable exceptions, the British are particularly bad at this. We tend to take it for granted that the rest of the world either already speaks English or can learn to do so.

Similarly, some Americans seem to regard the rest of the world as simply an extension of their own boundaries. A senior American businessman once said to me, when we were discussing the issues involved in marketing in Europe, 'I completely understand what you are saying, Colin—in the States we have differences between the East and the West Coasts'. This remark showed that he did not begin to understand what I was saying!

There are many aspects of these cultural differences. We shall discuss the main issues below, but anyone intending to travel or work overseas is advised to prepare in much more depth for the particular countries to be visited.

National culture

This affects the way in which people communicate, interact with each other, treat foreigners and so on. It takes many visits, and, preferably, an extended period of living in a country, to begin to understand the subtleties of national culture. Where this is not possible, reading books and articles and talking to people with experience can help the visitor to avoid at least the grosser errors.

Business culture

This varies widely from country to country. The way in which decisions are made, the speed of the negotiation process, adherence to agreed meeting times and so on can be specific to a part of the world or even to a country. Even though 'the world is getting smaller', some deep-rooted differences remain. To treat a German businessman as if he were an American is crass ignorance. To assume that everyone in the Middle East, the Far East, Africa or South America acts like the archetypal Englishman is disastrous.

For these reasons, companies wishing to operate seriously in overseas countries, for example by opening an office or acquiring or setting up a subsidiary company, will probably prefer to use a trusted national of that country to head up the operation, not only because of the language but also because of the more subtle business issues. This is particularly important when legal and employment matters are involved.

Financial culture

A failure to understand the differences in financial culture can have disastrous consequences. For large capital projects, the source of the funding may be the overriding factor in the buying decision. In a repeat purchase situation, the way in which particular groups of customers obtain their finance is equally crucial. In the medical business, for example, it is pointless assuming that an American doctor in private practice, an English doctor in the National Health Service and a European doctor operating under a reimbursement scheme will have a similar basis for generating their income; extrapolating from one situation to another is inept.

Language

It is seriously recommended that people who are intending to take international marketing seriously should be fluent in at least some of the languages of the countries in which they will be working. It is not only a sign of professionalism it is also good business sense, because it generates respect, strengthens the negotiating position and helps to avoid costly errors. In particularly critical situations, where legal or financial issues are involved, it may be necessary to bring in a local expert for whom the language is the mother tongue. Fortunately there is now a vast array of crash courses, tapes, videos, programmed learning packages and so on to help business executives to learn languages in a practical and relevant way.

The fact of being 'foreign'

Transcending all these particular cultural differences is the fact that we are 'foreign' to potential buyers from another country. If their alternative to buying from us is to buy from an indigenous supplier, or from a supplier whose culture is closer to their own, we have to ask ourselves why they should take the risk of buying from us. However good our product or service may be, the dice is loaded against us from the start. We have to take steps to overcome this.

The exception to this is where the fact that a product is 'foreign' is actually a status symbol. If our product belongs to this category, we will obviously want to exploit the fact to the full.

Global marketing

The term 'global marketing' adopted by many internationally operating companies has good features but also some serious limitations. Where possible, it is obviously helpful to the supplier to have a common product with common back-up resources. As customers are becoming more international in their outlook, there is an advantage to them in knowing that they will obtain exactly the same product and service with the same brand personality and positioning ('international branding') anywhere in the world.

However, there is a danger that we achieve the worst of all worlds and not the best. It might be better to sell the same product to the same type of people (market segments, socio-economic groups, etc), but to do so in different ways in different territories. For example, in countries where they expect to take time to negotiate, where they want to feel they have gained a concession, or where they hold human courtesies in high regard, it is not appropriate to ask for a breakfast meeting at an airport with a pre-printed contract being signed the same day. We need to gain the benefit of an international approach while at the same time actually taking advantage of local differences.

Conclusion

The existence of these major differences between countries leads us to state a principle of international marketing which we shall be reinforcing throughout this chapter—take international marketing seriously or don't do it at all! Realize that the marketing effort and the marketing message have to be targeted to each country at least as specifically as they do to a market segment, a member of a decision-making group or a member of a distribution chain as discussed in Chapter 2 (see Exercise 10.1).

10.2   A step-by-step approach to international marketing

Let us assume that we are a UK-based company which has decided that it would be good to do some exporting. This may be either for the positive reason that we believe that there are further opportunities outside the UK or for the negative reason that the home market is not large enough to satisfy our aspirations.

We might try to exploit the overseas potential in a number of ways. These are set out below in a sequence which represents an increasing degree of commitment and which brings corresponding degrees of risk and reward.

Home-based

This implies that we and all our activities are firmly based in the home country. Our export activities consist of flying visits to various overseas markets, often on a somewhat random basis. We might visit an exhibition or even take a stand ourselves; we might visit certain contacts and potential customers, and perhaps engage in limited advertising or direct mail.

While this may work in some situations, and it certainly limits the exposure in terms of finance and effort, it can rarely do more than scratch the surface of the opportunities. It is virtually impossible to establish credibility with customers in this way. Although, in principle, we can communicate extremely quickly by telephone, fax and aeroplane, there is always the feeling that we are at a disadvantage compared with a local competitor.

If we intend to take international marketing seriously, this remote approach is probably only of value in the initial stages to test the potential of a particular market. We would then decide whether or not to increase our commitment.

Agent or distributor

The remoteness which is an inevitable feature of the home-based approach can be a real problem in the minds of our customers. We can at least begin to overcome it by appointing someone on the spot to handle our business.

Broadly speaking, there are two ways of doing this: via an agent or a distributor. These are distinguished by the contractual relationship between the principal, the agent or distributor and the customer. Although these descriptions are not 'watertight', the normal difference would be as follows.

An agent is someone who seeks business on the supplier's behalf, and is trained and briefed on the products and business objectives of the supplier. His or her job is to find 'qualified leads' (see Chapter 7). A good agent should be in a position to help to formulate plans for selling in the territory. When possible opportunities are found, the supplier is put in touch with the customer.

If a visit is required, the agent would arrange and probably attend it, but is not contractually involved in the sale. The order is placed by the customer on the supplier, the title of the goods passes directly from supplier to customer, and the contractual debt is from the customer to the supplier. The agent may be paid an ongoing retainer and would normally receive a percentage commission on sales in the territory.

The situation with a distributor is usually quite different. The important distinction is that the distributor purchases the goods from the supplier and sells them on to the customer. The distributor would normally stock an agreed quantity of the products for demonstration and sale, carry spares where appropriate, and have qualified and trained service engineers. The contract is between the customer and the distributor; the distributor is responsible for collecting the payment. The supplier would have an agreed basis for receiving money from the distributor, even if the ultimate customer had not yet paid. Further notes on distributor agreements are given in the appendix at the end of this chapter.

The key to success in such an arrangement is that each party must need the other. Even so, the principal should aim to create a situation where the distributor needs the principal rather more than the principal needs the distributor. To have a partner who simply passes on requests in a reactive manner is to play at exporting. We need someone who is 'hungry' on our behalf, and who is prepared to commit substantial time, resources and management effort to ensure success. The distributor should feel that we can find another distributor more easily than they can find another principal. The distributorship needs to be large enough to have the necessary resources but small enough for our business to be important to it.

The distributor is normally allowed to sell non-competing products to cover the cost of the sales and service teams, workshop, administration, etc., but the arrangement works best when the principal is the major supplier of the distributor. This means that success with the principal's products is the main factor influencing the profitability of the distributor's business. This may be difficult to achieve when we are selling into a niche market, but it is worth bearing the principle in mind (see Exercise 10.2).

Strategic alliance

This form of relationship is becoming increasingly common, and has some great advantages. The assumption is that both parties have something to contribute which brings mutual benefit to the relationship. Typically, the supplier would have products or services to offer and the strategic partner would have market knowledge and access.

A strategic alliance is normally a much deeper relationship than that between a principal and distributor. Both parties may invest equity in the operation, and the level of commitment should be high. In a good strategic alliance, the process may work in both directions so that each partner gains access for their products to the other's market. Joint manufacturing and other agreements are then possible, in a way which would not normally be relevant to a distributorship arrangement. A wise choice of partner is even more crucial than in the case of an agency or distributorship, because the commitment is that much greater.

There should be major long-term strategic benefits for both parties in a strategic alliance. It should not be seen as a 'quick-fix' solution to a short-term problem. Many companies set their sights too low in terms of what they expect from such an arrangement, or have an alliance which is not equally balanced in terms of benefits to both parties. In these circumstances, they do not achieve the degree of commitment which is implicit in such a situation and therefore do not reap the rewards which they should.

Setting up a subsidiary

It is a common feeling in a principal/distributor arrangement that the distributor receives a disproportionate share of the profit. The principal has incurred all the risk and expense in developing a product, manufacturing and marketing it; the only thing the distributor has to do is to sell it!!

The time may come when the supplying company feels that it would be better to do the distribution itself. The distributorship agreement is terminated (with care!), and the company sets up in its own right. The subsidiary may start by being relatively small, with one senior person who has to act as local general manager, sales manager, accountant and everything else; a more substantial structure may be built on this foundation once some initial success has been achieved.

It is essential that the person running the subsidiary understands the legal, employment, financial and other issues involved. Employing people and particularly attempting to terminate their employment in another country can lead to very deep waters.

The supplier very quickly finds out that 'just selling the products' is not quite as easy as they had supposed! The subsidiary has a habit of demanding more and more investment and management time. Embarking on this course should be undertaken with care, after proper consideration of all the issues involved and the possible alternatives which are available.

Acquisition

While the acquisition route to international marketing obviously requires the greatest investment it can also bring the greatest rewards. At a stroke, we become the owner of a market share in that country. Assuming that we do not fall into the trap of changing the name of the acquired company, we immediately take on board all the goodwill, image and reputation which it possesses. Some companies that have tried all the other approaches to exporting have concluded that the only way to achieve real success is to make acquisitions in key countries.

There is a problem which needs to be understood before embarking on the acquisition route. A company of any value is likely to be sold for considerably more than the net asset value in the books. This means a write-off in the accounts of the acquiring company which, in some cases, can be large enough to affect the corporate balance sheet. In these circumstances, 'bean-counters' will question why the acquisition was made at all. I recall one case where we had to pay $50 million for a company where the tangible assets were only $25 million. We were asked why we were recommending 'wasting' the second $25 million. The answer was, of course, that it was the second part which was the whole objective of the acquisition, because it represented customers, market share and brand equity. We didn't particularly want more factories, or stock which had been dressed up by creative accountancy!

If the acquiring company is already a household name in the new market, it may be possible to change the name of the acquired company at an early stage but this should be done with great care. Numerous examples exist where the acquiring company is either not known or is completely misunderstood. Our assumption that 'everyone knows what we do' should be carefully tested. In most cases, at least in the early stages of an acquisition, saying that the acquired company is 'a Division of XYZ' is probably the furthest we should go.

It is important that the acquired company should not immediately be stifled by the imposition of new systems, procedures and so on. The number of visits ('I'm from head office—I'm here to help you'!) should be severely limited, especially in the early stages. This requires a mature understanding by the senior management of the acquiring company. There have been cases where an acquired company has either failed to meet its potential or has actually been killed in the process, because of disproportionate interference and unnecessary change by the acquiring company (see Follow-up 10.1).

10.3   Key markets and the problem of dissipated resources

One of the prime reasons for a company to move along the step-by-step process described above is the growing realization that serious exporting requires tremendous commitment. Below a certain 'critical mass' of activity and investment, the success rate may be negligible.

For this reason, it is better to concentrate our limited resources on a few key markets than to spread them thinly over the whole world.

This is particularly true if the product or service we are selling requires locally available support, such as trained service engineers and spares, which must be rapidly delivered. One company, which had good penetration in the USA and Europe, told me that they had sold one system in India and one in the Middle East. They had to admit that the consequences were disastrous, both for the customer in terms of support and for the supplier in terms of expense. In these circumstances it is counterproductive to sell one unit in a territory, unless it is part of a planned process to penetrate the territory before moving on to others in stages.

This is a good example of the possible conflict between sales and management objectives. The salesperson wants to get the turnover whatever the implications. More responsible management and marketing has to take account of the broader issues involved (see Follow-up 10.2 and 10.3).

Exercises

10.1 Do the people responsible for international business in your organization have sufficient understanding of the cultural issues involved in their territories? Are you taking exporting seriously? Should some more experienced export staff be recruited?

10.2 Which overseas partnerships are working well? Which are not working well? What conclusions do you draw from this analysis?

10.3 If you have any distributorship or agency agreements, examine them against the checklist in the appendix to this chapter. What improvements can you make for the future and negotiate in existing agreements? Do your agreements ensure that these partners are committed to you and are 'hungry' on your behalf?

Follow-up

10.1 Select a small group of colleagues, and familiarize them with the progression described in Section 10.2. Arrange to meet regularly, say every two weeks for a period of three months, perhaps over a sandwich lunch, to explore the implications of moving towards the next stage in the process. At the end of the exercise, write a brief report to senior management with some clear and supported recommendations.

10.2 Visit a key overseas territory and examine the potential for increased business which could be obtained if more effort were devoted to it. Ask yourself whether the total export resources should be increased to achieve this, or whether effort should be diverted from a less worthwhile territory. Repeat for other key markets if you feel it would be worth while.

10.3 If appropriate, read a book on International Marketing such as Paliwoda S. (1994) *International Marketing*, Butterworth-Heinemann, Oxford.

Appendix: Distributor agreements

It is a great mistake to think that a distributor agreement is merely a legal document which is the prerogative of the legal department. Of course it is a legal contract which must be vetted by suitably qualified experts, but we lose a great deal of the benefit if we do not also see it as a marketing and business aid. It is a means of gaining ongoing commitment from the distributor. We can use it, for example, to require the distributor to purchase a stock of products and spares, and to provide the agreed sales and support resources. It can also play an important role in the negotiation phase; if we are aiming for our invoices to be paid within 45 days, we might put 30 days into the first draft and (reluctantly) allow ourselves to be talked up (in exchange for some other concession)!

The agreement is a summary of the privileges and responsibilities of both parties. In the outline below, it is accepted that the distributor may want to place further obligations on the principal (which may or may not be acceptable.) These are not listed—there is no point in doing their negotiation for them! Many of the privileges of one party correspond to responsibilities of the other.

The example below is written for stockholding distributors who buy our products and resell them to their customers. This contrasts with agents, who would normally identify selling opportunities in return for a fee and/or retainer but who would never own the title to the products (see Section 10.2); only parts of the agreement will be relevant in this case.

It is important to emphasize that the list is not necessarily complete or appropriate to every situation. Our purpose is to highlight the management and negotiating issues involved. *We would stress that appropriate legal safeguards must also be incorporated, using advice which is based on an expert understanding of the legal situation in each particular territory.*

1. *Introduction*
1.1 Parties to the agreement, date of the agreement

1.2 Territory

1.3 Definitions of products

1.4 Basis of pricing, discounts, commission, etc.

1.5 Limitations on appointment (e.g. the distributor does not have the right to bind the principal)

1.6 Termination conditions *(appropriate legal wording required)* or restriction of territory or exclusivity if insufficient sales or service effort is being provided (see 5.3 and 5.8)

1.7 Other legal matters

2. *Privileges of the distributor*
2.1 Exclusive rights to the sale of the products in the territory (see 3.1). Receives commission on direct sales into the territory (see 4.1)

2.2 Duration and renewal conditions

2.3 Rights to all new products within the agreed product areas (see 5.16)

2.4 Will receive necessary parts free during the warranty period (see 3.3)

2.5 Will receive training for sales and service staff, and appropriate manuals (see 3.4 and 3.5)

2.6 Will receive text and artwork for promotional literature (see 3.6)

2.7 Will receive people to assist in staffing exhibition stands and to give other marketing, sales and technical support (see 3.8)

3. *Responsibilities of principal*
3.1 Will not sell the defined products to other distributors in the territory (see 2.1)

3.2 Will not sell direct to end users in the territory without the knowledge of the distributor and payment of an agreed level of commission (see 2.1 and 4.1)

3.3 Will provide any necessary parts free of charge during the warranty period (see 2.4)

3.4 Will provide training to sales and service staff at the principal's site, and will pay for accommodation and subsistence of trainees (see 2.5 and 5.6)

3.5 Will provide training, service and user manuals in English (see 2.5 and 5.7)

3.6 Will provide text and artwork for promotional literature (see 2.6 and 5.7)

3.7   Will provide spares for 7 years after the last sale of the product

3.8   Will provide people to staff stands at agreed exhibitions in the territory (see 5.15), and will provide other agreed marketing, sales and technical support (see 2.7)

3.9   Will deliver products and spares within agreed time scales

4.   *Privileges of principal*
4.1   May deal with unsolicited enquiries about the products from the territory, and will pay the distributor an *ad hoc* commission on each occasion a sale is made (see 2.1 and 3.2)

4.2   May change prices at any time for products not yet ordered from the principal

4.3   Can agree end-user selling price

4.4   Can negotiate commissions, discounts, etc. within limits defined by agreement

4.5   Can change the specification of products not yet ordered

4.6   May use other distributors in the territory for other product ranges

4.7   Can terminate distributorship if terms of agreement violated by distributor

5.   *Responsibilities of distributor*
5.1   Will buy all products in the defined fields from the principal and maintain the agreed stock level. Will not sell competing products in the territory

5.2   Will use their best endeavours to sell the products in the territory *(but see also 5.12)*

5.3   Will provide the agreed number of full-time equivalent sales staff dedicated to the sale of the products (see 1.6)

5.4   Will provide premises for receiving customers and demonstrating products

5.5   Will provide any necessary labour at their expense during the warranty period (see 3.3)

5.6 Will release sales and service staff for training, and will pay for their travel to the principal's site (see 3.4)

5.7 Will obtain a linguistically and technically accurate translation of promotional literature, training, service and user manuals and arrange local printing or over-printing (see 3.5 and 3.6)

5.8 Will provide the agreed number of full-time equivalent qualified service engineers and workshop facilities (see 1.6)

5.9 Will purchase demonstration stock from the principal *(although the principal may agree to provide these on consignment for an initial period of, say, 1 year)*

5.10 Will purchase all spares from the principal, and maintain an agreed stock level appropriate to the cumulative installed base of products in the territory

5.11 Will check and install all products, train users and maintain a record of products installed in the territory by serial number to enable products to be traced

5.12 Will agree a (non-contractual) sales forecast with the principal on an annual basis

or

Will agree the minimum quantity of each product to be purchased during the coming year as agreed with the principal

5.13 Will pay all invoices to the principal within ... days, irrespective of when the distributor is paid by their customers

5.14 Will provide to the principal a regular report on the marketplace and the competition

5.15 Will take, pay for and staff an exhibition stand at the main events as agreed with the principal (see 3.8)

5.16 Will take and promote new products in the relevant product/market areas, or allow the principal to make alternative arrangements (see 2.3)

5.17 Will not promote or sell the products outside the territory *(possible legal problems here)*

5.18 Will possess appropriate cover for public and product liability *(but may expect some indemnity from the principal)*

5.19 Will assist with and monitor appropriate product trials in the territory

5.20 Will indemnify the principal against any liabilities incurred by the distributor *(appropriate legal wording required)*

5.21 Will keep confidential all information and intellectual property provided by the principal (see Exercise 10.3)

The same issues are involved when we are the distributor for an overseas principal.

Part III
THE ROLE OF BUSINESS DEVELOPMENT

CHAPTER 11

What does the market want?

Market research, marketing research

Key business issues   *Section*

- Business decisions depend on researching the market. The cost   11.1
  of acquiring the information increases rapidly with the accuracy
  sought.

- We should be 'disciplined entrepreneurs'.

- Market research information is divided into 'primary' and
  'secondary' data.

- Market research can be qualitative or quantitative.

- Interviews and group discussions can be used very effectively   11.2
  for qualitative research if certain principles are followed and
  risks avoided.

- Existing in-house market intelligence is often underused
  because it cannot be accessed.

- Information from the salesforce can be useful but must be
  treated with care.

- Quantitative research based on small samples should be left   11.3
  to the experts, but is a good investment in the right situation.

- Some types of market research do not require a large budget.   11.4

- Alternative marketing activities should be researched to   11.5
  evaluate the comparative effectiveness of each.

11.1 Business decisions depend upon researching the market

The whole emphasis of this book is that we start with the needs of the
marketplace and work back to our own resources. While this is partly an

attitude of mind, market research is obviously an important formal ingredient to this approach. In some cases it can provide us with information on which to base the whole of our business strategy.

A problem with which we are immediately faced is that the cost of the research rises rapidly with the precision of the information which we wish to obtain. A relatively small sample and a low level of research activity can yield some apparently useful results, but there is a danger that the sample is unrepresentative and that the conclusions are therefore suspect.

A guiding principle is suggested. With a particular level of under-standing of the marketplace, we are able to make business decisions with a certain degree of confidence. The question is 'would these business decisions be significantly better if we had more precise information?' If so, we should perhaps go at least to the next step. If not, why spend any more money? We cannot afford information just because it is interesting.

The reader is cautioned against the attitude which appears to prevail in some companies, that no business decision will be made until it is thoroughly ratified by research. This may be perfectly appropriate in major fast-moving consumer goods situations, where the rewards for success and the penalties for failure are enormous. In other cases, it may be an excuse for not making decisions. Management is weighing up imponderables; we often have to make decisions when we have about half of the information we would really like to have.

This raises the issue of management style, as illustrated by the spectrum shown in Figure 11.1. The question for each of us is 'where should we be on that line?' Again, it depends upon the rewards for success and the penalties for failure. If we are building power stations, we will be at the right-hand end. If we are working in a rapidly changing fashion market, there will be no time for long-drawn-out decisions and we will be at the left-hand end. One seminar delegate said to me 'our company is about two yards to the right of 'discipline'—we never make mistakes, but we never make any progress either!' The answer for many of us is to be 'disciplined entrepreneurs': we do whatever research is appropriate, give

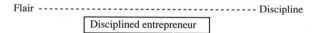

Flair -- Discipline

| Disciplined entrepreneur |

Risk-taking	'Safe' decisions
Entrepreneurial qualities	Slow decision making
'Seat of the pants' management	Thorough decision-making process
Few formal procedures	Involved procedures

Fig 11.1 Management style

a sensible amount of management time to the decision, and then back our judgement (see Exercise 11.1).

Primary and secondary data

There are two types of data about the marketplace—primary and secondary. Secondary data is information which is already potentially available. The process of acquiring it is described as 'desk research'. It might be found in our own internal records of sales and customers, or it may have to be sought from various external sources such as government statistics, industry and trade journals, economic studies, libraries, professional and academic reports, directories and so on. It takes time to search out the data, and it is not always in the form we would most like. Nevertheless, the cost compared with studies which we have commissioned is relatively trivial, and it is irresponsible not to make use of it. A key to the effective ongoing use of secondary data is the design of a suitable acquisition, storage and retrieval system (see Section 11.2). This can be supplemented by the use of on-line subscription databases if appropriate.

Primary data is information which results from new research studies which we ourselves have commissioned. It may be possible to reduce the cost by commissioning a 'syndicated' or shared project with other suppliers, but this has the disadvantage that the information is not exclusive to us and it may not be in the form which we would ideally have chosen.

A confusing fact is that secondary data should be considered first! It is much less glamorous to sift through secondary data than to commission a new primary research project, but the cost is also much less. We should therefore start with secondary data, and then commission a more expensive primary research study if the secondary data is not adequate.

Methods of sampling

If the number of potential customers is small—if we are selling to car manufacturers, for example—it may be possible to carry out a census, i.e. to study the whole marketplace. In most cases, however, we have to study a small sample and use the results to represent the whole. There are two methods of doing this:

1. A random sample. To avoid unacceptable risk, the sample must be statistically large enough and must have been obtained in an unbiased way. A random sample is not the first ten or hundred people we happen to meet. Nor is it likely to be found within our company, where our colleagues may be totally unrepresentative of the market in both socio-economic terms and in their attitudes towards our product.

2. A structured quota sample. In this case the structure of the whole marketplace is carefully analysed and particular groups are differentiated by socio-economic status, buying patterns or other parameters. A certain number of interviews are then held within each group, and the significance of the feedback is weighted according to the size or buying power of that group.

Qualitative and quantitative market research

Market research can be divided into two types—qualitative and quantitative. In the first case we are looking for information about things such as the desires, attitudes and behaviour of potential customers; in the second we are quantifying specific aspects of the information, in terms of either numbers or percentages.

11.2   Qualitative market research

Objectives

1. *Opportunities for new products or services.*   In most businesses the cost of developing products and services is extremely high, and it makes good business sense to evaluate the prospects as far as possible before investing in the product itself. The feedback may show that the product will be well received, or it may indicate some areas for improvement. Sometimes the research will convince us that we should not proceed with that particular product; although this will be disappointing, it is extremely valuable information which avoids further abortive investment.

2. *Characteristics of buyers and users.*   Important input to our marketing strategy and tactics can be obtained if we study issues such as:
   - the way in which the product is to be used
   - the issues which surround the buying decision
   - the role of different members of the decision-making group in the buying process

3. *Image and perception.*   Image research should not be dismissed as being of no value just because the subject is intangible. As we have discussed in Chapter 2, the perception of our product, our brand, our company or even ourselves as people can override all other considerations in the buying decision. I recently saw an image survey which included a question on the installation lead time of sophisticated electronic equipment. The rational part of us says 'there

is no point in carrying out image research on installation time—it is a fact, not an opinion'. Wrong! The key issue is not how long it will take but how long people *think* it will take. If their perception is that one company will take twice as long as another, they will react accordingly. This is true even if their perception is wrong, or if it is out of date. In this particular case, there *had* been a problem with one company but they had put it right; the survey showed that the perception remained and that they were losing business as a result.

4. *Market segmentation.*   As discussed in Chapter 4, our products and our marketing messages need to be targeted to particular segments. It may be necessary to do some market research to enable us to segment the market in the most effective manner, in order to decide the most appropriate message for each.

Methods

1. *Individual interviews.*   The most effective form of qualitative research is a discussion with a sample of respondents, probably in the interviewee's office. This will take the form of a 'depth' interview, using topic guides as prompts to open-ended questions to get the respondent talking in the desired direction. The process may be carried out on a single occasion in order to obtain a 'snapshot', or it may be repeated after a period of time in order to observe trends during the intervening period. Careful structuring of the questions is essential. Ambiguity must be avoided because this would invalidate the whole study. The respondents must feel that the questions are relevant or they will lose interest and either terminate the interview or give their answers less thoughtful consideration.

   The questions must be asked on a uniformly structured basis so that the answers can be correlated and consolidated. The safest route is perhaps to use a well-briefed consultancy for the whole project; the advantage of this is that they are specialists in the area and are aware of the pitfalls. However, it is my experience that, with carefully worded questions, one can obtain valuable information at a much lower cost (see Section 11.4).

2. *Group discussions.*   Such sessions may be run by consultants using 'focus groups' or other formal techniques. In this case, one is paying for specialized experience and facilities. Alternatively, it can take the form of a discussion panel or 'brainstorming' session. With certain safeguards, we can carry out such research ourselves on a relatively low budget as discussed in Section 11.4.

3. *In-house information*   There is one source of market information which is 'under our nose'. It is to be found in our sales and invoicing records, our customer correspondence files, the minds and reports of our salesforce, and in various other places. The problem is that we cannot access this information easily or draw statistically significant conclusions from it if we have not first set up some system to categorize and analyse it. We should also be aware that salespeople tend to react disproportionately to the last thing that happened; we perhaps need to receive similar reports from a number of salespeople before we attribute great significance to the information.

A little effort to design a suitable system can give useful results. Someone needs to be given the responsibility of maintaining it, and everyone who receives the information from the marketplace must conscientiously pass it through to be entered on the system according to the agreed guidelines. The system then provides a structured database of customers who can be approached under various circumstances. We might ask their opinion on a proposed new product, or visit a sample of them to discuss their longer-term needs.

Risks

The risks must be very carefully evaluated before any form of market research is undertaken. Without this, the results can be not only useless but actually misleading. Those setting up and carrying out the exercise must clearly understand issues such as bias, sample size and statistical significance. The main risks are:

1. *An unrepresentative group.*   Methods of obtaining samples have been mentioned in Section 11.1.

2. *The interviewer influences the discussion.*   The essence of all market research is that it must be totally objective. It is not only a waste of time and money but it is actually a delusion to conduct research which simply confirms our prejudices. If there is bad news, we need to know it! The danger is that interviewees or members of a panel tell the interviewer what they think he or she wants to hear. The essential skill is to devise appropriate questions and to probe in an unprejudiced manner so that we learn what the respondents really think.

3. *The analysis and the report is biased.*   This is a subtle trap. Some people pay consultants to tell them things they already know and want to hear, and the consultant is anxious to produce a report which will be welcomed (am I becoming cynical?!). It can also arise when the study is carried out by internal staff who want to reinforce their own views or impress their superiors. Ruthless objectivity is essential, and, indeed, some of the most valuable research comes when we find out information which is, at least at first sight, surprising or even unwelcome (see Exercise 11.2).

11.3 Quantitative market research

Quantitative research is used either separately or in conjunction with qualitative research when we want to put numbers on the information. As we have said, the cost of the research rises rapidly with the precision of the information we wish to obtain. With the exception of research on individual customers, discussed in Section 11.4, the whole area of quantitative research is not for the amateur and should be left to specialists.

Objectives

Common objectives are to obtain figures on market size, market shares and trends. If the marketplace is at all sophisticated, the amount of information required and therefore the cost of obtaining it can be extremely large, and we may have to be selective. If we have a broad idea of the market size and the share of ourselves and our major competitors, the most useful information is probably the trends. Uncertainty in market size and share may not significantly affect our business decision making, but it may be absolutely crucial to our future investment plans to know whether the market is increasing or decreasing by a certain percentage each year.

The classic users of this type of research are the major consumer marketing companies. They will know within a few days of the end of each month what market share they and their main competitors have achieved during the month. If we are a brand manager and our share has fallen from 33.7 per cent to 33.4 per cent, we may need to look for another job! The marketplace is almost treated as a computer model on which certain changes can be imposed, so that the effects can be measured of a new product launch, a price change, a promotion, an advertising campaign and so on. Past activities can be evaluated and decisions made about future programmes. The cost of this regular research is very high, but it makes eminent sense in this type of situation in view of the very high rewards for success and the penalties of failure.

Methods

The consumer market information described above comes from regular (usually monthly) audits. The market research company visits a structured quota sample of customers. For example, if the client is selling to the housewife, the sample will include the major retail multiples, the symbol groups, large and small independent shops and so on. Originally the researcher had to count the stock on the shelves and in the warehouse, record the deliveries received by the shop and thus obtain a measure of the sales made during the period. With the increasing sophistication of computerized check-outs, the information available from the point of sale can make the task much easier.

As with qualitative market research, some forms of quantitative study can also be carried out on a 'one-off' basis, possibly repeated after a period of time in order to measure trends. This might take the form of face-to-face interviews, or telephone or postal questionnaires.

Risks

The risk of a wrongly structured sample is so great that the task should not be undertaken by those who do not have specific expertise in this area. Having set up the sample, the target list of respondents must be rigorously pursued; if they or a legitimate equivalent are not found, the whole exercise may be biased (see Exercise 11.3).

11.4   Market research on a low budget

'The easiest answer to all market research problems is simply to commission a consultancy with the appropriate expertise, pay the fee and all our problems will be solved!' Apart from the fact that this is not true, it is not very helpful advice for companies with little or no money available to spend on professional market research. While there are some areas of research which should only be performed by professionals, there are four approaches which I have used successfully (and I would not claim to be a specialist in market research). These are as follows.

A group of opinion formers

Assembling a suitable group is a useful means of gaining an informed view of the longer-term trends in a particular industry. The group might typically consist of between three and six people whose opinion can be trusted and who have played a significant part in the development of the industry. It might include leading academics and research workers (as long as they have their feet firmly in the real commercial world), a senior representative of a professional or other body if appropriate, an informed journalist or other commentator on the scene and some senior representative users or recently retired users who are not prejudiced or restricted by commercial confidence.

The key to such an event is to have a really effective moderator, facilitator or chairman. The first task is to attract the members of the group. I have seen senior people willing to give up two or three hours, without payment of a fee apart from their expenses, simply because of their respect for the person leading the session. The chairperson should be well aware of the objective of the session, so that the right balance can be steered between allowing freedom of expression and wandering off into unproductive sidetracks.

Some consultants would record or video the discussion, but I personally prefer to do without such intrusions. The essential point is that the session should be unthreatening so that people are free to express their views without any inhibitions. One or two senior members of the company might be present, unobtrusively taking notes and participating from time to time but not in any way dominating the discussion. After the event they then quickly 'capture' all the key thoughts which have been developed, and record them for further consideration.

As with all market research, it is essential that the participants do not simply say what they feel the company would like to hear. It must not be regarded as a political or selling event, and the views expressed must be as objective as possible.

Users' groups

These are somewhat similar to the above, but the members of the group are all existing users of the company's products or services. They meet from time to time in order to advise the company on future lines they might follow. In terms of time scale, whereas the first group is looking very much to the long-term speculative future, a users' group is looking at more immediate issues such as the next version of the product they are already using. It is therefore more pragmatic and possibly more technical than the first type of discussion.

Again, it is important that the meeting is not seen as a commercial or selling event. It is also essential that it does not become a forum for criticism. If a member of the group is likely to complain about the company's performance, legitimately or otherwise, the issue should be dealt with outside the discussion; if it is not, the complainant will act as a 'rotten apple in a barrel', and the whole event will be counterproductive.

In my experience, users are often happy to host such events on their own site and, indeed, are quite proud to show their facilities to non-competing visitors. Again the cost to the company is trivial—perhaps some modest refreshments and expenses. Compared with the cost of commissioned research, the cost/benefit ratio is extremely favourable.

Image research

We have stressed the importance of knowing how we are regarded by the marketplace. There are obviously times when a major externally commissioned image study is worth while, but there may also be times when a relatively modest exercise can yield useful results.

One such example is an institution which had had a disappointingly low success rate with the award of technical contracts. They decided to visit a sample of the potential clients to find out the reasons for rejection. The feedback from the first four respondents was unanimous and therefore highly statistically significant. The problem was not the price or any doubts about technical ability. It was a perception that the people who would carry out the projects were not sufficiently attuned to the highly competitive commercial environment in which the companies had to operate. This perception was not accurate, but that is not the point—images do not have to be true to affect buying decisions positively or negatively. The logical outcome of the research was therefore to address the cause of the image problem. This is an important lesson which many companies need to learn. It might sometimes be useful to carry out a 'pilot' study in order to decide whether or not to invest in a more major research project.

Quantitative research on individual customers

As with all market research, it is essential that the study is not regarded as 'selling in disguise'. Unless the responses are objective and free from bias, the exercise is not only useless but may actually be misleading, quite apart from the fact that this is not a proper use of market research.

The aim is to find out specific data on individual customers. Let us suppose that we are a leading manufacturer selling high-value capital products such as computer installations used in industry. We might choose a representative sample of existing users of our own and competitive equipment. We would then visit them with a questionnaire, asking for information such as:

When are you proposing to install a new system?
Within what price bracket is the new system likely to lie?
For what reasons will you be wanting a new system (higher capacity, greater precision, ability to interface with other equipment, improved flexibility, etc.)?

The quantitative aspect of this research comes when the results of individual interviews are combined in a way which will provide a numerical input to future product strategy.

The risk of this type of research is that it costs the respondent nothing to be optimistic. If asked 'would you like a machine which has twice the capacity of your present equipment?' most people would say 'yes'. To persuade them some time later to buy a machine is a totally different matter! The questions must therefore be very carefully posed, and there is an advantage in using an external interviewer who is not seen to belong to one of the supplying companies. The information received can be extremely valuable compared with the cost of achieving it. As with other forms of market research, the results of a 'pilot' study might lead us to commission a more detailed study to resolve crucial issues.

Where the potential target market is small, the research can actually take the form of a 'census'—i.e. covering the whole marketplace. In this case, there are obviously no problems of extrapolating from a small sample to the whole market, and bias of this particular type is eliminated (see Exercise 11.4).

11.5   Marketing research

So far we have used the expression 'market research' to describe research into the market. This includes research into the competition. However, there is another extremely important area of research which we might call 'marketing research'. This is researching and testing our various marketing activities. It involves doing experiments in the marketplace, measuring the results, drawing conclusions and thus obtaining an input to future decision making. (It must be said that this distinction between market research and marketing research is not universally used; some people refer to the whole subject as 'marketing research'.) Some of the activities which can be researched in this way include the following.

Advertising

The degree to which it is worth researching our advertising depends very much upon the cost of the advertising. If we are planning to spend millions of pounds on a television campaign, it makes good sense to spend, if necessary, tens or even hundreds of thousands of pounds to attempt to ensure in advance that the ultimate investment will produce the maximum results. In these circumstances, our agency might produce several versions of a proposed advertisement and test them with a panel, measuring such aspects as impact, recall, recognition of the company name, motivation to purchase, and so on. The advertisement might then be tested in one television region before being released nationally.

On the other hand, if we have an advertising budget of only a few thousand pounds, marketing research might be confined to trying different forms of advertising and logging the responses against the date and place of the advertisement. This would help us to decide which journals to use, which time of year to advertise, whether to use pages in the journal, front or back covers, 'bingo cards' (where readers tick boxes for further information), inserts and so on.

In favour of this latter more pragmatic approach, it must be said that the only real test of an advertisement is whether it works. Impact, recall and so on are not ultimate objectives of advertising, and they do not always correlate as precisely as we would hope with the level of orders or enquiries which they generate. Advertising which wins prizes at film festivals does not always do the best job for the advertiser!

Selling

Again, because a large amount of money is involved in the selling process, it may be worth researching the effectiveness of different methods of selling and various ways of combining them. Options might include:

- *Specialist versus generalist sales staff.* For a newly introduced product, there might be an advantage in dedicating part of the sales team full-time to exploiting the opportunities for an initial period. The rest of the team might be asked to pass on sales leads to the specialists during this phase. Some might say that the commission arrangements would not permit this, but who is making the rules?!

- *Full-time versus part-time sales staff.* Some companies, such as those involved in consultancy, have to use fee-earning staff for the selling process, because they have no one else. This has advantages and disadvantages, as discussed in Section 8.6. These options might form the subject of a marketing research study.

- *Selling direct versus selling through distribution channels.* This a more fundamental decision, in which we are testing whether the discount/commission/mark-up allowed to the distributor is more or less favourable than the cost of selling direct to the end customer through our own resources. If we are considering a change, a pilot experiment might be set up as part of a marketing research exercise.

Literature

Different versions of a particular item of literature can be tested at the draft stage before committing to the final version. Alternatively, we might test the effectiveness of having a whole hierarchy of literature with each component having a specific purpose. This could involve targeting different market segments or different members of the decision-making group.

Exhibitions

I once took an exhibition stand where the cost had been recovered by 10.35 a.m. on the Monday week following the exhibition. This is a rather precise measurement which is not available to everyone! The point is, however, that unless we have a specific and measurable objective, it is impossible to determine whether an exhibition was worth while and whether we should attend on the next occasion. Marketing research might therefore test one exhibition against another, and could test the relative effectiveness of spending money on exhibitions compared with other ways of spending the same amount of money.

Price

As price can have such a significant effect on the volume of sales and their profitability, any research which will assist us in determining the optimum market-based price can be very valuable. As discussed in Chapter 6, many companies underprice in some areas and over-price in others, because they do not know the price the market will bear. In a large consumer marketing operation, price can actually be tested by selling at different prices in different regions of the country (assuming all other factors are equal). In a consultancy situation, where the price is decided for each individual project, the broad effect of increasing or reducing prices can be judged.

Packaging and presentation

The perceived value of a product or service can be significantly affected by its packaging and presentation. Various forms of packaging can be researched in the marketplace, either by using a representative panel or with a sample of customers in an actual purchasing situation.

Test markets

A highly sophisticated form of marketing research is the test market, where the whole package involved in the launch of a product is tested on a limited scale before committing to a national or international launch (see Section 12.4).

Conclusion

Marketing research is almost an attitude of mind. It means that we recognize the fact that there is rarely a completely 'right' way to market a particular product, and are constantly trying new approaches and learning from our experience. As with normal market research, the cost need not be very great if we use the resources we already have with imagination and intelligence (see Exercise 11.5 and Follow-up 11.1 and 11.2).

Exercises

11.1 Where do you think your company lies on the spectrum in Figure 11.1? Is this appropriate for your type of business? What changes need to be made?

11.2 What subject would you most like to research qualitatively in the marketplace? How would you go about it? What size of sample would be required? How much would you be willing to pay for such a study? What three (or more) main questions would you ask?

11.3 What subject would you most like to research quantitatively in the marketplace? Would you need to use external resources? With what precision would you like to know the result? How much would you be willing to pay for such a study?

11.4 What type of 'low-budget market research' as described in Section 11.4 might be appropriate to your operation? What subject will you research? Who will organize it? What risks will you specially consider? When are you going to do it?!

11.5 Which parts of your operation would be useful subjects for marketing research? What alternatives will you want to test? Who will do it? How will it be done? When are you going to do it?!

Follow-up

11.1 Cultivate the habit of asking yourself, every time you consider a particular form of marketing expenditure, whether you have sufficient evidence to say that this is the most cost-effective way of achieving the desired objective.

11.2 If appropriate, read a book on market research such as Crimp, M. (1990) *The Marketing Research Process*, Prentice Hall International (UK) Ltd, Hemel Hempstead, UK.

How do we achieve profitable innovation?

Market-led innovation

Key business issues	*Section*

■ New product development is not the only route to business   12.1
development. New markets for existing products may give
quicker returns even though the work is technically unexciting.

■ The marketing cost of innovation may exceed the technical cost   12.2
and should be included in the appraisal process.

■ More products fail for marketing reasons than for technical
reasons.

■ Proposals for new products or new markets should be put   12.3
through policy, marketing, financial, management and technical
filters before project expenditure is approved.

■ Probable winners should be identified as early as possible. We   12.4
should not 'start developing now, think about the market later'.

■ An R&D department should be regarded not as a cost centre   12.5
but as a 'value-generating centre'. Differentiation should be
built in at the concept stage.

■ Under- or overspecifying or changing the specification can be   12.6
disastrous and are often signs of immature marketing.

■ Income and expenditure forecasts for new products should be   12.7
analysed for risk and sensitivity.

■ Delay in time-to-market can make a whole project unprofitable.
Management attention is often directed at the wrong targets.

■ Impending failure should be recognized, and projects terminated   12.8
before even more money is wasted.

■ Unwillingness to 'lose face' inside the company or at corporate
level is a common cause of wasted investment.

12.1   Options for business development

Ansoff (1957), defines a diversification matrix which offers four possibilities for business development. We can sell new or existing products into new or existing markets, and so the options are:

- *Penetration*   existing products into existing markets
- *New product development*   new products into existing markets
- *Market development*   existing products into new markets
- *Diversification*   new products into new markets

Penetration

This involves selling more of our existing products in our existing markets, and is the routine daily activity of most businesses. Whether or not this is sufficient to meet our corporate targets depends upon the size of the market, our market share, the strength of the competition, the merits of our products and so on. If the potential is sufficient, it may be wise not to divert management time and money into new areas.

However, although such a favourable situation can exist, it may not remain for long. If the market is sufficiently attractive, new competitors will come in until potential supply exceeds potential demand, and everybody has to engage in a constant battle to defend their own share. In these circumstances, something more has to be done.

New product development

This involves developing new products for our existing markets. The first reaction of many managers when thinking about business development is to turn to the new product development department. 'In order to grow, we must have new products,' they say. This may be right, but it is an expensive and risky process (see Chapter 13), and it is important to realize that it is not the only option open to us.

Market development

This involves selling our existing products into new markets. These may be new geographical markets or they may be new market segments where a product which has been tried and tested in one segment is seen to have potential in another. The product or service may have to be adapted slightly to the new marketplace, but this route avoids the cost and delay of fundamental new product development.

Experience with a large number of companies shows that this is an increasingly common activity, particularly in the field of services. In many cases, the market in which the company has been operating has either plateaued or is actually declining. Examples are the defence, nuclear and space industries as discussed in Chapter 4. The market will continue to have potential for evermore, but it is inadequate to satisfy all the participants. In these circumstances, companies have no option but to seek to sell their skills elsewhere. Scientifically, this seems to offer no problem. However, we need to consider the very substantial process described in Section 4.8 as 'establishing a track record'.

At certain stages in the evolution of a company, market development may bring greater and quicker rewards than new product development. The problem is that market development is not very exciting for the R&D department. It takes them away from the stimulation of new product development, and requires them to undertake unchallenging tasks such as adapting the product to new standards. Some companies overcome this problem by assigning different staff with different motivations to the two very different operations.

In many cases, product development and market development are used in combination. A new product is due to appear in, say, two years' time, but in the meantime we have to maintain the profit stream; entering a new market with an existing product may be the best means of doing this.

Full diversification

This involves selling new products into new markets. It requires two steps into the unknown, and the combined risk may be very high indeed. There may be nothing wrong with having a small element of full diversification as part of a total portfolio, but it is very risky to be in a situation where this is the only option remaining. Such a position should be anticipated many years in advance and corrective action taken. It is no use waiting until the demand for one's product has ceased, perhaps as part of the 'peace dividend', and then sitting back and blaming the government! Marketing is making the future happen, and this includes preventing the unacceptable consequences of predictable future situations as well as exploiting the profitable ones (see Exercise 12.1).

12.2   The role of marketing in innovation

If you ask most companies what they spend on innovation, they will quote the percentage of their turnover which is allocated to the R&D budget. This reveals a very inadequate view of what marketing is there to do. Many market-led companies would recognize that the marketing cost of innovation may have to be at least as high as the technical cost. In other words, new product development is not something which goes on solely or even mainly in the R&D department. If this is so, we might feel that the marketing cost of innovation is so expensive that we cannot afford to engage in it. Successful marketeers would say the opposite. Without in any way denigrating the importance of the technical content of innovation, the key to business success may lie as much in identifying and exploiting profitable market opportunities as in developing the products themselves.

Serious problems arise in large companies when the total cost of innovation is not taken into account when making investment decisions. Senior technical staff are sometimes authorized to decide on suitable R&D projects without reference to marketing. A senior technical director told me that projects were prioritized on a technical basis; this has to be wrong! One of the specific purposes of this book and the seminars on which it is based is to enable 'non-marketing managers' to understand the role of marketing, particularly in innovation, and to be able to interface synergistically with their marketing colleagues. The benefit of collaboration between strong marketing and strong technical staff has been discussed in Section 3.3 (see Exercise 12.2 and Follow-up 12.1).

More products fail for marketing reasons than for technical reasons. This needs to be recognized when investment decisions are being considered.

12.3   Make decisions before spending money

It is sometimes easier to understand the technical implications of a new product than the marketing factors which are likely to be involved. The technical specification can be accurately defined, and the course of the project and the way in which it is managed can be understood in a logical manner. Sophisticated techniques can be used during the project review procedure. The marketing issues, on the other hand, are usually much less clearly defined, even in a market-led organization. The needs of the customer are not precisely known and the activities of the competition may be unpredictable.

For this reason, companies tend instinctively to start by spending their time and money on the areas with which they feel most comfortable. They embark on the technical part of a project in order to show some progress and to test the technical feasibility of the product concept. They advance with a large number of projects in parallel, in the hope that some of them will eventually achieve commercial success. The marketing department is brought in at the end of the process with the task of selling a product which it is hoped will meet market needs.

The saddest obituary I ever read in a development report was 'Project successfully completed, Marketing not interested'. This statement reveals a total misunderstanding of the role of marketing in innovation. Marketing do not have the option of 'being interested' once the project is complete. Their obligation is to commit themselves to marketing the product (subject to successful technical development) *before* any money is spent on R&D. The technical specification—the description of *how* the product requirements will be met—should not even be written until marketing have signed off on at least the key parts of the user requirement or marketing specification—the definition of *what* the market will want the product to do. In the situation where strong technical staff are interfacing with weak marketing staff, they do not receive this authoritative and definitive input; they therefore go ahead with development, making 'marketing' decisions as they go, and hoping that the results will sell!

It is useful to consider a number of 'filters' through which all new ideas should pass before money is spent on them. This may seem to be a counsel of perfection, but why not?! There are enough business problems which are outside our control; we should at least try to address those which are within our control.

1. *The policy filter*
    Is there a positive policy to go into this area?
    If not, does the policy allow the freedom to do so?
    Is there a policy not to go into this area?
    Is there a policy that another part of the company should do it?

2. *The marketing filter*
    Is there a market for the product?
    Is it large enough?
    Is it growing at a sufficient rate?
    Do we have sufficient customer benefits to create a demand?
    Do we have sufficient meaningful differentiation to overcome the existing and future competition?
    Do we have both the calibre and quantity of marketing resources?
    Do we have both the calibre and quantity of selling resources?
    Do we have the appropriate sales channels, or is there enough in the budget to set them up?

3. *The financial filter*
    Have we done a full financial appraisal (all areas of expense, including marketing, not only R&D)?
    Are we able to commit the necessary financial resources—capital and revenue?
    Is the predicted profit stream adequate?
    Can we stand the initial profit and cash outflow?
    Have we evaluated the risks and sensitivity (see Section 12.7)?
    Is the worst case acceptable?
    Have we avoided the trap of self-fulfilling delusion (see Section 12.7)?

4. *The management filter*
Do we have the necessary quality of management skills?
Do we have the necessary quantity of these management skills?
Have we resolved conflicts of priority for these management resources?
If we are entering a new area of business, do we have the right style of management?
Do we sufficiently understand the new business?
Are we in danger of extrapolating too far from the known to the unknown in management terms?

5. *The technical filter*
Is the project technically feasible?
Do we have or can we acquire the necessary technical skills and resources at all levels?
Do we have the necessary spare capacity to devote to the project?
Have we resolved conflicts of priority for these technical resources?

The more we can apply these filters at an early stage in the decision-making process, the greater will be our chance of success and the less will be the amount of management time and money which is wasted.

The sequence set out above seems to represent a logical train of thought but, if possible, it would be best to identify and tackle the hardest filters first. If the project then fails at the first filter we apply, at least we will have saved the management time involved in applying all the others; if it passes, the rest of the process should be that much easier (see Exercise 12.3 and Follow-up 12.2).

12.4   Identify winners as early as possible

The process of choosing the projects in which to invest may go through a number of distinct stages. We are thinking particularly of new products and services, but the same criteria apply to marketing activities such as entering new markets. Money spent on marketing decisions early in the process can reduce the amount invested in projects which are ultimately aborted.

Produce a 'long-list'

Initially, it is useful to list as many ideas as possible. This can be done by using all likely sources of ideas within the company, perhaps by means of a 'brainstorming' session. A 'marketing purist' would say that all ideas have to come from the marketing department because that is their prerogative, but this is arrogance. All ideas should go through filters, including the marketing filter, but the number of ideas should not be limited at this stage. Sales staff, R&D engineers, production staff, senior managers, customers—indeed almost anyone—may have ideas which are worth considering. The art is to reduce the list as early as possible in the process in order to identify the relatively small number which should become committed projects.

Screen the ideas

The initial screening of these ideas may reduce the list to perhaps a half or a quarter of the original total. This screening may be done inside the company, but only if those who are making the decisions have a good understanding of present and future marketplace needs. The criteria must be based on market and financial considerations as well as technical ones. The cost of screening each idea at this stage may be relatively low, possibly of the order of a few hundred pounds.

Test the concepts

The ideas which have survived the first stage now need to be tested, albeit on a theoretical basis, in the marketplace. This may be done using formal or informal panels, arranged by ourselves or by a market research consultant, or we may visit a number of key potential clients or opinion formers (see Chapter 11). The purpose is to judge whether the concept on which the possible new product is predicated is soundly based.

The cost of a concept test will be considerably higher than that of the initial idea-screening. It is for this reason that we are proceeding in stages. Each stage covers a smaller number of products, and the cost of implementing each stage rises rapidly.

Develop the product

This represents the actual technical content of the innovation project. It is significant that this is the third item on the list and not the first. The cost of the project may vary from a few thousand to millions, tens of millions, or even hundreds of millions of pounds depending upon the nature of the project. A very little arithmetic shows the benefit of the first two preliminary stages. If the relatively small amount of money spent on idea-screening and concept testing can improve the success rate of the R&D department by even a small percentage, it will be amply rewarded.

Carry out a test market

Test markets are a standard procedure in the consumer marketing industry and in many others. The cost of a national launch can be millions of pounds; an international launch costs many times more. A small proportion of this amount of money spent on validating the programme before commitment makes eminent sense.

The test market will seek to test not only the acceptability of the product but also the effectiveness of pricing, advertising, point-of-sale display material, literature and any other parts of the marketing programme which can be tested on a limited scale. For consumer products advertised on television, the test is normally carried out in one television region. Where other media are used, an appropriate small but representative sample of the marketplace is chosen. This process is to be contrasted with the relatively low-key efforts of many companies during the phase between development and launch of a product.

Various results of a test market are possible. If everything is favourable, we can launch with even greater confidence, using lessons learned during the test. Alternatively, the test market may reveal inadequacies in the product, the message, the media, the price and so on; if such feedback is potentially available, it is disastrous not to take steps to find it out (see Exercise 12.4).

12.5   Product differentiation should be built in at the concept stage

A research and development department is normally regarded as a cost centre. However, the ultimate purpose of R&D is not so much to develop new products or services as to create value. This value benefits the company funding the R&D, and also its customers and, where appropriate, their customers in turn. It is therefore more healthy to regard it as a 'value generating centre', irrespective of the way it is treated in the company accounts.

A key indicator of value is differentiation. When customers perceive a meaningful differentiation from competitors' products which they value, they are prepared to pay a premium price for it.

The cost of adding differentiating features to the product depends very much upon the stage in the development process at which it is done. Most of us can think of situations where a product development programme has been virtually complete and then someone has come along with a 'bright idea'! If that same idea had been introduced at the concept or specification stage, the incremental cost of including it might well have been lower or even zero. Once designs have been completed, software written, long lead-time components ordered, tooling made and so on, a change in specification not only costs a great deal of money but also may seriously delay the launch date.

The instinct of many small companies is to copy the industry leader. It might be better if they did something different, either in the product or in the way it is marketed. The aim is to define a new market segment in which they can become the leader, even if it is smaller than the original segment which is dominated by the competition.

This again illustrates the point that innovation is not something which takes place solely or even mainly in the R&D department. Marketing and business decisions made at the concept stage can have a 'make or break' effect on profitability (see Follow-up 12.3).

12.6   Under- or overspecifying or changing the specification can be disastrous

Underspecifying

In many product fields, particularly the fast-moving high-technology areas, the life cycle of a new product in the marketplace can be shorter than the time required for development. This represents a trap—we have to be thinking about the Mark 2 and Mark 3 versions before Mark 1 is even launched.

In these circumstances, the launch of a new product must represent a distinct advance in the mind of the customer. Underspecifying, by developing a product which really only brings us up to the level of where the competition were on the previous cycle, will not create a winning opportunity.

Overspecifying

Conversely, and this is a more subtle trap, overspecifying can lead to commercial disaster. The instinct of the technical enthusiast is to include every possible feature in the specification, whether or not the customer is likely to value it. Equally, low-calibre marketing staff who are not willing to make difficult decisions compile a long-list of everything which any customer might conceivably want. The motivation is obvious—if the product will do everything, they are more likely to be able to sell it!

There are two major problems with this approach. First, the unit cost of the product may become excessive, and the only customers who will buy it are those who are prepared to pay a top price for an absolutely top specification. Much higher sales volumes and profits might have been achieved if the specification had been restrained. Second, the elapsed time needed to tie up all the loose ends of a highly complex specification may mean that the product misses a critical time window.

A 'wish-list' is not a product specification—it is a sign of marketing immaturity. Experienced marketing staff have learned the difficult art of saying 'no'—of settling for an optimum commercial specification rather than a maximum technical specification.

Changing specification

Another common fault is the so-called 'changing specification'. There are, of course, times when a change may be legitimate. Technology may change and render the original approach unnecessary or obsolete. The competition may come out with some unexpected new product which undermines the original strategy. The price of major components or finished products may change in the marketplace. We can all make mistakes (but not too often!). These are legitimate reasons for having to change a specification.

However, in my experience, a much more common cause of a 'changing specification' is that marketing had not 'done their homework' properly in the first place. The initial specification was based upon their first, rather casual, thoughts; the changes became necessary when they realized that there were issues which they had not previously taken the trouble to address. This is another sign of marketing immaturity. Marketing cannot have the privilege of determining market-led specifications for new products without also bearing the responsibility for getting it right (to the extent that there is a 'right' answer!) (see Exercise 12.5).

12.7   Risk and sensitivity

The normal starting point for any business plan or marketing plan is a sales forecast. The period of time which this covers depends upon the nature of the business, but a five-year period is common. This sales forecast is then combined with production costs and indirect expenses such as R&D, marketing and general and administration to give a net profit.

All these figures are, by their nature, estimates. A risk and sensitivity analysis asks 'how much does it matter if any one of these figures turns out to be wrong by a certain amount, and is there anything we can do to minimize the risk of this happening?'

In Table 12.1, the turnover has been based on a unit selling price of £100. The cost of sales is then subtracted to give the gross margin in each of the five years. (Note that 'cost of sales' is the cost of providing the product—assumed to be £50 per unit—it is nothing to do with selling expenses which appear lower down.) The gross margin is the amount of money which is available for two things—covering the fixed expenses and, we hope, providing a profit. For simplicity in this example, the indirect expenses are expressed as a total figure. The brackets indicate that they are negative figures.

There is a danger that managers engage in the self-fulfilling delusion of putting in sales figures which give them the answer they want. A profit

Table 12.1

Year	1	2	3	4	5
Units		50 000	150 000	250 000	300 000
Financial (£million)					
Sales @ £100		5.0	15.0	25.0	30.0
Cost of sales @ £50		2.5	7.5	12.5	15.0
Gross margin		2.5	7.5	12.5	15.0
Expenses	(3.0)	(3.0)	(5.0)	(7.5)	(8.0)
Net profit	(3.0)	(0.5)	2.5	5.0	7.0

projection of this kind acquires a legitimacy and a sense of authority which many recipients are prepared to accept without question.

What can go wrong with such a forecast? The answer is—everything! The volume of sales may not be achieved, the unit selling price may become depressed by the activities of competition, the unit cost of sales may be exceeded by unforeseen problems in production or supply of raw materials, and every area of expense may eventually turn out to be over budget. The question is—how serious are these variances?

It would not matter if 'swings equalled roundabouts'—for example, if we failed to reach the unit price but exceeded the sales volume in a way which still gave the same bottom-line profit. While a purist would like the profit to be achieved in exactly the planned way, a realist will be thankful that the planned profit had been achieved at all.

The key to this exercise is therefore to evaluate very critically the risk of each figure being wrong by a certain amount, and the sensitivity of the profit to this variance. This can be done on a computer model, but it can also be done very simply and effectively with a basic calculator. We can calculate the effect on profitability of a sales shortfall of, say, 10 per cent, 20 per cent, 30 per cent .... Similarly, we can evaluate the effect of adverse variances in all the other factors. This very quickly shows where the sensitivity lies. In the example quoted above, the profit is completely eliminated if any one of the following situations occurs:

- A price shortfall of 15 per cent
- A delay of 9 months
- A sales shortfall of 30 per cent
- A unit cost increase of 30 per cent
- An expenses overrun of 40 per cent

In reality, the variance will not be restricted to one factor but will be found in most if not all of the elements which contribute to profit.

Where do we go from here? We start by examining the areas where a variation is most likely to put the planned profit at risk, and then look for ways of containing this variation.

For example, in the case quoted above, a delay is absolutely critical. A little arithmetic will show whether it would be worth spending more money in the development phase—by bringing in subcontract staff, for example—to increase the probability of reaching the target time-window.

Further work to ratify the sales forecast and unit selling price would also be very worth while, although it is accepted that these figures will always be estimates. The figures are particularly important in cases such as this one where most of the income is generated in the latter part of the period; this is, of course, the time for which the forecasts are least likely to be accurate.

The sensitivity of the profit to time-to-market has been estimated by calculating the effect of a one-year delay and then taking a proportion on a pro-rata basis. Even this is too optimistic—it assumes that the competition do nothing during the intervening period and that the customers are happy to wait, neither of which is true. The danger is that we become neurotic if the R&D budget is exceeded even by a small amount, but are not sufficiently concerned if the product misses the time-window for which it is intended. Very simple arithmetic shows that these priorities may be completely wrong. Having said this, good management will adhere to expense budgets as well as planned time scales!

The above calculations contain a basic fallacy in that they have ignored the time value of money. A pound today is equivalent to 75p in three years' time if we use a 10 per cent interest rate. The cash flow statement should be discounted, using the well-established DCF technique, to bring the expenditure and income back to present day terms, in order to calculate a net present value (NPV). In most cases, and this is certainly true in the above example, we are spending the high-value pounds now and earning the lower-value pounds a few years later. The effect of this is to bring the net present value of the project down to, perhaps, one half or three quarters of the arithmetical sum of the profit stream or even less, depending upon the discount rate used. A brief description of the DCF technique is given in the appendix at the end of this chapter.

The analysis may show that there is a possibility of favourable variances, so that our profit forecast will be exceeded. This may create problems, with production capacity for example, but let's have a few problems like that (see Follow-up 12.4)!

12.8   Dealing with impending failure

We have been arguing the case for a thorough investigation of market-place needs and an analysis of the competition in order to arrive at a sound marketing specification. We have also urged that a critical financial appraisal of the investment is made before substantial funds are committed to research or development work.

In spite of all these precautions, it has to be accepted that projects sometimes go wrong. The technical problems prove to be greater than anticipated, and the cost of solving them appears to increase drastically. Marketplace needs may change, alternative technology may be developed and competitors have a nasty habit of doing unpredictable things.

In these circumstances, the best course of action may be to terminate a project. Herein lies the trap. We hear statements such as 'We have already spent £5 million on this project—we can't stop now!' 'The solution is just round the corner.' It always is, but the corner seems to get further away! The most insidious reason for not wanting to terminate a project is 'We have told corporate headquarters about it, the president/managing director has taken a personal interest in it—there will be too much 'egg on our face' if we stop now'. Managers carry on in the vain hope that the problem will go away, only to end up by terminating the project at a later date when still more money has been wasted.

Money already invested in a project is a 'sunk cost'—nothing can bring it back. Unless there are sound reasons for believing that the prospects of success have significantly increased, the wise course of action may be to take the loss and get on with something else which can be more profitable (see Exercise 12.6).

Exercises

12.1 Analyse the business development activities of your company over, say, the last two years, in terms of the four categories in Section 12.1. How much future income (or, preferably, profit) has been generated by each? What unexploited opportunities does this analysis suggest?

12.2 Estimate the marketing cost of innovation for the last financial year, and compare it with the technical cost. Are these two figures in a sensible relationship? (See Follow-up 12.1 below).

12.3 Put your current new product development projects through the five filters listed in Section 12.3. Does this lead you to change your investment decisions in any way? (See Follow-up 12.2.)

12.4 Carry out the process of 'identifying winners' described in Section 12.4. (This will involve assembling an appropriate team, and ensuring that they can devote the necessary time to the exercise; the project should first be 'sold' to senior management, so that it is done with their backing.)

12.5 Select a recent development project which has not gone as smoothly as it might have done, and assess the extent to which the specification problems described in Section 12.6 have been a contributory factor.

12.6 Ask yourself (honestly!) whether you are falling into any of the traps on impending failure described in Section 12.8.

Follow-up

12.1 For your business plan period (3 to 5 years?), set out the estimated marketing cost of innovation beside the technical cost. Consider ways in which your innovation could become more market-led, and estimate the cost of doing so. What would be the effect on long-term profitability of this changed emphasis?

12.2 Incorporate the five filters in Section 12.3 into your future new product evaluation procedures.

12.3 Incorporate the idea of 'value generation' in Section 12.5 into your R&D assessment procedures.

12.4 Incorporate the 'risk and sensitivity' analysis described in Section 12.7 into your investment appraisal procedures, using discounted cash flow (see appendix) unless you already have an equivalent procedure.

Reference

Ansoff, H. I. (1957) *Harvard Business Review*, Vol. 35, No. 5, Sept.–Oct.

Appendix: Discounted cash flow (DCF)

Although the DCF technique was introduced many decades ago, it still represents one of the simplest aids to investment appraisal. Such investments might include building a new factory, installing a new machine or, in the context of this chapter, developing a new product or service or entering a new market segment. Although it is possible to use a computer model, a programmed calculator or DCF tables, the calculation can be done with a basic calculator (or even with pencil and paper!).

The basis of the technique can be understood by asking 'would we be willing to lend someone £100 if they promised to repay us £100 in a year's time, with a guarantee of no risk?' No, because we could put the money into a bank and earn some interest. Suppose they offered to repay us £105, £110, £115, £120 ... ? The point would come where we would agree to the deal because it was better than other ways of investing the money. In other words, we have a certain view of what we expect our money to earn for us. If the figure were 10 per cent, we would say that £110 in a year's time was equivalent to £100 today, or that £110 in a year's time had a *net present value* (NPV) of £100.

It is important to note that this is nothing to do with inflation, but relates to the time value of money. Inflation is obviously a complicating factor, but it may be possible to eliminate its effect by assuming that we can raise prices in line with inflation, i.e. we do the calculation at present-day prices and assume that inflation will cancel out.

Let us now apply this thinking to an investment. We have a number of sources of cash outflow and cash inflow. If we simply added up the outflows and subtracted them from the inflows to see whether we had made a gain or a loss, we would be ignoring the time effect. The problem is that, in most cases, we are investing the valuable pounds at the start and in the early years of the project, and receiving back the less valuable pounds in the later years of the project. This gives us an artificially favourable view of the value of the investment, particularly when the majority of the sales come late in the time period. Let us apply the DCF technique to the investment in Section 12.7:

	Year 1	Year 2	Year 3	Year 4	Year 5
Cash sources (£million)[*]					
Sales revenue	0	5.0	15.0	25.0	30.0
Total cash inflow	**0**	**5.0**	**15.0**	**25.0**	**30.0**
Cash uses (£million)[†]					
Cost of goods sold	0	2.5	7.5	12.5	15.0
Development cost	2.0	0.5			
Sales & marketing expenses	0.75	1.75	3.75	6.0	6.5
General & admin expenses	0.25	0.75	1.25	1.5	1.5
Total cash outflow	**3.0**	**5.5**	**12.5**	**20.0**	**23.0**
Net cash inflow	**(3.0)**	**(0.5)**	**2.5**	**5.0**	**7.0**

[*]   Other cash sources might include:
   Increase in creditors/payables
   Buildings and equipment sold
   Royalties
[†]   Other cash uses might include:
   Increase in debtors/receivables
   Buildings and equipment purchased
   Increase in stock/inventory
   Tax

It could be argued that the above figures do not strictly represent the overall cash flow, but they will suffice to illustrate the technique. Refinement of the figures is unlikely to lead to significantly different conclusions.

If we simply added the figures, the cumulative cash inflow would be £11 million and we would feel favourably towards the project. However, if we discount the cash flows at 10 per cent, the picture is very different. To do this, we need to divide the cash flow:

In year 2 by 110/100 = 1.1
In year 3 by 1.1 × 1.1 = 1.21
In year 4 by 1.1 × 1.1 × 1.1 = 1.33
In year 5 by 1.1 × 1.1 × 1.1 × 1.1 = 1.46

These figures can be obtained from DCF tables, but they can easily be calculated by putting 1.1 into the memory of a calculator and dividing the year's net cash inflow the appropriate number of times. This changes the net cash inflows from

Undiscounted:	(3.0)	(0.5)	2.5	5.0	7.0
to					
Discounted at 10 per cent	(3.0)	(0.45)	2.07	4.13	4.78

We can now add these *discounted* figures to give the net present value:

NPV at 10 per cent = £7.53 million

This is significantly different from the original sum of £11 million without discounting, and may cause us to revise our degree of optimism in the project.

If we were to use a discount rate of 20 per cent, the figures would be:

Discounted at 20 per cent	(3.0)	(0.42)	1.74	2.89	3.38

NPV at 20 per cent = £4.59 million which is less than half of the undiscounted total

Some might say that a discount rate of 20 per cent is much too 'greedy'; by looking for this sort of return on investment, worthwhile projects might be rejected. Against this argument, we must remember that some projects fail to reach their expected potential or even fail altogether. The 'successful' projects have to pay not only for themselves but for the unsuccessful projects as well. We may therefore have to use a higher discount rate, depending upon the risks in our particular type of business.

An alternative to using the net present value based on a predetermined annual interest rate is to calculate the interest rate which would give an NPV of zero. This rate is known as the internal rate of return (IRR). This can be an aid to ranking a number of projects which are competing for limited resources, but we must not forget the magnitude of the cash flows; a very high per cent IRR is not much good if the amount of money involved is small.

As we said at the start, much more sophisticated evaluation techniques can be used, but the DCF method can be used by anyone. Certainly no product managers reporting to me would ever have submitted an investment proposal without a risk and sensitivity assessment (see Section 12.7) and a DCF calculation—they knew that it would be referred back to them if they did (see Follow-up 12.4).

How do we manage the future?

CHAPTER *13*

Marketing management and business planning

Key business issues	*Section*

■ Sales is part of marketing, not vice versa; job titles and responsibilities should reflect this. — 13.1

■ Strategic business units (SBUs) have the advantage of defining clear profit responsibility for achieving results in the marketplace.

■ At different stages in a product life cycle we may be selling a different product to a different type of customer, at a different price with different profitability, with different strategic objectives, marketing emphasis and marketing expenditure. We ignore this at our peril. — 13.2

■ Life cycles should be extended by various means in order to maximize return on investment. — 13.3

■ Plans should be regarded as essential working documents, not theoretical exercises. — 13.4

■ The business plan sets out a viable future for the business and ensures that everyone is working to the same objective. — 13.5

■ It is a standard against which to monitor progress.

■ The marketing plan shows that marketing strategies and tactics have been clearly thought out, and ensures that everyone understands the commitment to marketing which the plan requires. — 13.6

■ Internal business proposals are marketing documents. Some key factors which would lead to early approval are often ignored. — 13.7

■ Models and techniques can assist us in understanding our business situation. — 13.8

- They are only worth using if we treat them realistically and act upon the findings.

- Many companies set their sights far too low in their under-   13.9
standing of the role of product management and marketing management.

13.1   Organization of the marketing function

The organization of the marketing function often follows the three aspects described in Section 1.11—sales, strategic marketing/product management and marketing services. There is a problem with the meaning of the word 'marketing'. The whole area is properly called 'marketing'. Within that we have the 'sales' part of marketing and the 'marketing' part of marketing, the latter covering the strategic and marketing management issues discussed in this book.

Company organization

There can be an ambiguity of job titles at a senior level, depending upon the way in which responsibilities for selling and the broader aspects of marketing are allocated. In a small or medium-sized company, the preferred route is normally to have a 'marketing director' who is responsible for both sales and marketing (see Figure 13.1). There is a serious problem when the position is reversed—when 'marketing' reports to 'sales'. This usually indicates a very inadequate view of the marketing role, where it is regarded as little more than sales support, and the crucial strategic and business aspects of marketing are ignored.

   If there are two board directors, one responsible for sales and the other for marketing, the two functions can only be brought together at chief executive level. This is not ideal, as the other responsibilities of CEOs make it unlikely that they will have sufficient time to create synergy and resolve conflicts between the two parts. In a very large company, where the sales force may run into hundreds or even thousands, a sales position

Fig. 13.1   Company organization

at board level may be necessary, but the issues involved in integrating sales and marketing still have to be resolved.

It is fairly common for people to be given the title 'sales director' when they are not in fact members of the board of directors. This is because customers like to feel that they are dealing with a senior person. A formula which is used internally in some companies is that 'director of X' is not a board position while 'X director' is.

Marketing organization

The hierarchy can vary enormously with the size of organization, but in a large marketing orientated company the structure might be as shown in Figure 13.2. To reflect the emphasis given to branding in consumer marketing companies, the 'product managers' might be called 'brand managers'.

Sales organization

As with marketing, the structure will depend upon the size and complexity of the company's operation, but the general pattern shown in Figure 13.3 will act as a guide. Many companies based in the UK would now regard the whole of (Western) Europe as their 'home' market, and reflect the fact in their organization (see Exercise 13.1).

Strategic business units

Modern management thinking prefers 'flatter' organizations without as much hierarchical structure as that shown in Figures 13.2 and 13.3. One way of doing this, which has great advantages in terms of marketing and management resources, is to divide the company into a number of strategic business units (SBUs).

Fig. 13.2 Marketing organization

Fig. 13.3 Sales organization

An SBU is a part of the business which, in principle, could exist as a separate company in its own right even though, in practice, it may share a number of common facilities with other SBUs. Each SBU has its own product range, market segments and competitors.

An SBU is managed by an SBU manager (or sometimes a business unit manager—but beware the acronym!), who is responsible for strategic planning and profit performance for that part of the company. In the simplest case, the SBU manager is responsible only for the marketing activities of the unit, normally including line responsibility for the selling function. Beyond this, it is quite normal for a number of SBU managers to share common resources such as R&D, manufacturing, personnel, buildings and so on. These functions can be included in or excluded from the SBU in an almost infinite variety of ways. The SBU manager may be very happy to share the fixed costs of other functions. If, for example, a company had five SBUs, it might be unnecessarily expensive to have five separate manufacturing or R&D units, and each might suffer from the problem of being too small to reach 'critical mass'. Obviously there may be conflicts of priorities between the demands of the various SBUs on these common resources, but management is there to resolve such issues!

We said initially that the SBU manager would normally have direct line responsibility for the selling function. It is possible for this also to be carried out by another part of the company for which he or she is not responsible, but this can lead to enormous conflicts rather similar to those described in Section 6.8 on in-company transfer pricing.

The great merit of SBU management is that it delegates profit authority and responsibility to senior middle management who are able to focus exclusively on the exploitation of their particular marketplace. SBU managers are, in effect, 'champions', who are paid to put all their effort, enthusiasm and resources behind the achievement of a clearly defined goal. At a stroke, this organization overcomes many of the problems of bureaucracy, delayed decision making and wasted expense which one often observes in more hierarchical organizations.

In an organization in which SBU managers have full responsibility for the whole of the sales and marketing operation, there is probably no role for a central marketing function unless it is to coordinate the SBUs for activities such as a major tender, a company open day or a company-wide piece of promotional literature. My own preference wherever possible would be to delegate the marketing responsibility as far as possible towards the individual marketplaces (see Follow-up 13.1).

13.2   The product life cycle

Although we normally speak of 'the product life cycle' it is perhaps more correctly described as a 'marketplace life cycle'. The product may well have to be adapted to meet the changing needs of the marketplace.

The life cycle is normally designated as shown in Figure 13.4. Some people would give different titles to the phases, and some would have five phases rather than four, but the principle is the same. Before the phases shown, there is, of course, also the pre-launch phase as discussed in Section 7.4.

The essential point to realize is that, at different stages in the life cycle, we may be selling a different product to a different type of customer, at a different price with different profitability, with different strategic objectives, marketing emphasis and marketing expenditure. If we do not realize this, we might not only fail to take the right actions—we might actually do the opposite of what we should be doing.

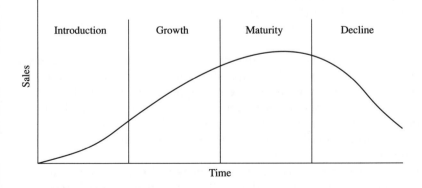

Fig. 13.4   The life cycle

Product

Introductory	Basic
Growth	Improved
Mature	Differentiated
Decline	Rationalized

The product is basic at introduction for two reasons. First, more sophisticated versions and enhancements have not yet been developed. Second, there is actually a strategic argument for not launching a product with all the possible features but saving some of them to be added later. Marketing people love to have something new to say, and our private and business experience shows that marketing campaigns are often based on relatively trivial advances. It is difficult to keep going back to the marketplace with exactly the same claim (although there are some notable examples of where this has been done well).

In the growth phase, the product is improved in various ways. In the mature phase the product may be differentiated, i.e. different variants will be sold into different market segments. In the decline phase it may not be profitable to maintain all of these differentiated variants and only the most successful are likely to remain. Product rationalization is a paradox which presents an agonizing decision to management. If we rank our products by profitability and consider eliminating the least profitable, the result in the short term may be that we are worse off. This is because the associated indirect expenses still remain. The art of product range management is to bring new products in to take the place of the old, so that we are gradually refining our portfolio and generating an increasing level of profit through the fixed resources of our operation.

Customers

Introductory	Innovators
Growth	Early mass market
Mature	Late mass market
Decline	Conservative

The innovators are those who always want to try new things. Their need may be tangible—they need the capabilities of the latest product, software and so on. Alternatively, it may be intangible—they want to be seen as being in the forefront of technology, or they want to own the latest gadget so that they can impress their friends. They are prepared to put these benefits ahead of the fact that the product might be unproven and possibly unreliable.

In contrast to this, conservative customers will not buy until the need has been thoroughly established and all the defects have been ironed out. The early and late mass markets fall between these two extremes.

It is clear from this analysis that the claim we make for a product is absolutely crucial. 'New' is a positive advantage to buyers of type 1 but a real disadvantage to buyers of type 4. Customers of type 1 are likely to be influenced more by intangible factors, whereas those of type 4 require more solid proof.

Price

Introductory	High
Growth	Low
Mature	Lowest
Decline	Rising?

In the introductory phase the price may be at a level which, viewed some time later, seems incredibly high. Some of the early versions of the ballpoint pen cost more than a day's average salary. There are three possible reasons for pricing high in the introductory phase. First, there is little or no competition and therefore no reference point by which price comparisons can be made. Second, people may be prepared to pay a high price simply because the product is new. Third, there is always an element of uncertainty about the price which the market is prepared to pay, particularly in the case of a new product which has not yet become established. There is an argument for pricing at the upper end of the range of uncertainty—it is much easier to bring a price down than to put it up. As the market grows and matures, competition increases and prices are likely to be forced down.

Surprisingly, prices may actually rise during the decline phase because competition has been reduced. In some fields there might be a scarcity value, as with prized models of old cars.

Profitability

Introductory	Negative
Growth	Peak
Mature	Risk of decline
Decline	Low or possible opportunity to increase

The point which many people are reluctant to accept is that the pre-launch and introductory phases incur a loss of profit. As we have discussed in Chapter 12, the marketing cost of innovation is often at least as high as the technical development cost. The profit outflow gradually decreases to zero, after which a positive inflow is achieved.

In the growth phase the profitability may peak. In a mature market there is a risk that profitability will decline because competition has reached a maximum and prices may fall as the product begins to take on the characteristics of a commodity (see Section 6.5). This loss of profit may be partially offset by a reduction in costs, as the development investment has been recovered and production efficiencies are achieved, but the net result may still be a reduced profitability.

It is very difficult to generalize about the decline phase. What it means is that there is not enough residual demand for everyone to achieve the same levels of sales or profit as before. However, if a number of competitors decide to abandon the market, the business that remains can actually be quite profitable. The dilemma is whether to stay in or get out; ideally we want everyone else to get out, leaving the rich pickings for ourselves! Prices may rise and marketing costs may be low, and this phase should not be ignored.

Strategic objectives

Introductory	Create and expand market
Growth	Develop market
Mature	Defend market share
Decline	Optimize the situation

In the introductory phase, particularly if we are the first to enter a new marketplace, customers may not know that the product exists. We therefore have to create a market out of nothing, selling the concept rather than the product. In the growth phase the task is to develop the market, by continuing to increase its total size and increasing our brand share. In the mature phase, when competition is at its highest, we see the constant battle for defending share. Massive amounts of marketing money are poured into this operation, even though no growth may be achieved. The penalty for losing sales in a mature market can be very high. Unit profitability has decreased, and, effectively, the whole of the profit comes from the last few per cent of sales, with most of the turnover being required to cover the fixed costs. Again, the optimum strategy in the decline phase depends upon the actions of the main competitors.

Marketing emphasis

Introductory	Product awareness
Growth	Brand preference
Mature	Brand loyalty
Decline	Selective

In the introductory phase, the emphasis is to make the marketplace aware of the product and to convince customers of why they need to buy. In the growth phase, strong branding is crucial. The need for the product is reasonably well established, and the task is to show why our particular brand is to be preferred. In the mature phase, we again have the battle for brand loyalty. In the decline phase, the emphasis will be directed as opportunities permit.

Marketing expenditure

Introductory	High
Growth	High but lower percentage
Mature	Falling
Decline	Low

A product launch is an extremely expensive marketing operation, and this expenditure continues during the introductory phase. At first, when sales are low, it can reach a very high percentage of turnover.

In the growth phase, marketing expenditure remains high, because we are continuing to penetrate the market and gain market share. However, for the first time in the life cycle, the percentage of turnover spent on marketing comes down and approaches a reasonable figure. In the mature phase, the marketing task is reduced in some respects. It is no longer necessary to sell the concept or to create the market—these tasks have largely been accomplished by ourselves and by our competitors. The emphasis is more on continued selling and promotion than on major new marketing initiatives. In the decline phase, significant marketing expenditure is not justified. If ever there is a time for reactive 'order taking' it is now, but proactive selling in selected areas may still be worth while.

Failure to appreciate the significance of the different phases of the life cycle is the cause of a great deal of ineffective marketing and wasted expenditure. We might be prioritizing the wrong customers. We might be putting prices up when we should be bringing them down. We might be making claims about the product when we should be making claims about the concept. We might be pouring money into a quest for growth when all the market forces are moving in the opposite direction. An intelligent study and comprehension of these life cycle factors is essential to a professional marketing approach (see Exercise 13.2).

13.3   Extending the life cycle

The previous discussion has assumed that we accept an inevitable progression through the life cycle. A key task of marketing is to attempt to extend the life cycle, particularly if this can be done before the decline phase has commenced. The aim is to give one or more 'mid-life kicks' so that the mature phase, or preferably the latter part of the growth phase, is continued for as long as possible. There are various ways of doing this.

Enhanced product or service

This can be achieved by a general improvement in performance or, more usually, by the addition of some new distinguishing features which rekindle the attractiveness in the mind of the customer. A product which was regarded as rather out of date suddenly assumes a new lease of life.

Ideally, a number of phased enhancements would be planned into the product at the concept and development stage. The incremental cost of enhancements is often very low if they are incorporated from the start, whereas a substantial amount of re-engineering expense may be incurred if they are introduced as an afterthought. This approach is an integral part of professional product range management.

New markets

A product which is mature in its original market may have growth potential in new markets. These might be new geographical areas. Although the position in the life cycle in different parts of the world is becoming more uniform as markets become more international, there are still opportunities such as transplanting mature products into developing countries.

Another approach is to introduce the product or service into a new market segment. Something which has become well established in its original segment may have considerable opportunities to progress in areas where it was hitherto unknown. An example is the fax machine which was originally sold for business use but which is increasingly being sold into the home.

New uses

Markets which have become saturated may be revitalized if new uses for the products can be found. An example is a mountain bicycle which is regarded as an exciting product at a time when the traditional bicycle has lost some of its attraction.

More frequent use or multiple use

Some markets become mature because most of the potential customers already own the product and new sales are confined to replacement. These markets can be enhanced if more frequent use can be promoted. For example, until relatively recently, very few homes had more than one telephone. A second telephone in the bedroom then became common, and many houses now have three or more instruments, some of them combined with facilities for answering machines, remote cordless operation, fax and so on.

Wider range of products or services

Consider, for example, a milkman making daily deliveries to the home. The opportunity for increasing sales is very small, and sales levels may have actually fallen because of competition from supermarkets, garages, and so on. If the milkman decides that he is really in the home delivery business rather than the milk business, he is able to deliver a much wider range of groceries at a relatively low incremental cost. If a petrol filling station decides that its main advantage is easy access and parking, with frequent visits already being made for petrol, it has the facility to become a mini-supermarket which is open at all hours.

Styling changes

Some products are regarded as mature because they appear to be old-fashioned in style. They are no longer attractive to innovators who are looking for something different. Relatively trivial styling changes, such as round corners rather than square, or horizontal car radiators rather than vertical, can give a product a more modern appearance and thereby delay or even reverse the progress along the life cycle curve.

Ideally, the enhancement should offer at least some real additional value to the customer. However, it has to be said that many so-called enhancements are relatively trivial and are simply an excuse for having something new to say. This is particularly true in products such as cars and home appliances but it can also apply to software and intangible services and, indeed, to most of the products we buy (see Exercise 13.3).

13.4 The planning process

Put very simply, the planning process addresses three questions:

Where are we now?
Where do we want to go?
How are we going to get there?

Although we have to start with where we are now—we can't change the present situation or the process by which we have reached it—the whole emphasis of our thinking should actually be the other way round. We should look to the long-term future and work back to the present. If we are too constrained by where we are, we are in danger of simply extrapolating the past. A series of short-term tactical decisions does not constitute a strategy. We cannot assume that the organization, staff and physical resources which we happen to have at the moment are correctly balanced for the future. We may have to make some changes, thinking laterally rather than linearly.

Marketing planning must be intimately linked with business planning. In a market-led company, senior marketing management will have had a major input to the business plan. The marketing plan develops those parts of the business plan which relate to the marketplace, the competition, the products and the marketing and sales function within the company. Although it must be 'owned' by the senior marketing member of the management team, it has major implications for R&D, manufacturing, finance, personnel and almost every other function in the organization.

We would urge readers to ensure that any plans which they develop are realiztic working documents. Too many companies engage in an annual ritual where the whole senior management team stops making money for several weeks and fills in bits of paper which nobody believes and no-one but 'head office' reads. If the planning documents are not the almost daily guide of the line managers in the profit centre which originated them, they have not achieved a major part of their purpose.

The titles of the various documents may vary, and companies, particularly those which are parts of larger corporations, have their own particular framework within which the various plans fit together. The plans are normally updated on an annual cycle. A typical structure is as follows:

Whole company

Business plan   *This is the long-range strategic plan*
Management plan   *This is next year's component of the business plan*
Action plans   *These are plans for specific activities (see below)*

Marketing department

                   The business plan and management plan both require a major input from marketing
Marketing plan   *This defines next year's marketing strategy and tactics*
Action plans   *These are plans for specific marketing activities (see below)*

In some companies, the business plan might be called the strategic plan or the long-range plan, and the management plan might be called the business plan.

The time scale for the long-range strategic business plan is typically 3 to 5 years. In some industries, where the impact of investments takes much longer to be measured, a 10- or even 20-year time scale may be necessary.

The annual management plan should be seen as a component of the long-range business plan. Each rolls forward in a consistent manner every 12 months. I have seen situations where the two planning exercises were entirely separate and did not even use the same figures for the first year of the plan period. This wasted a considerable amount of management time. It is understandable that senior management will need some time to approve or modify the long-range plan before the annual plan is written, but their review should not take so long that everything has changed in the meantime. Some companies also have a 'rolling 12-month plan', which moves forward every month irrespective of the year-end.

Action plans in the marketing area might cover activities such as developing a new product range, launching a product, entering a new market segment or setting up an overseas office. Other departments might have action plans for activities such as building a new factory or introducing a new job-evaluation and remuneration scheme. These action plans will be components of the annual and possibly the long-range plans, depending upon their significance to the company as a whole. It is essential that action plans define time scales and responsibilities; if we do not know who is going to do what by when, the planning process is pointless.

To summarize, the aim is to produce a series of documents which are realistic and internally consistent, are approved with the minimum of disruption, and are regarded as essential aids to the management process (see Exercise 13.4).

13.5   The business plan

The business plan defines the long-term strategy which should achieve a viable future for the business, and ensures that everyone is working to the same objective. It is a yardstick against which progress can be monitored during the plan period.

An outline for a business plan might be as shown below. Some of the key factors which make it more likely that the document will be approved by the recipients are discussed in Section 13.7 and marked with an asterisk.

1. **Executive summary**[*]
   Purpose of the plan
   Product and market description (*if necessary—very brief*)
   Key factors for success
   Risks
   Financial projections (£000 or £million) (*listed for 3, 5 or more years*)
   Revenue
   Cost of sales
   Gross margin
     R & D expenses

Marketing expenses
General and administrative expenses
Total expenses
Net profit before interest and tax

2. Background to the plan
Recent history
Key assumptions*
Core skills and expertise
Strengths and weaknesses of the company (*see SWOT analysis, Section 13.8*)
Main strategic initiatives
Alternative strategies rejected*
Changes since last plan*
Benchmark go/no-go decision dates

3. The market
Current size and share (by segment)
Projected size and share (by segment)
The competition (*see SWOT analysis, Section 13.8*)

4. Product strategy

5. Sales and marketing strategy
Key issues (*developed in more detail in the marketing plan—Section 13.6*)

6. Manufacturing strategy

7. Management, organization and human resources strategy

8. Capital investment
Cost and timing (*source of funding in financial schedules—item 10 below*)
Financial justification (*summarized, with details in individual proposals*)

9. Systems and administration

10. Financial schedules
Profit and loss, cash flow, capital investment, balance sheet, interest, tax, etc, projected for the plan period.
Risk and sensitivity assessment (*see Section 12.7*)
Control procedures

Large companies have their own standard structure for the financial and other schedules, so that they can be readily compared and consolidated throughout the organization.

Although a business plan may be a very long document, it is a good discipline before writing it to set out the key issues on a whiteboard or on one piece of paper. It is useful to try presenting a summary of the argument to a colleague in not more than five minutes. The instinct of many managers is to start 'filling in the boxes', and they never really step back and think what it is all about (see Exercise 13.4).

13.6   The marketing plan

The marketing plan defines in much more detail those aspects of the business and management plans which relate to the marketing function. As with the business plan, the logic is

Where are we now? (*analysis of the present situation*)
Where do we want to go? (*marketing objectives*)
How are we going to get there? (*strategies and actions*)

As with other parts of the planning process, the marketing plan is a means of ensuring that marketing strategies and tactics have been clearly thought out. Without this attention to detail, the plan simply cannot be written. The plan also ensures that everyone understands the commitment to marketing effort and expenditure which the programme requires. A typical structure is as follows:

1. **Executive summary**
   Key issues, strategic initiatives and their implications
   Non-marketing readers can be strongly influenced by the summary

2. **The present situation** (*Where are we now?*)
   The economic environment
   The marketplace (*size, shares and trends*)
   Company SWOT analysis (*see Section 13.8*)
   Competition (*size, market share, strengths/weaknesses*)
   The product range

3. **Key marketing objectives** (*Where do we want to go?*)

4. **Key assumptions** (*on which achievement of the plan depends*)

5. **Marketing strategy** (*How are we going to get there?*)
   Market segment strategy
   Product range strategy and product management strategy

Pricing strategy
Sales strategy
Distribution strategy
Promotional strategy
   Literature
   Advertising
   Exhibitions
   PR
   Other
These strategies will be amplified by individual action plans where appropriate

6. **Human resources implications of the plan**
Quantity and calibre, existing and required
Recruitment
Training
Secondments and transfers
Remuneration and incentive policy

7. **Profit and loss account** *(consistent with business plan)*

8. **Financial budgets required** *(breakdown of expenses in P&L)*

9. **Risk, sensitivity and controls** *(see Section 12.7)*
(What can go wrong? How can the risk be minimized? What are the implications if it does go wrong? How will progress be monitored and controlled?)

This structure should be our servant rather than our master, but it offers a checklist against which our own plan can be compared.

A marketing plan is a very good diagnostic indicator of the degree of marketing professionalism of a company and a senior marketing team. If you don't know where you're going, any road will get you there! However, the only thing that ultimately matters is the performance rather than the plan, and the document and its accompanying action plans must define very specifically who is going to do what by when (see Exercise 13.4).

13.7   Successful internal proposals

The principles of marketing discussed in this book can be applied to internal business proposals. In this situation one is, in effect, trying to sell an idea to senior management, usually with a view to gaining approval for spending money. The document might be a business plan, a marketing plan, or one of the specific action plans discussed In Section 13.4. It can apply to almost any situation where the idea is not so obvious that approval is immediately and automatically granted.

Many proposals are extremely pedestrian and do not excite the reader. Attention to the following points may make all the difference between a hard-hitting proposal that is likely to be approved and a sterile process which wastes a great deal of time and still leaves senior management undecided.

Executive summary

A good executive summary not only saves time for busy senior managers who have to approve proposals. It is also a test of clear thinking. It demonstrates that the writer has really thought through the argument. As an illustration of this, I recently heard that a major company insists that proposals for millions of pounds of research funding must not exceed one page.

Assumptions

If we say that a proposal is predicated on certain assumptions, the reader can challenge them as part of the decision-making process. The assumptions might relate to advances in technology, prices of components, actions of the competition, estimates of the size and rate of growth of the market and so on. Some readers may not be able to understand the technical intricacies of the conclusions, but can legitimately challenge the assumptions on which the conclusions are based as a test of the credibility of the report.

Alternative strategies rejected

Too many reports fall into the category of 'take it or leave it'. A particular strategy is proposed, and the reader is invited to approve it. However, the reader may not be certain that the suggested strategy is necessarily the best. The report might be referred back for reconsideration and resubmission. Other approaches might be suggested.

If the writer anticipates this by describing several alternative strategies which have been considered and rejected, the writer is, in effect, doing some of the reader's homework. This shows that the writer has made a mature business appraisal of the situation and has not simply latched on to one particular idea which happened to be attractive at the time of writing.

Changes since the last plan

Proposals, particularly annual plans, often refer to situations which have been described in earlier plans. The careless proposal writer forgets to read last year's plan, and becomes ready prey for an astute recipient who takes the trouble to do so! I recall a meeting when a senior manager with a twinkle in the eye said to one of my colleagues 'I was very interested to read your proposal, particularly since you said the opposite last year; are you sure you know what you are doing?!'

There are inevitably times when circumstances change. The wise approach is to acknowledge this by saying 'Last year's proposal was based on the assumption that ...; circumstances have now changed and this modifies our recommendations along the following lines ...'. This makes the document much more credible.

A well-written internal proposal, which clearly demonstrates how new profit opportunities can be created, is a sign of professional marketing management (see Follow-up 13.2).

13.8   Models and techniques

There are a number of models and techniques which can help us to understand our business situation and make business decisions. In my experience of using them, I have found that there is a danger that the technique becomes the objective of the process, and very little is done to make decisions as a result. Senior managers spend days 'filling in boxes' and writing down things which everyone already knows, send the results off to head office with a sigh of relief and then revert to running the business. This is a pointless exercise.

To overcome this problem, I would suggest the 'so what?!' approach. Having done the analysis, what are we going to do differently in future? What changes do we need to make in our policy, strategy or tactics? Should we change our organization or any of the managers in the organization? Should we change our competitive strategy or our product strategy?

The techniques do not, of themselves, answer any questions. What they do is to help us to clarify our thinking. They make us ask questions which we might not otherwise ask, and tackle important issues which we might otherwise not consider.

The two techniques described in this book are not new, but they have stood the test of time. Sophisticated computer models are now available which may be valuable when used by specialists, but the methods described here can be used by any experienced manager.

SWOT analysis

This exercise, as the initial letters imply, investigates Strengths, Weaknesses, Opportunities and Threats. It is normally expressed in the form of a grid as shown in Figure 13.5. We start by thinking very critically about our operation, listing the strengths and weaknesses. We must be

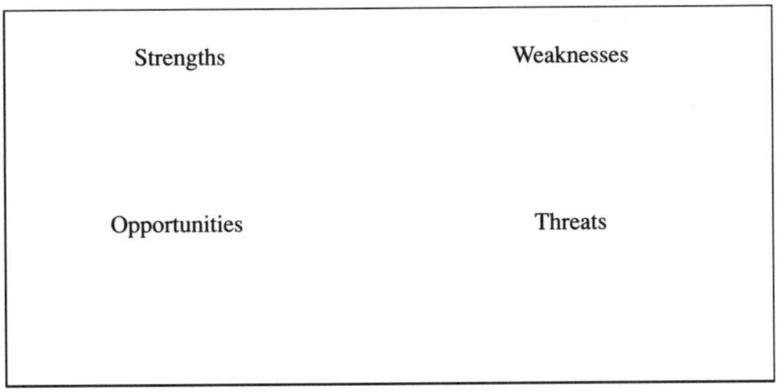

Strengths	Weaknesses
Opportunities	Threats

Fig. 13.5 SWOT analysis

willing to record the bad news as well as the good. We should try to see ourselves as the marketplace sees us, not as we would like to see ourselves.

We then write down the opportunities open to us in the marketplace, and the threats which might restrict those opportunities. The threats might come from economic, environmental or technical factors, or from the activities of the competition. The strengths and weaknesses of the main competitors can be considered as part of the analysis.

It is useful to do this exercise with a small group of colleagues, at or around our own management level but covering a variety of management disciplines. There is a benefit in doing it off-site where a more relaxed environment can be created and interruptions minimized. This can create a very vigorous forum where constructive argument can take place and vague generalizations can be critically challenged.

Having done the analysis, argued about it and clarified the issues, we now need to ask 'so what?' How can we use our strengths more effectively? What are we going to do about the areas of weakness which we have identified? How can we exploit the opportunities which are open to us? How can we overcome or minimize the effect of the threats? If we take this practical approach to the SWOT analysis, we should be able to gain a useful input to our strategic planning without spending too much time on the exercise (see Exercise 13.5).

The Growth Share Matrix

This technique was developed by The Boston Consulting Group (see Henderson, 1973) and has gained wide acceptance. It helps us to identify the relative role and stage of development of the various products which make up our overall product portfolio, or of the SBUs within our organization. As shown in Figure 13.6 the grid is a plot of market growth rate against relative market share (defined as our share divided by that of

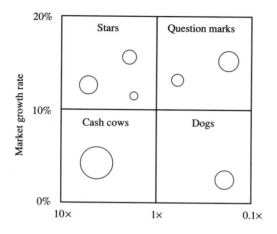

Fig. 13.6 The Growth Share Matrix. (*Source*: Henderson (1973): used by permission of The Boston Consulting Group, Inc., Boston, Massachusetts)

the market leader). The position of each circle represents the position of a particular product, product range or SBU, and the size of the circle indicates its monetary value.

As with the SWOT analysis, the Growth Share Matrix is a good subject for an off-site brainstorming session as an aid to determining business strategy. The grid defines four situations:

1. *Question marks*   This is a common starting point, where we have a low share in a high-growth market. A Question Mark has a potentially high demand on cash resources, and we may need to select the most favourable from a number of options. To summarize—invest in order to exploit the opportunity, or abandon it.

2. *Stars*   A Star has a high share in a high-growth market, and often results from a former Question Mark. A Star may still require investment of cash, but the best of the Stars are the Cash Cows of the future.

3. *Cash Cows*   These have a high share in a low-growth or declining market. They provide cash for promoting Stars, resolving Question Marks and divesting Dogs, and are a prime source of cash for the whole company operation. As 'Cows', they should be milked for as long as possible.

4. *Dogs*   These have a weak market share in a low-growth or declining market. They can cause a major diversion of management effort and

drain on profit. Some people retain Dogs for sentimental reasons, and brutal steps may have to be taken.

A typical life cycle might be that a Question Mark becomes a Star which becomes a Cash Cow which becomes a Dog. The whole process may take years or even decades, but in many fields (see Section 13.2), life cycles are becoming progressively shorter and management actions must reflect this.

The Growth Share Matrix may throw up some possible management errors. These include:

1. Concentrating on the short term to the detriment of the long term. Business development usually requires a profit outflow before it can generate a profit inflow, and short-term management focus may prevent some activities from becoming Stars and Cash Cows because they are starved of initial investment.

2. Expecting all SBUs to have the same growth rate or return on investment. Market place realities simply do not allow this.

3. Weakening Cash Cows by taking too much cash out of them. If we do not feed cows, they will stop producing milk!

4. Allowing Cash Cows to become complacent by leaving too much cash in them. Cows should not be allowed to become fat and lazy! (Nor should SBU managers!!)

5. Investing unrealistically in Dogs in the vain hope of turning them round. Our normal priority should be to reinforce success rather than trying to prop up failure.

6. Maintaining too many Question Marks and under-funding each. A Question Mark is not a stable situation; we should either invest to move towards segment dominance or drop or divest the activity concerned.

Intelligently applied, the Growth Share Matrix can be a cost-effective way of stepping back from our daily activities and asking ourselves where we are going (see Exercise 13.6).

13.9   The model product manager

Although this section is written as for a product manager, most of the comments apply to any marketing management or business development position.

Product management grew up in consumer marketing companies, which often have large and complex hierarchies of product managers or brand managers, product group managers, marketing managers and so on. These people have a vital role to play and are often dealing with issues which have major financial implications. Ironically, however, because of the importance of what they are doing, their individual freedom to make management decisions may actually be constrained by the organization and the system. Their proposals have to be ratified by more senior managers or by specialist committees. From my personal experience in both fields, I am convinced that a product manager in a less-structured marketing organization has much more freedom to take individual initiative and to exercise management responsibility.

In my view 'model product managers' should:

1. *Be managing their products*   This involves
   - understanding the products, their applications, the marketplace and the competition, and keeping this information up to date
   - perceiving trends and foreseeing future needs and opportunities
   - knowing market sizes, market shares and product life cycles
   - understanding business and financial aspects (profit, ROI, cash flow, etc.)
   - on the basis of the above, producing *definitive marketing specifications*

2. *Be managing themselves*   This involves
   - making and keeping commitments on time, and being consistently reliable
   - responding well to crises
   - managing conflicts of priorities
   - keeping on top of paperwork
   - documenting decisions, proposals, results of meetings, etc.

3. *Be customer oriented*   Proposals must be based on existing or potential customer needs. Those which are mainly designed to optimize company resources or to achieve internal aspirations are doomed to failure. There must be regular contact with a sample of opinion leaders and basic customers.

4. *Speak and write with authority*   They must be regarded at the most senior levels as people who know what they are doing. The reaction we want is 'if *they* have written the proposal, I reserve the right to challenge it but my experience shows that they will have "done their homework"'.

5. *Be world oriented*   Fewer companies these days can experience continued profitable growth if they are restricted to the UK market.

6. *Manage a product throughout its life cycle*   Too many products are launched like ships and then left to disappear over the horizon.

7. *Understand how decisions are made at board level*   Directors of other functions need to be supplied with facts and figures on which they can rely. They do not all want to be flooded with technical information—they want the appropriate *business* issues to be addressed.

8. *As far as possible, present their managers with proposals not problems, answers not questions*   While readers will argue that this applies to any business discipline, marketing when properly understood is an almost infinite subject. Clear thinking and decisive commitment are essential. There are times when a genuine cry for help is a sign of maturity, and managers should certainly be informed of disasters so that they are forearmed, but in general product managers should do all the 'pre-digestion' and produce material which their managers can use as their own.

9. *Be totally confidential*   Product managers deal with information which is denied to more senior people in other functions. They may be the only people outside the board who have so much information on items such as profitability and corporate strategy.

Points 1 to 9 seem to paint a picture of a rather self-opinionated over-confident arrogant prig! However, they must also:

10. *Be good team members*   Interfaces, especially with engineering/development/design and sales, are crucial to success. Mutual respect for each other's role and expertise is essential (even if good marketing people do feel they are 'rather more equal than the others'!).

Conclusion

This final section is much more than a job description. It encapsulates the essential ingredients of marketing management. I hope it will help readers—marketing and non-marketing managers alike—to become more professional in their own marketing activities (see Follow-up 13.3).

Exercises

13.1 Does your sales and marketing organization give an appropriate balance to the two functions?

13.2 Consider your product ranges in the light of the discussion on life cycles in Section 13.2. What changes do you need to make as a result of this analysis?

13.3 What opportunities for extending the life cycle of your existing products or services are suggested by Section 13.3?

13.4 What improvements can you make to your planning process in the light of Sections 13.4 to 13.6?

13.5 Carry out a SWOT analysis on your company and on your major competitors as suggested in Section 13.8. What are you going to do with your findings? Incorporate the technique into your annual planning procedure.

13.6 Complete the Growth Share Matrix as described in Section 13.8. Consider the six 'management errors' listed. What new inputs to your strategic planning does this exercise suggest?

Follow-up

13.1 If you do not already have them, consider the implications of setting up strategic business units in your organization.

13.2 Use the guidelines in Section 13.7 to prepare your next internal proposal.

13.3 Use the description of a 'model product manager' to test existing job descriptions and as a basis for future recruitment or internal appointment of marketing staff.

Reference

Henderson, B. D., 'The Experience Curve Reviewed: The Growth Share Matrix or the Product Portfolio', *Perspectives* (The Boston Consulting Group, Inc., 1973).

Author's contact address

Dr Colin Sowter can be contacted at:

MARKETING SEMINARS
PO Box 274
Shamley Green
Guildford,
Surrey
GU5 0NE

Fax: (from UK)   01483 892894
         (from outside UK) +44 1483 892894

INDEX